WHITEHEAD'S RELIGIOUS THOUGHT

WHITEHEAD'S RELIGIOUS THOUGHT

*From Mechanism to Organism,
from Force to Persuasion*

DANIEL A. DOMBROWSKI

Cover art: Coast of Porto courtesy of iStock by Getty Images.

Published by State University of New York Press, Albany

© 2017 State University of New York

All rights reserved

Printed in the United States of America

For information, contact State University of New York Press, Albany, NY www.sunypress.edu

Production, Diane Ganeles
Marketing, Anne M. Valentine

Library of Congress Cataloging-in-Publication Data

Names: Dombrowski, Daniel A., author.
Title: Whitehead's religious thought : from mechanism to organism, from force to persuasion / Daniel A. Dombrowski.
Description: Albany, NY : State University of New York, 2017. | Includes bibliographical references and index.
Identifiers: LCCN 2016031445 (print) | LCCN 2016040661 (ebook) | ISBN 9781438464299 (hardcover : alk. paper) | ISBN 978-1-4384-6430-5 (pbk.: alk. paper) | ISBN 9781438464312 (e-book)
Subjects: LCSH: Whitehead, Alfred North, 1861-1947. | Religion—Philosophy. | Philosophy.
Classification: LCC B1674.W354 D66 2017 (print) | LCC B1674.W354 (ebook) | DDC 210.92—dc23
LC record available at https://lccn.loc.gov/2016031445

10 9 8 7 6 5 4 3 2 1

To Marie

CONTENTS

INTRODUCTION

It is widely assumed both inside and outside of academe that there are two primary worldviews that are open to us in the period in which we live. One is the classical theistic worldview wherein God supernaturally hovers over a mechanical world and arbitrarily (and often violently) intervenes into the workings of the world machine. The other worldview is that defended by religious skeptics wherein at the anthropocentric level the (besouled) ghost is exorcized from the human machine and at the cosmological level the (divine) Ghost is exorcized from the cosmic machine. The present book is an attempt to explore a third alternative between these two extremes by way of an original interpretation of the process theistic thought of the great mathematician-philosopher Alfred North Whitehead (1861–1947).

It is the responsibility of philosophers both to clarify nonempirical concepts and to use such concepts, along with empirical data, to illuminate problems of value. This book will attempt to clarify and apply the four major concepts mentioned in the subtitle of this book: mechanism, organism, force, and persuasion (see Hartshorne 1970, xiv).

Readers of the present book will notice that the subtitle is also the title of a chapter from Alfred North Whitehead's *AI*: "From Force to Persuasion" (also Henning 2005, chap. 1). My thesis is that the move from force to persuasion (hereafter, FTP) is not a minor one in Whitehead's thought, in particular, nor in what is commonly called process thought, in general. Indeed, as I see things, the transition from FTP is a topic that illuminates much that is going on in contemporary academe, both in English-language philosophy, theology, and religious studies, on the one hand, and in various tendencies in postmodernism influenced by well-known continental thinkers, on the other. To put the point more energetically, not to examine carefully the theme of FTP is to fail to understand not only Whitehead but also several important thinkers who have either been heavily influenced by Whitehead or who have recently been dialogical partners with Whitehead: David Ray Griffin, Isabelle Stengers, John Rawls, Charles Hartshorne, and Judith Butler. I will also treat William Wordsworth, who heavily influenced Whitehead and Hartshorne. The thesis can be put as follows: the transition from FTP is a necessary condition for the flourishing of (or perhaps even for the continued existence of!) our civilized life together.

In a way the topic of FTP is a perennial one, as is witnessed by the fact that in Plato's *Timaeus* (which Whitehead viewed as one of the two greatest works in the history of cosmology, the other being written by Isaac Newton) the creation of the world of civilized order itself is "the victory of persuasion over force" (*AI* 25; also *PR* xiv, 71–72), with "force" referring to what the antecedent volume of the world of fact contains. In this sense the victory of persuasion over force involves nothing less than the adventure of an idea with a creative power always on the verge of actualization (*AI* 42). In cosmology, religion, and ethics, recourse to force is a disclosure of the failure of civilization. If interaction between individuals must take one of these two forms—persuasion or force, or perhaps a mixture of both—then we should beware of theories or cultural forms (e.g., the dominance of men over women) that depend primarily on force (*AI* 83). Granted, persuasion can be powerful, but I assume that the reader will easily notice the difference between persuasive power, on the one hand, and coercive power or force, on the other.

Plato points the way toward the victory of persuasion over force when he denies omnipotence to the divine Demiurge, who can produce only such order as is possible through persuasive rather than coercive devices, a victory that Whitehead explicitly connects with the nonviolent devices of Mohandas Gandhi and the Quakers in the twentieth century. Plato's discovery of FTP is one of the greatest in the history of humanity in that the later effects of belief in an omnipotent God, who coercively disposes at will a wholly derivative world, were disastrous, as we will see (*AI* 148, 160, 166, 296).

Of course, both "force" and "persuasion" can mean different things when these terms are used in cosmology in contrast to their use in science or ethics or religion. In a Newtonian context, say, the force acting on a body is quite different from the force of belief that just *is* religion, on at least one of Whitehead's definitions of religion (*RM* 15; *IM* 17; *SM* 45). Even within religious discourse there is a difference between religion as the force of belief and the claim that the life of Jesus exhibits a persuasive power that is devoid of coercion or force (*RM* 57). Further, all of these uses of "force" differ from the analytic force of evidence in an argument, which as a mathematician Whitehead understood quite well (*RM* 65, 117). Although some uses of "force" in Whitehead have a positive connotation (as in the force of rational argument), some are neutral (as in the force of an accelerating body), and still others are treated with disapprobation. Regarding this last type, consider the following:

> God's role is not the combat of productive force with productive force, of destructive force with destructive force; it lies in the patient operation of the overpowering rationality of his conceptual harmonization. He does not create the world, he saves it: or, more accurately, he is the poet of the world, with tender patience leading it by his vision of truth, beauty, and goodness. (*PR* 346)

Presumably, if Whitehead were alive today, he would (along with Hartshorne, who lived long enough to see the merits of gender-neutral language regarding God) refuse to refer to God as "he," even if he would nonetheless continue to view God in personal terms.

The first half of the subtitle to this book ("From Mechanism to Organism") also refers to an important theme in that Whitehead's preferred label for his view was not "process philosophy" but "philosophy of organism." Although the science of mechanics had its origin in ancient Greece in the study of levers and various problems connected with the weight of bodies (*IM* 30), it was not until the seventeenth century that the great forces of nature (e.g., gravitation) were systematically described as machines. The mechanistic theory of nature has reigned supreme ever since. Indeed, Whitehead refers to it as "the orthodox creed of physical science" (*SM* 50), despite the fact that difficulties with this theory were apparent almost from the start, as in Giambattista Vico's criticisms of René Descartes. Whitehead compares what is sometimes seen as an oddity in traditional Chinese culture (that one can be an adherent to two religions, say Confucianism and Buddhism) with a significant and peculiar feature of Western culture (that one can be a mechanist *and* have an unwavering belief that humans and other animals are self-determining organisms). On Whitehead's view, "the only way of mitigating mechanism is by the discovery that it is not [really] mechanism" (*SM* 76).

Only relatively recently has the importance of organisms led to a significant challenge to mechanism, which, despite its dominance in intellectual life, "is quite unbelievable." We will see that the problem with mechanism is that it is based on high abstractions that are taken for concrete actuality; it commits the fallacy of misplaced concreteness. We will also see that Whitehead endorses "the romantic reaction" to mechanism by putting organisms first in that they are the truly concrete realities (*SM* 41, 54, 75, 79). The transition from mechanism to organism (hereafter, MTO) is found in many places in Whitehead in addition to his philosophy of science. For example, in *AE* he notes the mechanical tendencies found in educational institutions that merely impart information and the difficulty these institutions face in fostering zest for learning. This difficulty is connected to the pathos of organic life in general: "The tragedy of the world is that those who are imaginative have but slight experience, and those who are [mechanically] experienced have feeble imaginations. Fools act on imagination without knowledge; pedants act on [mechanical] knowledge without imagination" (*AE* 93).

Mechanism is often disguised as dualism, or, as Whitehead refers to it, the bifurcation of nature. Such a bifurcation is nothing less than a vice, he thinks. In *CN* he states that "if the reader indulges in the facile vice of bifurcation not a word of what I have . . . written will be intelligible" (*CN* vi, also 185, 187). Or again,

> another way of phrasing this theory which I am arguing against is to bifurcate nature into two divisions, namely into the nature apprehended in awareness and the nature which is the [mechanical] cause of awareness. The nature which is the fact apprehended in awareness holds within it the greenness of the trees, the song of the birds, the warmth of the sun, the hardness of the chairs, and the feel of the velvet. (*CN* 30–31).

Whitehead confuses matters a bit when he at times refers to his own view as "organic mechanism" (*SM* 80, 107), but he clears up the confusion later when he calls his view an "organic realism," wherein in Heraclitean fashion "all things flow" or "all things are vectors" (*PR* 309). To be precise, "organism" means two different things in Whitehead: there is a microscopic meaning and a macroscopic meaning. On Whitehead's usage, physics studies the former and biology and psychology study the latter. Regarding the latter, it should be noted that a nexus of many microorganisms can obviously be treated as an organism in its own right (*PR* 128–129, 287; *SM* 103).

With the foregoing as a background, I would now like to state three goals I have in the present book: (1) to highlight the MTO and FTP transitions so as to use them as searchlights in order to see various features of both intellectual life and the world in which we live in the early twenty-first century that might not otherwise be seen and (2) to link MTO and FTP in a novel way that leads to (3) an enlargement of our view of the world, both metaphysically and ethically. Another way to state the aims of the book is to say that I hope to better comprehend Whitehead by putting him in dialogue with six major thinkers so as both to better understand the world we live in and to contribute to its improvement.

Regarding (3), it is crucial to emphasize the fact that on a Whiteheadian basis the *size* of our (mechanical) metaphysical and ethical concepts is very often scandalously narrow such that a philosophy of organism is meant to enlarge them (*PR* 204; also see Loomer 2013). Machines can be pushed around and manipulated, even exploited, and we do not much mind. But organisms, because they feel and hence are capable of internal relations, matter. To put the point succinctly, force may be needed when dealing with machines, but persuasion is more appropriate when dealing with organisms. The very activity of valuation, which is found in all concrete singulars, is itself a persuasive factor in the development of the universe. "Persuasion" here refers to both "incitement toward" value and "deterrence from" disvalue. Further, we will see that one of the key functions of God in Whitehead is the persuasive coordination of value among many values and valuers (*IY* 686–687, 694).

In chapter 1 I defend the MTO transition by way of the most notable analysis of this transition in Griffin's *Unsnarling the World Knot*. I will argue that his panexperientialism is significant *both* because he makes progress regarding the perennial difficulty, dating back to Plato, in understanding the relationship between mind and body *and* because he advances this understanding by taking his Whiteheadian panexperientialism directly to the heart of the debate regarding the mind-body problem in contemporary philosophy of mind. As before, the MTO transition is propaedeutic to the FTP transition in that in philosophy of organism (or more loosely, in process philosophy) the real is not constituted by tiny machines, nor are we super-machines constituted by the tiny ones. As a result, there is less of a need for force than is commonly thought and more of a need for the persuasion that is appropriate when dealing with living organisms. That is, the *res verae* are not, as is often thought, inert, lifeless cogs that are composed only by external relations (see the still-magisterial work by Lucas). If reality were so constituted, it could, as a result, legitimately be manipulated at will.

I try to show in chapter 2 how *not* to understand MTO and FTP. Granted, Stengers (who is the most important of the recent European thinkers who have vitalized Whitehead on the continent) is very much interested in these topics, especially MTO, but her disinterest in panexperientialism, along with her antipathy toward the persuasive God of process theism, makes her efforts to articulate Whitehead's achievements regarding both MTO and FTP open to criticism.

In effect, chapters 1 and 2 together exhibit a unity-in-difference in that these two great thinkers, Griffin and Stengers, although they are interested in largely the same subject matter, exhibit vastly different levels of success in understanding it, in my humble opinion. The theoretical achievements in chapters 1 and 2 are brought to bear on several crucial practical matters in chapters 3, 4, 5, and 6.

Chapter 3 *introduces* issues surrounding FTP by arguing for a Rawlsian version of political liberalism. This theory helps to illuminate Whitehead's and Hartshorne's own nascent version of political liberalism. In turn, Whitehead and Hartshorne offer metaphysical support for Rawlsian political liberalism. In this chapter the transition from FTP can be seen in terms of the development of convivial relations among citizens who do not share the same comprehensive doctrine, indeed who defend quite different comprehensive doctrines, whether religious or nonreligious.

FTP is the *focus* of chapter 4, where I argue that Whitehead and Hartshorne are not necessarily the best interpreters of their own theories, which have a life and logic of their own apart from the thinkers who brought them into existence. Neoclassical (or process) theism involves, as Stengers realizes, a devastating critique of the omnipotent God of classical theism, who lies behind both just war theory and the belief that coercive power is required in order for civilization to flourish. But Stengers does not realize (nor do Whitehead and Hartshorne themselves fully realize) the extent to which the God of neoclassical theism points us toward the appropriateness of both nonviolent methods of resisting evil and the fostering of pacific, rather than anesthetic, civiliz*ing* ideals.

Whereas chapters 3 and 4 explore the FTP transition as it relates to interactions (specifically disputes) among rational human beings, chapter 5 explores the FTP transition as it relates to interactions with nonrational human beings and with nonhuman animals. Here I will be in dialogue with several of Butler's concepts that have a family resemblance to each other: precarity, vulnerability, grievability, and mourning, which, in turn, have a family resemblance to Whiteheadian concepts like tragedy, sentiency, anesthesia, and perishing. Chapter 5, like chapter 2, brings process thought into dialogue with some of the most prominent trends in continental philosophy in the early twenty-first century. This is fitting, given the fact that many process thinkers, including Griffin and myself, think of themselves as postmodern (albeit constructively postmodern) in that they are explicitly moving beyond the deleterious features of modern philosophy and its mechanism.

In chapter 6 I explore both Whitehead's own "romantic reaction" to mechanism as detailed in *SM* as well as the implications of this reaction for the FTP transition. I will argue that we should take seriously the positive influence Wordsworth had on Whitehead and Hartshorne and that we should not give in to the popular (even in intellectual circles) identification of romanticism with a type of syrupy sentimentalism. Rather, a Wordsworthian view of nature, including the deeply interfused place of the divine in nature, dovetails with panexperientialism or panpsychism, as Whitehead and Hartshorne realized.

Chapters 3, 4, 5, and 6 together signal a notable advance in ethical theory and in the cosmological/metaphysical backing for such theory, on the one hand, and provide, on the other, a model or a lure for a way forward beyond our commonly accepted manner of negotiating our relationships with fellow rational human beings (both nationally and internationally), with nonrational human beings and nonhuman animals, and with the natural world, respectively. The commonly accepted norms I am criticizing are characterized by coercive power rather than by persuasive power, broadly understood. That is, these four chapters point the way toward a future realistic utopia, if the Rawlsian oxymoron be permitted (see Rawls 1999a; Dombrowski 2011).

The entire book presupposes the rejection of belief in divine omnipotence, a rejection that is a commonplace in process thought. Whitehead often criticizes omnipotence and Hartshorne even wrote a book titled *Omnipotence and Other Theological Mistakes*. Because excellent work has already been done on this topic, I will not duplicate such efforts here. But because the critique of omnipotence is a central assumption of the present book, I would like to at least list the types of reasons that could be used in arguments against omnipotence. My brief comments in this regard are not meant to substitute for detailed argument, which is a crucial point to notice given the fact that many (or most) theists are still unfortunately committed to belief in divine omnipotence. Rather, my aim here is to accurately depict my starting point so as to make intelligible the chapters that follow. Omnipotence is problematic for at least five reasons.

First and foremost, there are *metaphysical* problems with omnipotence. As we will see in chapter 1, process thinkers have historically been fascinated by, and have typically defended their own version of, the definition of being in Plato's *Sophist* (247e) as the dynamic power to be affected by causal influences from the past and to creatively affect others in the future, in however slight a way. That is, if being just *is* power, then no being, not even the greatest conceivable being, could have *all* power as long as there are other beings that exist. To say that God has the power both to be persuasively influenced by all others and to persuasively influence all others is *not* to say that God has all power (see Dombrowski 2005, chap. 2).

Second and relatedly, the concept of omnipotence seems to be integrally connected to the concept of creation out of absolute nothingness, in that it is one thing to create or to persuade order out of the disorderly stuff that is already in existence and quite another thing to create the disorderly stuff out of "absolute nothingness." The latter would require omnipotence. The problem is that creation *ex nihilo* is unintelligible hence the foregoing scare quotes. Even to talk about "it" (absolute nothingness) is to no longer speak about *absolute* nothingness but about somethingness. This is why process thinkers hold that Plato was wise in the *Sophist* (256–257) to interpret nonbeing in relative terms or as a rough synonym for otherness (e.g., this dog is nothing like that one), rather than in absolute terms in that the latter are unintelligible. It is noteworthy that creation *ex nihilo* is not a biblical idea but rather seems to be due to a political effort in the intertestamental period to make sure that God surpassed even Caesar's coercive power (PR 342–343).

Third, the most familiar criticism that neoclassical or process theists receive from classical theists is that the process God *lacks* power and hence is an unfitting candidate for the greatest conceivable being. However, it is not often noticed that this criticism succeeds only if the previous two points are groundless. It assumes that the words "*omnipotence*" and "all power" make sense in a world where there are other beings in existence with powers of their own. And because of the tight connection between omnipotence and creation *ex nihilo*, it assumes that sense can be made of the phrase "absolute nonbeing *is*" the substratum out of which God brought the world into being through His (the male pronoun is needed here) totalitarian coercive power. But there is no "lack" of power in the neoclassical or process God if these assumptions are defective.

Fourth, there is also a *moral* critique of omnipotence. Here the salient idea is that even if the concept of omnipotence made sense, it is not clear that it would be compatible with belief in divine omnibenevolence. Neoclassical or process theists have argued at length that it is by no means obvious that coercive power is more admirable than persuasive power, that to be a divine substance that needs nothing else in order to exist is superior to divine relational existence (How could God be omnibenevolent if there were no one else to love?), or that we have greater ignorance of divine goodness than we do of divine coercive power. It is precisely because the neoclassical or process God does not possess *all* power that such a divinity can possess *ideal* power, as we will see in chapter 4 (see Loomer 1976).

The fifth sort of reason to be opposed to omnipotence is related to the fourth. The *theodicy objection* to omnipotence is a powerful one that emerges directly out of David Hume's famous query regarding why an all-powerful God who is also all-good does not destroy evil, or at least destroy as much of it as possible and still preserve creaturely freedom. Of course, an *all*-powerful God could presumably destroy all evil and still preserve creaturely freedom. The debates regarding theodicy are well known and very complicated. The point here is to emphasize the tendency on the part of neoclassical or process theists to return to the Platonic concept of God as all-good yet not all-powerful (although ideally powerful). The problem with classical theism here is its apriorism: it starts with the assumption that God *has to be* omnipotent and then tries (unsuccessfully) to try to understand the existence of evil or tragedy on this basis. Whitehead and Hartshorne, by way of contrast, are more empirical by starting with the experiences of intense suffering, tragedy, and evil and then allowing these experiences to help shape discourse about God. It is not viewed as a defect by neoclassical or process theists that their view is that even God, although necessarily existent, is in some sense a tragic being. Indeed, in one sense God is the most tragic being in that there is no loss that is not felt by such a being, in contrast to our feeble assimilation of loss.

In short, on the classical theistic view there simply is no FTP transition in that in the final analysis everything that happens is either due to, or at least permitted by, divine coercive power. That is, in classical theism there is no real FTP transition in that we are left merely with "F." In this book I will argue that the price for this parsimony is too steep.

ABBREVIATIONS OF WORKS BY WHITEHEAD

AE	*Aims of Education*
AI	*Adventures of Ideas*
AN	"Autobiographical Notes"
AS	"An Appeal to Sanity"
CN	*Concept of Nature*
DW	*Dialogues of Alfred North Whitehead*
EC	*An Enquiry Concerning the Principles of Natural Knowledge*
ES	*Essays in Science and Philosophy*
FR	*The Function of Reason*
IM	*Introduction to Mathematics*
IY	"Immortality"
MG	"Mathematics and the Good"
MT	*Modes of Thought*
PR	*Process and Reality*
RM	*Religion in the Making*
SM	*Science and the Modern World*
SY	*Symbolism*

ONE

Griffin's Panexperientialism as Perennial Philosophy

THE NEED FOR A RADICAL APPROACH

The title to David Ray Griffin's book *Unsnarling the World Knot: Consciousness, Freedom, and the Mind-Body Problem* alludes to a rope metaphor from Arthur Schopenhauer to the effect that the key philosophical problem since the seventeenth century (the mind-body problem) is, on prevailing assumptions, unsolvable. At the risk of mixing metaphors, one can highlight several different prominent contemporary philosophers of mind to illustrate why we are tied in a "world knot": William Seager claims that we have no idea whatsoever how consciousness "emerges" from (mechanical) matter; Jaegwon Kim holds that we have reached a "dead end" regarding the mind-body problem; Colin McGinn alleges that we will *never* be able to understand the emergence of consciousness from the brain (viewed as a machine); John Searle suggests that most of mainstream philosophy of mind is "obviously false"; and Galen Strawson maintains that only a "revolutionary" new way of thinking will enable us to respond adequately to the mind-body problem. Although Daniel Dennett is a bit more optimistic regarding a solution to the mind-body problem on prevailing assumptions, even he sees consciousness as a "mystery" (Griffin 1998, 1, 4–6).

In full light of the enormity of the difficulty, Griffin hopes to "unsnarl" the world knot. It might be assumed that this unsnarling is an instance of the new, *revolutionary* thinking called for by Strawson. But

1

Thomas Nagel's phrasing of the same view may be more helpful when he says that *radical* speculation is needed in order to unsnarl the world knot (Griffin 1998, 5). I am taking the etymology of the word "radical" seriously in that it comes from the Latin *radix* for "root." That is, Griffin has offered an oxymoronic *radically new* approach to the mind-body problem, just as he is trying to revitalize an old solution to it. In the present chapter I will be attempting to find for Griffin a place of honor within a perennial tradition regarding MTO and FTP that goes back to Plato. As Josiah Royce once suggested:

> Whenever I have most carefully revised my . . . standards, I am always able to see . . . that at best I have been finding out, in some new light, the true meaning that was latent in old traditions. . . . Revision does not mean mere destruction. . . . Let us bury the natural body of tradition. What we want is its glorified body and its immortal soul. (Royce 11)

Whitehead once made a similar point: "Undoubtedly, philosophy is dominated by its past literature to a greater extent than any other science. And rightly so. But the claim that it has acquired a set of technical terms sufficient for its purposes, and exhaustive of its meanings, is entirely unfounded" (*AI* 229). But this gets us ahead of the story. Or better, it prematurely puts us behind it.

It will serve us well to get clear at the outset regarding what the problem is: How can experience arise out of, and act back upon, mechanical nonexperience? The two major contemporary responses to this question—dualism and mechanistic materialism—engage in thinking that is both wishful *and fearful*. I see this addition (and fearful) to be one of Griffin's most significant achievements in that both of these responses are often driven by fears that are frequently not acknowledged. One does sometimes hear dualists express their fear that life would not be meaningful if human beings were put on a material par with clocks or computers, but it is also instructive to note that mechanistic materialists are often fearful of a return to belief in supernaturalism and miracles if dualism is accepted. Hence, dualism is to be avoided at all costs, according to fearful materialists like Dennett (Dennett 37), even if Dennett is apparently oblivious of the fact that there are defenders of theistic metaphysics like Griffin who are also opponents to supernaturalism and miracles, as the title to one of his books makes clear: *Reenchantment without Supernaturalism* (see Griffin 2001). That is, Griffin's work in philosophy of mind is not unrelated to his overall Whiteheadian cosmology. By at least acknowledging the existence of wishful and fearful thinking in both forms, Griffin suggests, we might more easily work our way to a better solution to the problem.

Once again, some notable philosophers of mind like McGinn think that the mind-body problem is *permanently* unsolvable because of the persistent mystery regarding how mechanical, insentient neurons (assuming that there are such) can give rise to conscious experience in organisms. If McGinn is correct, it makes sense for Kim to claim that mechanistic materialism, in particular, is a "dead end" (also see Griffin 2000, chap. 6).

SOURCE OF THE PROBLEM

The root of the difficulty, if not of the solution, infamously goes back to Descartes and his enormous influence. Unlike most critics of Descartes, however, Griffin locates the problem not with Descartes' view of mind but rather with his view of mechanistic matter. This is another signal contribution from Griffin. Indeed, there are problems with Descartes' view of mind as constituted by a purely temporal inside with no spatiality, but even more problematic on Griffin's insightful reading are the issues concerning Descartes' view of matter as strictly outside, and hence devoid of internal relations, and purely spatial in the sense that it can be understood in an instant without temporal (and hence causal) relations (Griffin 1998, 46–49).

The problems unique to dualism are well known. It cannot account well, or even plausibly, for interaction between mind and body, and it violates the understandable assumption that there is continuity in nature. And the problems unique to mechanistic materialism are also well known, even if they are typically not proclaimed as loudly as those with dualism. Mechanistic materialists have a devil of a time explaining the unity of experience if it is composed of billions of insentient neurons, it typically either leaves consciousness out of consideration or treats it as an (emergent or supervenient) afterthought, and it contradicts what Griffin calls certain hardcore commonsense notions like belief in human freedom (Griffin 1998, 49–60). By the way, this is another one of Griffin's significant contributions: he distinguishes between certain "soft" commonsense notions, which apply only contingently in some circumstances but not others, and "hardcore" commonsense notions, whose denial is inevitably contradicted by our practice, such as belief in an external world, belief in human freedom (and hence responsibility), and belief in efficient causality from the past (Griffin 1998, 15–21).

Contemporary philosophers of mind tend to emphasize either the problems unique to dualism or those unique to mechanistic materialism. But from Griffin's radical panexperientialist standpoint, which lies outside the provenance of either dualism or mechanistic materialism, it is clear that there are some problems that are common to *both* dualism and mechanistic materialism. Among these are difficulties in determining where the line should be drawn between experiencing and nonexperiencing beings (a difficulty that is avoided in panexperientialism, as we will see), in accounting for consciousness in some fashion other than as the Great Exception in nature, and in explaining how experience could emerge out of machine-like nonexperience (Griffin 1998, 60–76).

All of these problems (those unique to dualism, those unique to mechanistic materialism, and those shared by dualism and mechanistic materialism) can be traced back to Descartes' views, especially to his view of machine-like matter. If mind is supposed to be pure temporality with no spatiality, and if matter is supposed to be pure spatiality with no internal duration and no experience of temporal passage, then the remarkable view of Whitehead embraced in a nuanced way by Griffin stands in stark opposition:

> The mutual structural relations between events are both spatial and temporal. If you think of them as merely spatial you are omitting the temporal element, and if you think of them as merely temporal you are omitting the spatial element. Thus when you think of space alone, or of time alone, you are dealing in abstractions, namely, you are leaving out an essential element in the *life* of nature as known to you in . . . experience. (*CN* 168—emphasis added)

It should be emphasized that there is one sort of emergentism that is acceptable to Griffin: the emergence of complex experiences out of the simple experiences of actual occasions or events or microscopic organisms. What is unintelligible is the emergence of an experiential "inside" out of nonexperiential bits of machinery governed strictly in terms of external relations. The latter sort of emergence would involve "sheer magic," as the panexperientialist geneticist Sewell Wright put it. Even the materialist J. J. C. Smart points out colloquially that no enzyme can catalyze the production of a spook (Griffin 1998, 63, 71). That is, the conscious experience that arises out of the primitive, preconscious, yet experiential organic reality of brain cells is, at least in principle, understandable. What is unintelligible is the idea that complex, conscious experiences arise out of completely insentient, nonexperiential mechanical constituents (IY 695). Once again, the root of the difficulty is to be found in Descartes' view of matter as vacuous actuality devoid of temporality, experience, and internal relatedness to the past.

The debate between dualism and mechanistic materialism is a family quarrel, on Griffin's view, in that the latter takes its meanings of both mind and matter from the former. Another way to put the point is to say that mechanistic materialism just *is* dualism in disguise. Once the dualistic ghost in the machine is exorcized by the materialist, what is left is the same mechanized nature that characterized almost all of reality on the dualist's own terms, the exceptions being the relatively infrequent "ghosts" in a predominantly mechanical world (Griffin 1998, 77–80).

We will see that Griffin's way out of these difficulties involves not only avoiding the view of matter as vacuous actuality (i.e., as devoid of any sort of internal becoming or experiential "mattering") but also avoiding the view that insentient aggregates of sentient constituents (e.g., rocks, telephones) are the most concrete realities. This view is an instance of the fallacy of *misplaced* concreteness if the *res verae* are concrete occasions of momentary experience (Griffin 1998, 117–124, 167). Another case of the fallacy of misplaced concreteness is found when high-level consciousness is seen as the primary, most "concrete" reality, when in point of fact such consciousness is rather rare and abstract in contrast to ubiquitous organic feeling of a more primitive sort. Both bottom-up (mechanistic materialism) and top-bottom (dualism) approaches to the mind-body problem ultimately lead to insoluble problems regarding the initially excluded reality. Panexperientialism promises a higher degree of integration of our knowledge than its alternatives, but not at the expense of explanatory adequacy.

The Cartesian view of matter (as well as the reductionist's view of matter) as vacuous actuality is, it should be noted, never *experienced* by us. Belief in matter of this sort is the result of high-level abstraction involving *concepts* like extension and mass. It is precisely this "pulpy" character of vacuous actuality that makes the emergence of experience out of it difficult, if not impossible, to understand.

BEING IS POWER

The thesis of the present chapter is that Griffin's unsnarling of the world knot is a highly original (indeed courageous) presentation of a very old view that goes back to Plato. At one point in his book Griffin acknowledges this in a reference to Plato (that unfortunately did not make it into the index of the book—see Griffin 1998, 230). The passage in question is from the *Sophist* (247e), where the Eleatic Stranger (presumably Plato) offers the following definition of being:

> I suggest that anything has real being that is so constituted as to possess any sort of power either to affect anything else or (*eite*) to be affected, in however small a degree, by the most insignificant agent, though it be only once. I am proposing as a mark to distinguish real things that they are nothing but power (*dynamis*).

Two terminological observations are needed. First, it is no accident that the Greek word for power (*dynamis*) is also the root of our word "dynamic," and it is precisely this identification of being with organic, dynamic power that makes Plato's later metaphysics so appealing to process thinkers like Whitehead (see, e.g., *AI* 5–6, 25, 83, 118–122, 129, 166–169, 179, 197; *MT* 119), Hartshorne (see Dombrowski 1991b), Griffin, and myself (see Dombrowski 2005, chap. 2). In these thinkers, dynamic power is the organic drive of the universe. Second, Plato's use of "or" (*eite*), however, would have to be changed to "and" (*kai*) in order to be congruent with Griffin's view. This is because the mind-body problem cannot be solved as long as it is assumed that there are some beings that can act on others but nonetheless remain completely unmoved by others, on the one hand, while there are other beings (vacuous actualities) that can supinely be acted upon by others but that exert no agency, on the other. On Griffin's view, the primary beings are actual occasions that have *both* the dynamic power to receive influence from the past *and* the dynamic power to creatively render determinate in the present what were once future determinables.

Mainstream philosophers of mind need to be reminded that Griffin's view is not panconsciousness, but panexperientialism. Consciousness, when seen as a type of specialized experience that involves a contrast between affirmation and negation and that emerges only in those beings with central nervous systems, involves not only a high level of experience but also of spontaneity. Even though experience and spontaneity are distributed throughout nature, consciousness is not. This point is worth emphasizing because of the alleged implausibility of Griffin's panexperientialism, an implausibility that would be quite understandable if panexperientialism were to be equated with panconsciousness.

I suspect that panexperientialism would have fewer critics if they realized that it is a view that is part of the effort to thoroughly naturalize the mind, to rid it of both supernaturalism and its anomalous status when it is interpreted by the Siamese twins joined at the hip: dualism and mechanistic materialism. That is, "naturalism" and "physicalism" are not synonyms for "materialism." Griffin's view is both naturalistic and physicalist. But it is not a type of "materialism" if this term refers to the Cartesian belief that matter consists in purely external relations with no internal relations or experience. That is, Griffin's view is not materialist if "matter" refers to vacuous actuality.

Further, panexperientialism is not only a type of naturalism; it is a type of monism in that on its basis there is only one sort of actuality: actual occasions with a physical pole, which has the dynamic power to receive influence from the past, and a mental pole, which has the dynamic power to bring about at least a partially novel advance into the future. Because experience, which at its highest level gives rise to consciousness, is not the Great Exception to everything else that is going on in nature, panexperientialism provides hope that the mind-body problem can be solved (Griffin 1998, 77–92).

Griffin starts from the realization that our experience is itself a part of nature. It is nature known from the inside (which does not commit Griffin to the dualistic implications often found in introspectionist psychology). Generalizing from this (experiential) nature that we know best, we can claim that experience is the very nature of nature. The feelings one has of what happened in one's past a second ago provide an analogy for what happens all the way down in nature. This view avoids the problems that are created in dualism and mechanistic material-ism when experience is, in effect, placed outside of nature. In a word, mechanistic materialism is halfhearted. Or again, Griffin agrees with dualists and mechanistic materialists that it is crucial that we observe nature, but he insightfully disagrees with them in claiming that the most direct way to observe nature is to observe it working in ourselves as experiencing beings (Griffin 1998, 124–132).

The Platonic view that Griffin defends is metaphysical or tran-scendental in the sense that he is offering an account of the univer-sal characteristics of *experiencing individuals* (which is something of a redundancy for panexperientialists). These characteristics would include *both* the dynamic power to feel causal influence from the past, to prehend the physical forces that impinge on an experiencing individ-ual, *and* the dynamic power to add something new, in however slight a way. Griffin speaks of a perpetual oscillation in that there is a dual-ity *within* each organic event wherein efficient causation from the past yields to a literal de-cision, a cutting off of some possibilities regarding the future, which then yields to efficient causation being exerted on future events, and so on *ad infinitum* (Griffin 1998, 151–162).

Because *each* event is subject for itself and an object for others, no event is simply a subject or simply an object, contra dualism and mech-anistic materialism. Reality is characterized by the power in subjects-that-become-objects. This stance is compatible with the view that every event has a physical aspect of receiving efficient causality from the past; hence, Griffin's position can be described as a type of "physicalism" even if it is not a type of "materialism" wherein there are vacuous actu-alities that are simply mechanical objects. Finally, this panexperien-tialist characterization of the real as constituted by dynamic centers of power applies to electrons, organelles, cells, simple animals, mammals, primates, and human beings, as the mental pole expands at each level, but never to the point where the physical pole vanishes (Griffin 1998, 194, 227–231).

The claim that being *is* power has clear theological implications. If there were an omnipotent being with *all* power, then such power would be exercised over absolutely nothing or over the absolutely powerless, neither of which makes any sense if any claim regarding what absolute nothingness *is*, is itself contradictory and if being *is* power, respectively. Hartshorne puts the point in an insightful way:

Whitehead does not "limit" the power of God as compared to some conceivably more powerful being; he merely points out that there is a social element in the very idea of power. . . . In Whitehead's terms every occasion is in some measure self-determining, and in some measure passive, receptive, toward the self-determinations of others. . . . Creativity is not a power, but just power. (Hartshorne 1972, 100)

In a sense, to be is to create, and belief in a so-called "inorganic" nature is the result of the very slight degree of creative power found there.

FROM PLATO TO DESCARTES AND FROM DESCARTES TO KANT

The question understandably arises: If Plato was close to a defensible position regarding the relationship between mind and body, what happened in the period between him and Descartes, and, by implication, between him and where we are today with the mind-body dead end? A short answer to this question would point to Plato himself as the culprit. To be sure, there is much in Plato's dialogues that is congenial to Griffin's panexperientialism, in addition to the preceding definition of being as dynamic power in the *Sophist* (see Dombrowski forthcoming). For example, there are passages in Plato's dialogues that hint at panexperientialism (*Phaedrus* 245E, *Laws* 896A, *Epinomis* 983D) in that psyche, defined in terms of self-motion, is required in order to understand the dynamism of the natural world. By contrast, there is also well-known evidence in Plato (and a great deal of it!) that supports the case for dualism. And it is this latter evidence that has been historically dominant, especially in terms of the efforts of St. Augustine and others to Christianize Plato or to Platonize Christianity. After all, the Cartesian dictum, often depicted as self-evident, that mind is unextended (in contrast to the more defensible view that experiences have *spatio*temporal relations) was Augustinian before it was Cartesian (see Hartshorne 2011, 68). In this regard Griffin is part of a tradition within process thought to uncover a lost, process Platonism, a tradition that includes Whitehead, Hartshorne, Leonard Eslick, and others (once again, see Dombrowski 1991b, 2005).

To be precise, Griffin's panexperientialism is prefigured in ancient philosophy in terms of a conjunction of three different concepts. Granted, no single ancient author put these three points together, but when they are configured by a contemporary scholar, one is able to see a strong resemblance to Griffin's panexperientialism: (1) Plato's discovery in the *Sophist* of the metaphysical concept that being *is* dynamic power, (2) his definition of psyche in the *Phaedrus* and *Laws* in terms of self-motion, a definition that is amplified, as we will see, by Aristotelian hylomorphism and *kinesis*, and (3) the Epicurean belief that ultimate reality is atomic in character. When these three concepts are put together, one derives a view wherein dynamic power and self-motion are seen to go "all the way down."

Because of Whitehead's frequent criticisms of the subject-predicate logic of Aristotle, based as it is on a metaphysics centered on the substance-accident distinction, some process thinkers have concluded that process metaphysics is completely removed from Aristotle and from those he influenced in medieval philosophy. But the situation here is just as complicated as it is regarding Plato (see Christian, chap. 5, regarding what is living and what is dead in Aristotle's concept of substance). For example, recently two very scholarly books have appeared, both written by Thomists heavily influenced not only by Aristotle but also by Whitehead (see Felt; Clarke). And both are somewhat favorably disposed toward Griffin's view. These process-enriched Thomists try to rescue Aristotle and Thomas from the charge that there is insufficient dynamism in metaphysics, with Whitehead providing the inspiration for their efforts. In the Aristotelian-Thomistic tradition, on their interpretation, matter is not the vacuous actuality it is in Descartes in that it is always in-formed. Or again, the whole point to Aristotelian-Thomistic hylomorphism is to suggest that matter without form and form without matter are the results of abstraction in that concrete reality is populated by "formbodies" or "mindbodies" or "soulbodies," to coin terms that try to capture the nondualistic character of hylomorphs. The Aristotelian idea that mind is, in a manner, all things is a protest against the view that mind is what is left over when one abstracts away from either behavior or matter; rather, matter in motion just *is* mind in some fashion (see Hartshorne 2011, 58).

Griffin's view is also "medieval" in the sense that Scholastic thinkers often distinguished (albeit inconsistently) between the categories, which were concepts that were applicable to all creatures but not to

God, and the transcendentals, which were concepts that were applicable to all beings including God. It is often noticed that among the transcendentals were oneness, goodness, truth, and beauty. In addition, there was *power*, the ability to influence others, and, in the process thinking exemplified by Griffin, the ability to be influenced. That is, one way to interpret what Griffin is doing is to say that the dynamic power to receive influence from others as well as the dynamic power to creatively advance beyond such influence (in that there are never sufficient causal conditions from the past to determine completely concrete actuality in the present, although there are necessary conditions of some sort) is a transcendental (see Hartshorne 2011, 113–119). The transition from mechanism to organism is facilitated by the realization that if power is a transcendental, so is *experience*. This is because each concrete singular in nature can both influence others and be *internally influenced* by others. This is precisely what Griffin means by the term "panexperientialism."

As before, it is Descartes and his legacy regarding matter that is Griffin's adversary, not premodern philosophy, whether ancient or medieval. Whitehead, it will be remembered, thought of his philosophy as a recurrence to pre-Kantian modes of thought (*PR* xi). In this regard, it is instructive to remember that no less an authority than Ivor Leclerc thought of Whitehead as a dynamic hylomorphist (Leclerc, chap. 21). My point here is to highlight the long tradition in philosophy that Griffin is not only revitalizing but advancing after a three-century slowdown due to Descartes' influential view of matter as vacuous actuality. As Whitehead once said, and as I think Griffin should affirm, "nothing in thought is ever completely new" (*CN* 26). Griffin is not being denigrated, nor is Whitehead, when they are seen as important footnotes to Plato (*PR* 39).

Although Griffin mentions only briefly the premodern roots of his panexperientialism (also see Griffin 2000, chap. 5), he pays careful attention to certain developments in modern philosophy that indicate the pushback that has occurred (or that could occur) with respect to the Cartesian view of matter and its effect on dominant modern and contemporary views of mind. For obvious reasons due to Gottfried Leibniz's own panpsychism, especially in *Monadology*, Griffin notes the importance of this great thinker, but Leclerc also alerts us to Leibniz's similarity to Aristotle. Newton insisted that an active principle had to be operative *in* nature, and not *ex machina* as in Descartes. But

Leibniz thought that Newton did, in fact, unwittingly fall victim to use of the *ex machina* device. Leibniz's defense of something fundamentally active in nature was seen by him as a return to the Greeks, specifically to Aristotle's idea that physical existents were characterized by *kinesis* and *dynamis*. On Leclerc's interpretation, which adds historical depth to Griffin's view, both Leibniz *and* Whitehead signal a revitalization of the Aristotelian doctrine of internal change and power in matter and a denigration of the Cartesian denial of internal change and power in matter, a denial, as Griffin notes, that has largely persisted to the present day (once again, see Leclerc, chap. 21). As Hartshorne puts the point, "If upon the wreckage of Newtonian materialism a new world view is to arise, then Whitehead's system is the most important single indication of what that world view is to be" (Hartshorne 1972, 39).

It is customary to emphasize the fact that Hume awoke Immanuel Kant from his dogmatic rationalist slumbers that were induced by Leibniz, Christian Wolff, and others. To view things exclusively in this way, however, is to fail to consider the possibility that the Leibnizean view may be more compatible with contemporary science than other modern views, including Kant's. Consider the idea that the usual classification of natural things as "inanimate" derives from a neglect of microscopic activity, as in the kinetic theory of heat or the view that even rocks are in motion in their microscopic parts (see Hartshorne 2011, 60). That is, scholars tend not to accentuate the degree to which Leibniz's panpsychism had an influence on Kant. As a result, there is a perhaps understandable tendency to read Kant's phenomena-noumena distinction as being almost exclusively under the influence of Descartes.

It is one of Griffin's signal achievements that he makes a convincing case for the claim that Kant in his *Dreams of a Spirit-Seer* came closer to panexperientialism than most scholars realize, specifically in his discussion of what will later be called noumenal things-in-themselves in contrast to the phenomenal world as it appears to us. In this early work Kant seems to think that *either* we should remain agnostic regarding things-in-themselves *or* we should agree with Leibniz that they are instances of psyche. As is well known, Kant eventually opted for the former alternative, but the prominent place given the latter alternative by Kant should not escape our notice, especially because it has not received the attention it deserves and hence may have unanticipated strengths. Kant appears to rebuke those who ridicule Leibniz's panpsychism because *if* we had to state what physical reality is in itself, we would have to follow Leibniz (see Kant, part 1, chap. 1; also Hartshorne 1972, 158–159, 206).

Consider the following: in *some* sense we know ourselves from the inside and other beings from the outside. What are the latter like in themselves? Because we have *some* knowledge from the inside, in that we are intimately aware of our own experiences, one wonders if others have insides as well. We need not assume that our purely spatial and external awareness of these objects exhausts what they are in themselves. Indeed, it would seem extravagant to make such an assumption. What it would be like to have no inside at all, what it would be like to be a vacuous actuality, is beyond our ken, as Griffin holds and as Kant indirectly intimates (Griffin 1998, 84, 98–103; also see Wilson). It is consistent with Griffin's view to emphasize that Kant refused to identify things-in-themselves with lifeless matter and left open the possibility that they were instances of experience (see Hartshorne 2011, 55; also see the remarkable work by Malone-France 2007).

We should be clear that when we experience green in a grove of trees, our immediate sources for this experience are events that take place in living cells in our eyes and in the brain. Some quality is abstracted from these events and transformed into what we experience as greenness; Whitehead speaks of "transmutation" (*PR* 27). This process of transforming many received data into one patch of experienced greenness is a mental operation that cannot be supposed to be enjoyed by cells in the optic nerve or in the brain in *exactly* the same way that it is found in human experience, but on the panexperientialist view there must be some quality *analogous* to greenness that the cells experience. Or again, if one has a toothache and if the transmission of the agitation from the cells in one's tooth to the brain is interrupted by an anesthetic, the cells may continue to have the same feelings as before, even if they are not transmuted into human experience (see Cobb 2007, 8, 149).

Because a single, unitary experience of a human being is molded out of many stimuli (evidence from the five senses, thousands of influences from the past relayed via memory, billions of experiences exerting their influence via brain cells), mechanical or automatic predictability is not likely. That is, prediction is limited not merely by our ignorance but is rather due to the creative synthesis that is experience itself. Those who might come to appreciate Griffin's panexperientialism may very well be like the character in Molière who did not realize that he had been speaking prose all his life (Hartshorne 1970, 4–6).

Of course, there are many other insightful thinkers who have defended panexperientialism or positions that have a family resemblance to it. David Skrbina details many (Skrbina), who would perhaps include Charles Peirce and other classical American pragmatists (also see Henning, chap. 1) and several of the German romantics. Time does not permit me to treat all of them, an effort that would duplicate Skrbina's book. But the last chapter of the present work does treat one of the English romantic poets who, through S. T. Coleridge, borrowed freely from the German romantics. The central point here is to locate Griffin within an overall tradition that is quite old, a tradition that is continued in various ways in contemporary analytic philosophy through thinkers such as David Chalmers, Nagel, Seager, Strawson, and others.

That is, I am well aware of the fact that my thesis that mechanistic philosophy of nature has reigned supreme since the seventeenth century requires several important qualifications, given numerous minority organicist voices. Even Kant, whose first critique embodies modern, mechanistic determinism, moves in his second and especially third critiques toward organism, teleology, and a romantic view of the world as beautiful/sublime.

ANTICIPATING THE FUTURE

Because panexperientialism and positions that have a family resemblance to it have been around since the time of Plato, it is unlikely that they will go away soon. Indeed, in part because of Griffin, it is not hyperbolic to suggest that not only will they continue to hang around, they will be positions that will likely be taken more seriously in scholarly circles than they have for quite some time. That is, having sketched the place of Griffin's panexperientialism in its historical setting, I would now like to indicate what its influence could be in the future. It makes sense in this context to gather together what I take to be his signal contributions to an understanding of the MTO transition and to suggest how they might collectively make a difference.

What is most important about Griffin's book is that he takes the case for panexperientialism directly to those analytic philosophers of mind who claim to be the intellectually respectable custodians for the mind-body problem. To cite just one example of a major figure in process thought who does *not* do this, consider Stengers' influential work

Thinking with Whitehead, where the author largely ignores panpsychism and is ambivalent toward it when the topic is discussed (Stengers 2011, 202). Stengers joins Whitehead in opposition to the bifurcation of nature (indeed, we have seen that Whitehead refers to the bifurcation of nature as vicious!—*CN* 187), but it is not clear what this means in the absence of a defense of panexperientialism or panpsychism or some cognate position. And Stengers seems to be completely indifferent to process thought as a version of *philosophia perennis*. As before, the first two chapters of the present book can be read together as an attempt to show how (Griffin) and how not (Stengers) to articulate the MTO transition.

Of course, Griffin will be accused of violating (soft) common sense. But when Griffin takes the case for panexperientialism directly to analytic philosophers of mind, he addresses both the concerns *and fears* of both dualists and mechanistic materialists; hence, it is difficult to claim that he does not "save the phenomena." He is intent to have his theory accomplish all of the good things accomplished by these two alternatives (e.g., dualism's attempt to save consciousness and mechanistic materialism's attempt to avoid the supernaturalism found in many dualists), which serves to make his view appealing, at least in theory, to former defenders of each of these two positions. The way forward is facilitated by Griffin's emphasis not only on Descartes as the source of our contemporary problem but on Descartes' view of matter, in particular. This is an especially insightful move on Griffin's part. One of the problems with *both* dualism and mechanistic materialism is that they do not assuage their opponents' fears (e.g., many dualists often fail to avoid the charge of supernaturalism, and mechanistic materialists typically fail to adequately save consciousness). Once again, explaining how complex types of experience emerge out of primitive types of experience is very different from, and is enormously easier than, explaining how experience of any sort emerges out of vacuous nonexperience.

By viewing the differences between dualism and mechanistic materialism as a family quarrel, Griffin is able to point toward the conclusion that in both positions matter is viewed as vacuous actuality. Further, in both positions mind is viewed as the Great Exception: in dualism as a Great Exception that is real and in mechanistic materialism as an illusory Great Exception. Along with Whitehead and Hartshorne, Griffin struggles mightily to disavow panexperientialism's critics of one of their favorite charges: that rocks and trees and automobiles are clearly not sentient; hence, panexperientialism or panpsychism is false. Griffin agrees that rocks and trees and automobiles are insentient, but they are insentient *as wholes*. Only some wholes bring together the experiences of the parts into experience as an integral individual. In fact, it is most notably animals, including human animals, with central nervous systems that do so. (However, some theists, including Griffin and Plato, see the natural world as a whole as *animated* by a divine World Soul—see Dombrowski 2006b.) Other wholes—like insentient rocks and trees and automobiles—are mere aggregates, even if there is experience in their subatomic or cellular parts.

The future success of Griffin's view depends in part on the degree to which scholars will be persuaded by his mereology (the theory of the relations between parts and wholes). In this regard it should be noted that he is more than willing to admit that much of reality consists of aggregational wholes that do not experience; hence, in this sense he saves the phenomena. The future success of his view also depends on the degree to which scholars are convinced that "panpsychism" is to be understood in panexperientialist rather than panconsciousness terms. That is, by appropriately managing the expectations of the critics, Griffin's defender is more likely to receive friendly response. The same could be said regarding Griffin's defense of hardcore commonsense, which involves the insistence that hardcore commonsense beliefs cannot rationally be rejected because their denial is inevitably contradicted by our practice. All of this is compatible with the view that primary beings are actual occasions that are both passive and active, as intimated long ago by Plato.

One of the obstacles faced by Griffin and his defenders is the fact that there is no uniformity in the terminology used in philosophy of mind. For example, although Griffin is a naturalist and a physicalist, he is not a materialist (because he uses the term "matter" to refer to what he sees as the mistaken Cartesian view of matter as vacuous actuality). However, Strawson, who holds a view similar to Griffin's, refers to panexperientialism or panpsychism as *real* materialism. It comes as a surprise to some people to learn that Griffin's panexperientialism is a type of naturalism in the sense that experience for Griffin is thoroughly natural and is at odds with supernaturalism. Likewise, with respect to the claim that Griffin is a sort of monist in that there is only one sort of reality, albeit exhibited at vastly different levels of experience, which goes all the way down. Experience is not the Great Exception.

Griffin's view might become more appealing to scholars as the lure of determinism fades due to various factors undermining it, including factors that are the result of the efforts of scientists themselves, who in the Newtonian era were its champions. It is not as difficult as it once was to advance the Platonic claim that reality is characterized by *both* the dynamic power to feel causal influence from the past *and* the dynamic power to add something new, in however slight a way. The fact that Kant came closer to this panexperientialist view than most think is one of Griffin's significant accomplishments in that the legacy of Kant is still enormous, and situating panexperientialism in a Kantian context might allow some thinkers to consider its strengths who might not otherwise do so.

I assume that in the future a theory's strength will still depend in part on its relevance to *all* the data and that the range of application of theories dealing with the mind-body problem will have to include the data of consciousness, including, ironically enough, the Cartesian *cogito*, properly understood in nondualist terms. We have seen that Griffin is well positioned in this regard when it is considered that the only way to avoid the problem of consciousness as the Great Exception is to rethink *everything*. This is what Griffin does, with the "re" part of "rethink" pointing us toward Plato, Leibniz, and even Whitehead's contemporary Arthur Eddington, whose version of panpsychism has had a large impact on Strawson. One can fruitfully wonder with Griffin about the cogency of certain standard views in philosophy of mind that suggest that experience (including conscious experience) emerges into existence over time when time itself *depends on* experience, as in the experience of "now," of nostalgia, of hope. As Whitehead insightfully put the point, "what we perceive as present is the vivid fringe of memory tinged with anticipation" (*CN* 73).

Griffin will also be helpful in the future in the effort to distinguish panexperientialism from Berkeleyan idealism: Panexperientialism holds that to be is to experience as well as to be experienced. George Berkeley's cutting off of experience at the human level is a type of anthropocentrism that should be increasingly suspect, given the environmental crisis we face and given the ever-strengthening case for non-human (at the very least, animal) experience. We have nothing to lose but the mind-body problem (to put a gloss on Karl Marx) if we *start* with experience and then explore the extent to which what we really know about matter (that it is capable of experience) can be expanded.

Our experiences are the privileged examples of reality (see Hartshorne 2011, 61, 76).

There are two points that I would especially like to emphasize regarding the future.

First, from a phenomenological point of view, everyone can attest to the experience of *localized pleasure and pain*, which offers strong support for the idea that experience occurs at least as far "down" as cells. Although this phenomenological evidence does not exactly prove panexperientialism, it does ably counteract the still-popular claim that panexperientialism is implausible. The hope is that even intuitions regarding implausibility will change over time once the most egregious caricatures of panexperientialism are removed: for example, that telephones and rocks are believed by panexperientialists like Griffin to experience or even to be conscious! As Griffin argues, one pays a very stiff price for failing to distinguish adequately between mere aggregates and compound experiencing individuals.

This phenomenological evidence indicates, at the very least, that experiences of a subhuman kind (cells or smaller) are real. It is not only *we* who suffer but also the microscopic living members of our bodies. "Our sensations are sympathetic participations in their feelings" (Hartshorne 2011, 3). Griffin's case for panexperientialism is more likely to be persuasive when we focus on a mode of perception other than vision, which tends to play into the hands of modern dualists or mechanistic materialists by giving us a static and apparently value-neutral concept of nature. By contrast, if we take as the quintessential example of direct perception a throb of localized pain or pleasure in an organism, we come to know that something is happening *in* the body that is not value-neutral. From this latter organic starting point it is much easier to consider the merits of the claim that there is no inanimate matter, if this means inactive matter. A panexperientialist defends the stance that in a material being's microscopic parts there is self-motion in response to influence. Cells in particular resemble us in having feelings (Hartshorne 2011, 4, 13).

It is true that we cannot quite discern the microindividual cells that constitute our bodies, but this should not conceal the fact that in vague outline we can demarcate localized feeling. In addition, it should not escape our notice that cells can in some vague way prehend us in that psychosomatic illness would be practically inexplicable on any other basis (see Ford). Experience occurs on both sides in that when we have experiences of purple or pain, the quality belongs *both* to the experience and to the experienced, otherwise we would not be able to explain the difference between these experiences and those of yellow or pleasure. The datum of pain experience is in the body, initially in cells and then in human experience or mind. "Hurt my cells and you hurt me" (Hartshorne 2011, 39, also 16, 38). A true solipsist would be someone who, if such were possible, never experienced localized pleasure or pain in that localized pleasure and pain signal feeling *of* feeling of a microscopic sort.

Griffin's view is captured well in Hartshorne's claim that the prosaic or apathetic fallacy is just as misleading as the pathetic one. Granted, we should not attribute pathos to entities that cannot feel (e.g., aggregates of sentient individuals or abstractions like threeness). But we should also avoid failure to appreciate microscopic sentiency when it is, in fact, present. Both primitive animism and seventeenth-century-inspired mechanism should be avoided in an accurate description of our own experiences and in our description of nature in general. And an accurate description of nature will involve not only theories in physics but also those in biology and psychology. None of us simply decides what our cells will do. Rather, because they are not entirely mindless or insentient, they make their own decisions, in however slight a way. Not only are cells within a body alive, they are alive *as animals* and possessive of a rudimentary spontaneity (Hartshorne 2011, 40–41, 75, 100, 140).

It will no doubt be objected that Griffin's theory might work as far "down" as cells, but it does not work when trying to explain inorganic nature. But if the bodily conditions of our feelings of "inorganic" nature are themselves feelings, then panexperientialism cannot be rejected as easily as these objectors suppose. If we learn about nature largely through sight, hearing, and touch receptors, and if these receptors genuinely relate us to things outside of the body, the relata cannot be entirely dissimilar. If sensation is human feeling of subhuman feeling, and if no feeling is solipsistic, then there is no radical difference in kind between cellular feeling and the self-movement in response to causal influence found in atoms. There is indeed "insentient matter," but this refers to a complex or aggregate whose constituents are primitive forms of sentience. As before, tables as unities are in fact insentient, but over a long stretch of time, the changes that are constantly occurring *in* the table will clearly manifest themselves. For example, the wooden boat exhibited at the museum at Giza in Egypt, allegedly the oldest in the world, is now hardly recognizable as a boat.

To say in seventeenth-century fashion that matter is *absolutely* insentient is to proceed as if cell theory and subatomic physics had not occurred. It is not hyperbolic to claim that we now know that nature is everywhere active. It is true that many materialists might try to conceptually sever the connection between activity and sentience by admitting that there is activity throughout nature, but there is zero sentience and zero novelty below a certain level. However, this distinction leaves the ubiquitous activity in nature unexplained. Panexperientialism provides such an explanation in terms of protean self-motion such that the slight level of novelty found in atoms should not be confused with the complete absence of such activity (see Hartshorne 2011, 14–15, 17, 51, 62, 129–130).

As before, our physical feelings of our own past just a moment ago provide a powerful analogy for what happens all the way down in nature. What is *really* implausible is either the placing of experience outside of nature (as in dualism) or the resting content with an explanatory scheme that leaves experience, especially conscious experience, unexplained (as in mechanistic materialism). If even our bodily cells are prehenders with inner durations and experiences of qualia, and if all the information we have about nature is mediated through them, then it can be said that understanding rests on our experiences *of* experiences at the microscopic level. To put the point in Platonic terms that Plato himself would never have used, human experience is re-collection of what is "collected" at the cellular level.

This takes us close to Griffin's panexperientialism. Once we are in the neighborhood of panexperientialism, there is no need to criticize physics, as long as one realizes that it deals with abstractions and needs to be supplemented by an "inner physics" (as emphasized by Strawson) analogous to the "inner biology" with which we are all familiar via localized pleasure and pain. Granted, our localized pleasure and pain is still *somewhat* abstract in that we cannot identify the specific microindividual cells that are harmed by intense heat, for example (see Plato's *Republic* 462c–d, regarding *neura* or "nerves"), but we do experience very small regions of cellular individuals and vicariously participate, via our central nervous systems, in their experiences.

In short, what we need is an enlarged conception of matter. Griffin will continue to help us figure out how to develop this concept.

It should be emphasized, however, that on the basis of this enlarged concept of matter we can still say that the physical has priority over the mental in the sense that even on a panexperientialist basis the mental pole in each actual occasion is derivative of the physical pole, but the physical pole involves powerful (Platonic) energy to be affected by others. To receive influence is oxymoronically a type of activity, as in working hard to hear the counterpoint in a difficult symphony or as in deliberately laboring to listen to what someone else is saying. *Purely* physical entities, on this view, are aggregates of active singulars. The robust character of the physical in panexperientialism, however, is expressed well by Whitehead when he says that "my theory . . . is ready to accept any outcome of physical research" (*CN* 160).

Second, it is still unclear if the resurgence of panpsychism in philosophy of mind will lead to long-term productive conversation between process thinkers like Griffin and *mainstream analytic philosophers.* It is clear that the "explanatory gap" between first- and third-person accounts of consciousness derives from at least somewhat inaccessible experiential "properties" (with the scare quotes to be explained momentarily), which are at least somewhat analogous to the self-motions of Platonic souls. Panexperientialism is the view that these properties are everywhere. Because they are everywhere, panexperientialism is capable in ways that dualism and mechanistic materialism are not of understanding experience as an evolutionary process. That is, Griffin's view is well equipped to bridge the gap between functional or causal theories of mind, on the one hand, and subjective accounts of experience (including conscious experience), on the other, in a way that dovetails well with evolutionary theory. Sequestering experience from the rest of nature prevents such a dovetailing, as Nathaniel Barrett notices in his insightful treatment of process panpsychism (or panexperientialism), which will inform much of what I have to say in the next several paragraphs (see Barrett; also see several excellent articles on Whitehead and analytic philosophy: Desmet and Rusu; Riffert; McHenry and Holmgren; and Shields).

Unfortunately, the resurgence of panpsychism in analytic philosophy of mind usually rests on tacit metaphysical assumptions that are at odds with those explicitly operative in process philosophy (including process Platonism), as Barrett notices. In analytic versions of panpsychism, the mind-body problem is typically framed in terms of *properties.* These may be phenomenal, physical, or functional. Further, these properties are seen to have various kinds of relationship to each other: identity, emergence, supervenience, or reductionist. The explanatory gap mentioned earlier involves a seemingly irreconcilable difference between phenomenal properties and the rest. Griffin's view is that these phenomenal "properties" (variously described as "what it is like to be an X," or as qualia) are ubiquitous in nature; hence, in one sense there is no gap to be bridged.

In Griffin's thought, however, feelings or experiences are not so much properties as they are the perspectives of momentary actual occasions. Feeling or experience is understood by Griffin within a framework that unfortunately tends to be ignored in analytic versions of panpsychism. Therefore, Barrett is astute to notice two different explanatory gaps: between process panexperientialism and analytic panpsychism and between first-person phenomenal and third-person accounts. Here we can see what could in the future be Griffin's major contribution to analytic panpsychism. When a "what it is like" feeling is *reified* into a special property, the particular perspective of an occasion of experience is in danger of being lost. Or again, if experience is viewed as a special property of the abstract entity "consciousness," what is lost is the distinctive dynamic perspective of a particular organic occasion. For example, notice the difference between focusing on the distinctiveness of categorical identity (e.g., what distinguishes red from green) and focusing on particular identity (e.g., what distinguishes lime green from forest green). One can imagine processes of extensive abstraction up to greater and greater levels of abstraction (as in Plato's isolation of the five most general forms in the *Sophist* 250a–259e: existence, motion, rest, sameness, otherness) and down to greater and greater levels of concreteness. The danger is that differences in perspective and uniqueness of perspective would become reified under the special property of "experience" or "consciousness."

Experience is not so much a property that is added to physical processes (a view that Whitehead called the theory of psychic additions and that Hartshorne called the annex theory of value—see *CN* 29; Hartshorne 1934, 94; 1970, chap. 15; Dombrowski 2004a, chap. 5), but it is the very (Platonic) dynamic power of what exists both to assimilate its causal influences and to exert itself in response to them. Granted, it makes sense to distinguish between what it is like to be "in here" and what it is like to be "out there" as long as one realizes that these are selective abstractions from a single stream and as long as one does not assume that the latter is more real than the former, as Barrett emphasizes. By contrast, for example, Nagel seems to think that the shift from subjectivity to objectivity is a transition from one type of property to another, rather than the passage in a concrescing actual occasion from the clutch of vivid immediacy in the present to its superjective influence on later actual occasions.

Griffin, along with Whitehead, also rejects the theory of psychic additions because there are no merely negative relations in nature in that every event that is, is only *partially* other than any other event that is. It makes no sense to say that mind is *completely* different from matter. That is, exclusion is as positive a relation as inclusion such that the two relations—exclusion and inclusion—are both positive contraries of each other (*CN* 186–187). We have seen that Plato intimated this, once again in the *Sophist* (258e–259b), in the idea that relative nonbeing or otherness, in contrast to alleged absolute nonbeing, should be seen as a type of existence (see Eslick).

"For process panpsychism, perspectivity is principally a matter of the particularity that belongs to the subjective experience of all actual entities" (Barrett 197). Respect for this particularity, however, need not involve an assertion of *absolute* uniqueness because, as Plato discovered in the *Parmenides* (137a–138e), to say that a one *is* absolute is nonetheless to put it in relation with other ones (dynamic centers of power) that *are*. Such a relation militates against absolute unity or absolute uniqueness. Nonetheless even "nonliving" things have *some* subjective reserves of particularity. We do not convert from one "property" to the next when we start talking about a physical object; rather, we just disregard the perspectival particularity found in the object. It is to Griffin's credit that he returns to the following theme often: To say that scientific descriptions are highly abstract is not to say that they are inaccurate, only that they tend to leave much that is real (in terms of dynamic power) out of the picture.

There are untapped possibilities within Griffin's view for bridging phenomenal, functional, even neurological descriptions. Because feelings always involve "something more," functional or reductionist descriptions all by themselves are especially incomplete. As Barrett emphasizes, in terms that seem to apply especially well in the case of Griffin's efforts to unsnarl the world knot, "process panpsychism indicates a way forward by understanding the 'something more' of conscious feeling in terms of perspectivity rather than special properties"

(Barrett 200). Experience, including conscious experience, develops *over time* in ways that reified properties do not. The explanation of such experience will in the future require an up-to-date version of Plato's view of the one and the many wherein a high degree of both integrity and diversity of participating neural populations are explicated, both philosophically and scientifically (see Edelman and Tononi).

Barrett captures well both the spirit of Griffin's panexperientialism and the contribution it could make to the perennial project initiated by Plato to understand the proper relationship between "the mental" and "the physical":

> Process panpsychism makes progress on the explanatory gap between functional and phenomenal accounts of consciousness because it registers not just the fact of qualitative experience per se, but the crucial additional fact that the qualitatively rich experience of consciousness is constantly changing. This dynamism arises from the particularity of conscious feeling, in both its clear and distinct aspects and its vast reserves of vagueness and triviality. In contrast, property panpsychism, like the analytic framework from which it is derived, deals only in static properties whose particularity is of no consequence. (Barrett 204)

A recent issue of *Journal of Consciousness Studies* devoted entirely to Strawson's panpsychist view indicates that, although Griffin's panexperientialism has exerted some influence on analytic philosophers interested in the topic, there is still considerable room (and, it is to be hoped, time) to get things right by adding yet a few more footnotes to Plato.

HISTORICAL THINKING

Griffin's panexperientialism belies the famous (or infamous) quip allegedly made by W. V. O. Quine that there are two quite different reasons why people enter philosophy: to do philosophy or to do mere history of philosophy. It has been the purpose of the present chapter to argue that regarding Griffin's panexperientialism, these two are not mutually exclusive. That is, thinking about the mind-body problem *is* historical thinking via Plato and Descartes, whether or not philosophers of mind realize it. To admit this much, however, is not necessarily to commit to the intellectually conservative claim that we stand on the shoulders of giants (like Plato) in that it is equally true to say that we stand in their (e.g., Descartes') dark shadow (cf. Mash). Once again, to be is to exhibit *both* the dynamic power to prehend causal influence from the past *and* the dynamic power to unsnarl knots.

It should be noted that what it means to be a process thinker in the wake of Griffin is to say not only that the reality of events is *successive* but also *cumulative*. Through prehension of causal influence, the present, in a way, includes the past; hence, we should be suspicious of thinkers who largely dispense with philosophers from previous centuries. Intellectual history is one of the principal sources for contemporary wisdom, including wisdom regarding what has come to be called "the mind-body problem." Or again, to be a process thinker in the wake of Griffin is to hold that becoming is both *cumulative* and *creative* in that the new at any moment is not already "in the cards" or entailed by previous events or conditions. Nonetheless, the cumulative character of process means that these conditions are in some sense contained in the new. In Hartshornian terms congenial to Griffin's project, each instance of becoming is a creative synthesis.

David Ray Griffin is to be thanked for alerting us to the fact that it is a new ballgame in philosophy of mind in that panexperientialism is now a reputable player. Understanding this fact, however, is extremely difficult without an awareness of earlier games and earlier players. Process thinkers, it should be noted, have defended this view throughout the twentieth century. That is, Griffin has shown that panexperientialism will not go away simply because it has been largely ignored for a mere three hundred years. To paraphrase Emerson for my own purposes, when the half-gods of dualism and mechanistic materialism depart, the gods of panexperientialism can arrive (see Hartshorne 2011, 23–24, 71, 101, 115).

TWO

Stengers on Whitehead on God

AGAINST CLASSICAL THEISM

One of the most significant developments in process thought over the past generation has been the surge of interest in Whitehead in Europe. Perhaps the most important work to come out of this surge has been the 2002 publication of Isabelle Stengers' *Penser avec Whitehead: Une libre et sauvage creation de concepts*. The significance of this book is evidenced by its translation into English in 2011 through Harvard University Press, titled *Thinking with Whitehead: A Free and Wild Creation of Concepts*. The purpose of the present chapter is to examine one part of Stengers' sprawling work: her treatment of Whitehead's concept of God. However, this is a significant part of her overall goal, which is to champion Whitehead's process philosophy, but without his theistic cosmology. My hope is to encourage a greater degree of engagement between neoclassical or process theists, on the one hand, and Stengers and those she has influenced, on the other. It will become clear how this chapter contributes in a significant way to the two themes of the present book—MTO and FTP—and prepares the way for my major treatment of FTP in the following chapters.

Speaking both for herself and for Whitehead (see *SM* 192), Stengers emphasizes the fact that classical theism can lead to barbarism; hence, whatever function God performs in Whitehead has to escape the despotic character of God in classical theism. The Christian version of classical theism, in particular, has caused great suffering, she thinks. In a memorable phrase she suggests insightfully that its (classical theism's) victims haunt the interstices of its ideals. One can agree with Stengers here without agreeing with her concomitant view that, by contrast, philosophers have not caused great suffering (Stengers 2011, 135, 225, 286, 334). One can easily imagine an account of Martin Heidegger's influence, for example, that would support the opposite view.

Stengers is correct to direct our attention to Leibniz, the classical theist who most influenced Whitehead. That is, Whitehead's criticisms of classical theism were not directed at a straw man. Even when the best versions of classical theism were on the table for discussion, Whitehead was willing to claim that Christian theology in its classical theistic formulation was one of the great disasters of the human race (see *DW* 143–145), as Stengers emphasizes. At one point Stengers leaves open the possibility that belief in divine omnipotence and divine monopoly of coercive power were the major causes of this disaster. This is because such beliefs cause the nastiest version of the theodicy problem, in that an omnipotent being could always eliminate evil, as we have seen. It is also because belief in divine omnipotence creates the intellectual atmosphere within which, even in an otherwise admirable character like St. Francis of Assisi, there is the belief that God will eternally punish people for their transgressions. But we will see that at other points Stengers contradicts this judgment by locating the disaster elsewhere, as in belief in divine omniscience or omnibenevolence (Stengers 2011, 314, 390, 451–454).

In any event, it makes sense for Stengers to suggest that Whitehead enters precisely at that point where classical theism has been disastrous. The problem regarding how a strictly permanent, unmoved mover could be altered by creaturely change and suffering is the central stumbling block in classical theism, a stumbling block that is often euphemistically described as a mystery. Inability to clear this stumbling block is a result of the failure to come to grips with the "barbarous brutality" of classical theism itself, which is also frequently criticized by Whitehead in the strongest terms. The classical theist, she thinks, will never be able to respond adequately to Job's lament in that, on a classical theistic basis, our cries may rise to the heavens, but no real re-sponse is possible on the part of the classical theistic, eternal, omnipotent God. Only an atemporal "inde-sponse" is possible (Stengers 2011, 378, 396, 479).

AGAINST THEISM

Unfortunately, Stengers' legitimate criticisms of classical theism, which are generally shared by neoclassical or process theists, culminate in an "excess of subjectivity" (one of her favorite phrases from White-head), wherein she criticizes not only classical theism but theism itself. Stengers (along with Bruno Latour) thinks it a "misfortune" that White-head has generated so much interest among theologians and philoso-phers of religion (although she does not distinguish these two). This is a misfortune, in part, because of the alleged paucity of attention paid to Whitehead's philosophy of science. (A brief perusal of past issues of the journals *Process Studies* and *Process Studies Supplements* would contradict Stengers' claim regarding the lack of attention paid to White-head's views on science.) In larger part it is due, Stengers thinks, to "what every serious philosopher knows today: it is illusory to deal in a positive way with the truth of God." To be frank, I think that the use of the word "every" here runs the risk of dogmatism and the use of "serious" could strike some careful readers as condescending (Stengers 2011, ix, 8).

Her overall view is that the speculative construction of God (as allegedly found in Whitehead) does not imply the existence of God. Indeed, such a construction is part of the general tendency toward demystification in philosophy. That is, there is nothing mysterious regarding ultimate reality. In response to Stengers on this point, I am tempted to ask: Nothing whatsoever? In a sense, it seems that Stengers buys into a strict Weberian disenchantment of the world without con-sidering attempts, such as Griffin's, to reenchant it on a Whiteheadian basis (see Griffin 2001). For Stengers, the question of whether God really exists is a crucial one *only if* one is concerned with the coercive force of the classical theistic God who demands and forbids and who has omnipotent political power. We are not told by Stengers why this question is not also a crucial one for neoclassical, process theists who deny that God is omnipotent. This is odd because many neoclassical, process (especially Hartshornian) theists *are* very much interested in this question (see, e.g., Hartshorne 1965a; Dombrowski 2006b; Sia; Viney). Further, Stengers does not give reasons for her claim that the previous question has no validity outside of a religious practice. This claim is also odd because neither Whitehead nor Hartshorne nor many other neoclassical, process theists are committed to religious practice as found, say, in some particular religious denomination. This is not surprising for philosophers. Or again, we are not told why the question of God (and of religion, in general) must be linked to the phenomenon of conversion if some religious believers have always just found themselves believing without dramatic *metanoia* or histrionic conversion experiences (Stengers 2011, 17–18, 36, 134, 282).

Although Stengers is in a way correct to emphasize the idea that "God" is a name for the efficacy religious vision has for human beings, there is quite a long jump from this claim to the conclusion that God is dead. The death of God is a fact (in fact, an irreversible fact) for Stengers. It is an unquestioned assumption concerning which any hesitation constitutes intellectual regression. This Nietzschean philosophizing with a hammer on Stengers' part is justified by her in terms of Whitehead's own "cavalier" approach to philosophy. Stengers thinks of herself as being made in Whitehead's cavalier image. Stengers offers no response to those who might see quite a difference between Friedrich Nietzsche's destructive hammer philosophy and Whitehead's efforts at tentative and fallibilist system building (Stengers 2011, 134, 255, 291–292, 498).

Another problem with Stengers' attack on theism is that it seems to be opposed to her endorsement of a Jamesian defense of an expanded empiricism that moves beyond the attenuated version of empiricism developed by the British "empiricists," with their bifurcated view of nature. Stengers is astute to see William James and especially Whitehead as opponents to the bifurcation of nature and its attendant mechanism. But she is not willing to concede that the expanded empiricism that she praises would have to include widespread claims (both across historical epochs and across cultural boundaries) to religious experience, as detailed in James' *Varieties of Religious Experience*. The problem is not merely that Stengers fails to appreciate the implications of the expanded empiricism found in James and Whitehead, it is also that she too aggressively interprets Jamesian/Whiteheadian pragmatism as avoiding altogether the idea that the task of metaphysics is to *understand* reality (see *MT*, chap. 3 on "Understanding"). Instead, she thinks the task is to *produce* reality. Somehow or other, however, Stengers nonetheless wants on this basis to retain the best in Popperian fallibilism (Stengers 2011, 340, 381, 405).

In the following section we will see that, on Stengers' interpretation, divine envisagement of eternal objects, which plays a significant role in Whitehead's philosophy, does not require a judgment concerning the existence of God. Once again, the importance of "God" consists entirely in the difference this word or concept makes for human beings. Stengers herself is often skittish when she talks about God, but her clear opposition to theism signals that she thinks that the historical damage done by the classical theistic concept of God cannot be repaired. That is, we should not hope that an improved concept of God as persuasive or a revised logic of perfection will do the repair job. This rules out in principle any version of neoclassical or process theism (Stengers 2011, 447, 451).

All monotheisms, not merely the classical theistic version of monotheism, point toward a coercive, despotic God, on her view. Sadly, as we will see in the following chapter, Stengers does not give reasons in favor of this conclusion. Nor does she give reasons for the claim that the very question "Is Whitehead a theistic philosopher?" is a peculiarly American one. In addition to being unsupported by argument, this approach also flirts with the *ad hominem* fallacy. From her (allegedly European) perspective, it is just obvious that God is not the ultimate. She thinks that Whiteheadians should be committed to the view that, if there is an ultimate, it is adventure (Stengers 2011, 254, 479, 491, 499).

One wishes that Stengers had paid closer attention to Whitehead's attempt to improve upon the Platonic connection between mathematics and the good, with the latter referring to an intradeical concept of the moral ideal. This connection does not involve a superstitious awe of infinitude, as Stengers might suggest. The infinite (the Greek *apeiron*), when considered abstractly by itself, is amorphous and has no properties; hence, all value is the result of an interplay between it and the finite (*peras*) whereby what would otherwise be a formless mass develops *pattern*. Mathematics is the assiduous study of finite pattern and herein lies its connection to the good. Because the infinite is a mere vacancy apart from the embodiment of finite values, the contribution of mathematics to the study of finite patterns is crucial in that civilization itself advances in terms of the fortunate modification of moral patterns of behavior. That is, the infusion of pattern in the flux of events is a necessary condition for a realization of the good in that the very recognition of the difference between good and evil involves some reference to the interweaving of diverse patterns of experience. Nonetheless it is also true to say that the finite needs the infinite in that any finite perspective already presupposes an infinite, unanalyzed background of possibility. It is not as easy as Stengers thinks to ignore the integral links among the infinite and the finite, the finite and mathematical pattern, and mathematical pattern and the recognition of moral pattern (MG 666–681). Whitehead puts a related point succinctly: "Philosophy is an attempt to express the infinity of the universe in terms of the limitations of language" (AN 14).

In every branch of knowledge, the infinite plays a role such that it *is* in a way within our experience: as in the infinite perspective behind the focal point in Renaissance paintings, or as in the temporally ever-lasting existence of the greatest conceivable being in theology, or as in Whitehead's famous method of extensive abstraction in mathematics (see *IM*).

STENGERS' INTERPRETATION OF WHITEHEAD

The God-function is at least implicit throughout Whitehead's philosophy; hence, one cannot ignore it. But this function is somewhat analogous to that of the Queen of England in British politics, on Stengers' (and Latour's) interpretation of Whitehead. Thus, Stengers tries to bring Whitehead scholarship up to date with current fashion. For example, God should not be referred to in terms of forceful masculine or even feminine pronouns but in neuter terms in that, on Stengers' interpretation of Whitehead, God is not personal. It should be noted, however, that to see God in personal terms is not necessarily to violate Stengers' quite appropriate desire not to go "beyond" experience but to understand and transform it. Or again, it makes sense for Stengers to emphasize Whitehead's belief that religion needs to face change in the same spirit as does science (*SM* 189), but I nonetheless wonder whether there is something hyperbolic in claiming, as Stengers does, that the future of religion is *completely* (Stengers' word, but my emphasis) distinct from the metaphysical question of the order of the natural world. The fact that philosophy of religion flourishes at present (even in Europe, as is evidenced in the excellent journal *European Journal for Philosophy of Religion*) seems to indicate that the two can be seen as closely linked (Stengers 2011, xiii, 23, 27, 46–47, 133).

As I see things, Stengers moves too quickly from the claim that Whitehead does not define himself as a Christian to the claim that he was an agnostic. Of course, he does not *define* himself as an agnostic either. His reticence to identify himself as a Christian can plausibly be interpreted as a reluctance to commit to the classical theism, and to the belief in divine omnipotence, that is often associated with Christianity. And I do not detect in Whitehead a reticence to be identified with theism of some sort. At the very least, the word "God" is all over the place in Whitehead, doing all sorts of intellectual and affective work for him. It is only on Stengers' tendentious interpretation of Whitehead that one could claim that he was an agnostic. I would like to emphasize that Stengers is *not* like Donald Sherburne, George Allan, and others in the Whitehead without God camp, who think that one could defend a thoroughgoing processual, Whitehead*ian* view without belief in God, or even that Whitehead's system is more coherent without God (see, e.g., Allan). Rather, Stengers is suggesting that Whitehead *himself* refuses to commit to theism in that when he repeatedly refers to "God" he is (like Stengers herself) not really referring to a personal, greatest conceivable being (Stengers 2011, 133–134).

Stengers is at her best when she contrasts Whitehead's treatment of God in *SM* with his treatments of God in other works. In the former, God functions as a construct that is required to solve a very particular metaphysical problem that arises once one breaks the disastrous habit of thinking (incoherently) in terms of the bifurcation of nature. This habit is analogous to the bad geocentric habit of positing epicycles in the period just before Nicolaus Copernicus. Once again, however, Stengers does not avail herself of the excellent work done by Griffin to unsnarl the knot tied by the bifurcation of nature (see Griffin 1998), as we have seen in the previous chapter. Because she traverses much of the same ground as Griffin, it would have been nice to see how she would have distinguished her work from his. But she does explicate well the reasons why Whitehead needed a principle of limitation in *SM*, a principle without which actual occasions would not have an individualized horizon from which to make literal de-cisions, wherein some possibilities are cut off so that others can become actual in the clutch of vivid immediacy in the present. It is not clear, however, how legitimately seeing God as a principle of limitation warrants the view that the God of *SM* has nothing in common with the God of religion. Nothing whatsoever? It will be remembered that chapter 11 of *SM* ends with a discussion of worship, which, as far as I can tell, is a religious concept and not a metaphysical one. Specifically, the power of God is the worship such a personal being inspires (n.b.: Whitehead uses a personal pronoun rather than "it"). The worship in question is not a rule of safety, as would be the case if one were dealing with a forceful, indeed vengeful, omnipotent God, but an adventure of the spirit, which belies Stengers' idea that Whitehead is opposed to *any* contemplative ideal (Stengers 2011, 126, 207, 220, 225).

When Stengers says that Whitehead is concerned with experience, not with something beyond experience, she is surely correct. But it is not clear to me that she can then jump to the conclusion that Whitehead is "obviously not religious" in that neoclassical or process theists, along with pragmatic theists, claim a theism that does not adopt a cosmological bifurcation that requires some sort of pole vault into another world beyond this one. By largely ignoring neoclassical or process theism, she continues the bad habit of assuming that theism is to be identified with classical theism. This truncated consideration of the theistic options leads to her suggestions that Whitehead's God is powerless, which works on the classical theistic assumption that if God is not omnipotent then God has no real power; that Whitehead's God is not a creator, which concedes the classical theistic case that only creation *ex nihilo* is appropriate for God, not a Platonic (or biblical) creation *ex hyle*; and that Whitehead's God is merely an *ad hoc* creature or accident of creativity, which buys into classical theistic monopolarity, as we will see (Stengers 2011, 244–245, 264–266, 500–501).

Throughout her book Stengers plays into the classical theist's hands by assuming that Whitehead and other process thinkers cannot offer a theistic alternative to classical theism. The implicit argument seems to go as follows: (a) either one is a classical theist or one is an agnostic/atheist, (b) classical theism is riddled with barbarous inconsistencies, thus (c) agnosticism/atheism is the only viable option such that any hesitation here is a mark of intellectual regression. The fact that Hartshorne spent over seventy years calling into question the first premise should not escape our notice, even if it largely escapes Stengers'.

Previously, I noted that at times Stengers sees belief in omnipotence as the key problem in classical theism, but there is also evidence that she thinks the main difficulty concerns omnibenevolence, or lack thereof. On this basis, the classical theistic God might be *able* to prevent evil and *know how* to prevent evil but *chooses* to permit it. Whitehead avoids this problem in *RM*, where the limitation of God by goodness means, on my reading, that the greatest conceivable being *would not* do or permit evil (see *RM* 153). In the transition from *SM* to *RM* Stengers rightly detects an expanded role for God in Whitehead, or added functions for God in Whitehead, but in her peculiar reading of *RM* Whitehead's God still remains utterly indifferent to human and other suffering. It is understandable why she would want Whitehead to avoid a God who was like the person who holds a carrot in front of a donkey. This is because the holder (God) might end up being responsible for the donkey's (humanity's) progress or regress. Or again, she wants Whitehead to avoid a God who spoon-feeds concrescence. But there is no great danger here if God does not know with absolute assurance and in minute detail what will happen in the future. I think Stengers agrees with me that the classical theistic (e.g., Leibnizean) version of omniscience might also be part of the problem with classical theism in that the classical theistic God *does* know the future with absolute assurance and in minute detail, thereby forcing creaturely freedom and novelty to dry up, as Leibniz himself admitted. Although, as indicated earlier, I agree with Stengers that classical theism should be rejected, until there is more clarity regarding exactly what the problems are with classical theism we will not be in a suitable position to assess the neo-classical, process theistic alternative that involves the FTP transition (Stengers 2011, 282, 285, 311, 315, 317, 378). I suspect that Stengers has objections to all three attributes (omnipotence, omniscience, and omnibenevolence); if so, these need to be spelled out more carefully.

Stengers also notes the obvious changes in Whitehead's cosmotheological economy in *PR*. In fact, she is worried by these changes in that a more prominent role for God as an eternal, changeless actual entity and for eternal objects, she thinks, runs the risk of crushing the temporal and everything else that is worthwhile in Whitehead. Her allusion to Homer in this regard is confusing, as she thinks that Whitehead moved from the Charybdis of an overly determinate God (?) to the Scylla of eternal objects, but her overall concern regarding eternal objects is understandable. If everything is mapped out in eternity, then it is hard to account for novelty. It should be noted that Hartshorne and many other neoclassical, process theists share Stengers' worry here, as well as her concern that an eternal (rather than a temporally everlasting) God would be at odds with the concept of divine providence. But Stengers thinks that Whitehead avoids the untoward possibilities that attend a view of God as a single, eternal actual entity in that Whitehead's God is not a coercing, all-determining Orderer. I am not sure why Stengers is interested in divine providence because, on her view, God is not personal and does not exhibit personal characteristics like patience. The "patience" of Whitehead's God, if there is such, consists, she thinks, in the idea that everything that happens is accepted without remainder. She handles Whitehead's language regarding God's acceptance or valuation of all that happens in terms of such valuation not being any sort of judgment, once again presumably so as to preserve the alleged nonpersonal character of God. Even in *PR* and *MT*, she thinks, it is God as a principle of limitation (as developed initially in *SM*) that is most important. And a principle of limitation, even an eternal principle of limitation, is not to be confused with the supernatural God of classical theism (Stengers 2011, 362–363, 383, 393–394, 418, 424, 427, 481; 2014, 43).

It is the fact that there is a cosmos that requires us to construct God, Stengers thinks. But she does not think that such a requirement points us toward a God who understands or cares for us. Her take on the problems associated with God in *PR* is that we are left with a literal di-lemma in that there are two paths open to us and there are potholes in each: (a) we could try to rewrite *PR* without God, or (b) we could try to make the God of *PR* coherent. Those in the Whitehead-without-God camp, who are surprisingly ignored by Stengers, take the first option, whereas Stengers takes the second one. Even this latter path is perilous, she thinks, because at the beginning of *PR* God functions as a nontemporal actual entity who can be rendered compatible with the *SM* God as a principle of limitation. However, by part 5 of *PR* God has become the persuasive Great Companion, the fellow sufferer who understands and who is therefore quite different from the God of *SM* (Stengers 2011, 447, 450–453; 2014, 59–60).

Stengers' path involves a hermeneutics of suspicion wherein God's two natures in *PR*—primordial and consequent—are seen as a "ruse" used by Whitehead to avoid rewriting the whole book. Despite this incredible interpretation, Stengers is nonetheless on the mark when she holds that these two natures are not separate, even if they can be abstracted away from each other. The two natures of the same God at the end of *PR*, according to Stengers, highlight the fact that Whitehead was not able to follow through on his effort to secularize God, an effort that she interprets as an attempt to defend agnosticism, despite his frequent use of religious-sounding language. When Whitehead's God exhibits "a tender care that nothing be lost" and a "love . . . for the world" at the end of *PR*, this failure becomes complete (Stengers 2011, 346, 455–456, 469), she thinks. Stengers does not take seriously the possibility that Whitehead was, in fact, a theist, albeit not an orthodox one, who was quite serious in what he said about God at the end of *PR*. For example, when he claimed that nothing is lost in the divine conse-quent nature, he was not so much throwing in the towel on the effort to secularize God (as Stengers interprets secularization), as he was con-tinuing his longstanding effort to think through the implications of his belief that the root of tragedy is the transitoriness of that which is good.

It is hard to make sense of the fact that, despite her obvious distaste for what Whitehead says about God in part 5 of *PR*, Stengers insists that Whitehead did not change his mind after the time of *SM* about God's *sole* value as a principle of limitation. For example, she holds that even in *PR* God is not a "Thou" who envisages what might be (even if God is said to care, love, etc.). Or again, Stengers thinks that White-head's God in *PR* is constantly growing even if this God has no past and "exists" as a single actual entity (not as an everlasting series of actual occasions). She compounds difficulties even more by referring at times to this God as everlasting, rather than as eternal. Her familiar escape route out of these difficulties is provided by a theory of "secularization" wherein God does not really exist (whether everlastingly or eternally), is not really a person, does not really care, and so on (Stengers 2011, 475–477).

I like the fact that Stengers holds that Whitehead attempts to *save* God. This view would make sense if she distinguished between the ideas *that* God exists in some manner or other and the *way* in which God exists. If God's existence is everlasting, then this existence has no need of being saved. But we *can* save, or at least contribute to, divine enjoy-ment (see Dombrowski 1997b regarding Nikos Kazantzakis' attempt to "save" God). But Stengers does not avail herself of Hartshornian dipo-larity in God. What she means by the view that Whitehead "saves" God is that God is a pure intellectual fabrication. To be precise, this claim is not so much argued for as asserted (Stengers 2011, 479–480).

It does not escape Stengers' notice that because Whitehead fre-quently uses theistic, personal, especially Christian, vocabulary, expec-tations run high in some quarters that he is defending theism. Further, she puts the points nicely that Whitehead's God lurks in the interstices of religious experience and that his God is not the triumphant or violent one of the missionaries, which puts her in alliance with those who defend the FTP transition. There is also some legitimacy to her view that Whitehead's God is that of mathematicians. My overall reading of her interpretation of Whitehead's God, however, veers away from Stengers precisely when she concludes from legitimate points such as these to the conclusions that Whitehead's God should in no way be construed as an existing, personal, loving agent, unless by "love" is meant something like the Stoic *amor fati*, wherein all that happens is impersonally accepted, thereby turning Whitehead into a pantheist (Stengers 2011, 484, 487–490, 492).

THE IMPORTANCE OF HARTSHORNE

It will be the purpose of this section to argue that Stengers either largely ignores Hartshorne's thought or misrepresents it when it is briefly mentioned. Such avoidance or distortion prevents her from understanding aspects of Whitehead's thought on God as interpreted by Hartshorne that are crucial for an understanding of the MTO and FTP transitions.

Stengers is ambivalent in her assessment of Hartshorne. At times she mistakenly indicates that he is a theologian, specifically one of the theologians whom Whitehead had the misfortune of influencing, and at other times she indicates that he is a philosopher who tries to base theism on rational arguments alone. These two tendencies are not only individually problematic, they are also jointly inconsistent. First, Hartshorne never thought of himself as a theologian, never attributed any special authority to scripture or to religious leaders, and so forth. Nor was he under the tutorial spell of Whitehead when it is considered that he had arrived at the major features of his philosophy in the 1920s, before he ever met Whitehead or read his Harvard philosophical works. Second, it is misleading to say that, as a philosopher, Hartshorne based his theism on rational arguments *alone*. For example, in Hartshorne's defense of the ontological argument, he makes it clear that St. Anselm's great discovery was the idea that the greatest conceivable being could not exist contingently. Hence, God's existence was either necessary or impossible, given the assumption in modal logic that necessity, contingency, and impossibility exhaust the logical alternatives. But is God's existence possible? This is a complicated question, even though Hartshorne and Stengers agree that the God of classical theism is impossible (for various reasons). In the effort to show that God's existence is at least possible (and hence, via the ontological argument, necessary), it is crucial to note that religious experience plays a role, along with rational argument (see Dombrowski 2006b, 148–154). And third, one cannot consistently claim, as Stengers does, that Hartshorne is both a theologian and a thinker who tries to base theism on rational arguments alone. That is, Stengers starts off on the wrong foot in her treatment of Hartshorne's thought (Stengers 2011, 5–6).

What would be needed on Stengers' part is a careful, critical engagement with Hartshorne's thought in order to redeem the barbed comment that Whitehead survived American theology and that American "theologians" like Hartshorne look favorably on a convergence between Whiteheadian theism and Christian doctrine. This issue is also complicated. Hartshorne (admittedly more than Whitehead) was committed to the task of trying to philosophically defend a concept of God that rendered intelligible the claim that God is love. That is, Hartshorne wanted to examine carefully the logic of perfection so that the concept of divine love could be defended. By contrast, the unmoved mover of classical theism cannot be a God of love. Like Thomas Merton, Hartshorne wanted to revitalize religious language in our mechanistic world, wherein "God is love" is as banal as "Eat Wheaties" (Merton 9).

But Hartshorne, like Whitehead, shied away from commitment to Christianity, despite the fact that both were sons of Anglican ministers. No doubt Stengers is correct that American process thinkers have often engaged in technical controversy regarding Whitehead's difficult texts, but to imply that Hartshorne was part of a "slightly secret school" is a real cipher, given the fact that Hartshorne is, by all accounts, much clearer than Whitehead (Stengers 2011, 5–6). Comments like these from Stengers nonetheless have the positive effect of forcing one to make sure that one's sense of humor is intact and that one is not taking oneself too seriously. I agree with Stengers that *homo ludens* should trump *homo gravis* (see Dombrowski 2009).

Several of Stengers' dearest concerns are also those of Hartshorne. For example, in chapters 4 and 6 of her book she frequently cites the example of birdsong to illustrate her critique of modern philosophy's bifurcationist theory that pleasure is a psychic addition to mechanistic reality. But she does not mention that Hartshorne wrote an entire book on this topic (Hartshorne 1973). In this book Hartshorne also challenged the bifurcationist—specifically, behaviorist—view. If one says that birds sing in order to attract a mate or to protect territory, as behaviorists allege, there is a crucial need to explain why birds sing when mating season is over and when territory is not threatened. Hartshorne defends the view that they *like* to sing. His anti-monotony thesis influenced some the world's most important ornithologists, if not Stengers (see Dombrowski 2004a, chap. 4).

Or again, when Stengers wonders in chapter 10 of her book (also 493, 496) about the defensibility of the reified character of Whitehead's eternal objects and about whether such reification is compatible with a genuinely processual view of reality, she does not consult Hartshorne's criticisms of Whitehead's eternal objects or Hartshorne's own theory of *emergent* universals. This theory could have aided Stengers in her attempt to reconcile abstract objects and temporal flux (see Hartshorne 1972, 31–33). Although Stengers defends Whitehead's "pole reversal" in God, she nonetheless thinks that God is utterly unimaginable because the initial pole is constituted by God's envisagement of the whole realm of *eternal* objects outside of time. If God is an *everlasting* series of actual occasions, however, God is, at the very least, imaginable, thereby averting Stengers' fear of a voyeur God who sees but who cannot be seen or imagined (Stengers 2011, 468).

To cite some final examples, when Stengers discusses the topics of synesthesia and Hume's missing shade of blue in the context of Whitehead's thought, she does not avail herself of Hartshorne's detailed and nuanced efforts (see, e.g., Hartshorne 1934, 77–86) to do the same (Stengers 2011, 351–363). In all of these areas (birdsong, emergent universals, synesthesia, Hume's missing shade of blue) one gets the sense that Stengers is groping toward resolutions to problems in process thought that, optimistically, have already been solved, or, more cautiously, have already received detailed analysis.

Hartshorne is most important in the effort to understand and criticize Stengers' approach to God in Whitehead in terms of Hartshorne's own dipolar theism, which he attributes to Whitehead as well. Unfortunately, Stengers does not do much in terms of critical engagement with Hartshorne on the concept of God. She dismisses without argument Hartshorne's view of God as the soul for the body of the whole world, a type of cosmic hylomorphism that one might think would be congenial to Stengers, were she a theist, in that classical theism consists in a type of cosmic dualism that exhibits the bifurcationism and mechanism that she opposes. Even more problematic is the fact that the contrasting pairs of divine attributes in Whitehead (*PR* 347–348) are viewed by Stengers as *contradicting* each other. This not only ignores Hartshorne's view that these *contrasting* pairs are mutually reinforcing and correlative, in that one cannot understand one term in the contrasting pair without understanding the other; it legislates out of existence the very possibility of the persuasive God of neoclassical, dipolar, process theism. Here Stengers is cavalier with a capital "C" (Stengers 2011, 379, 449–450).

For example, there is no logical contradiction, as Stengers thinks, between claiming that God is permanent *and* changing if these two attributes apply to different aspects of the divine nature. In Hartshorne (and, Hartshorne alleges—see 1953a, 273–285—in Whitehead), God permanently, everlastingly *exists* throughout all of time, but *how* God exists changes from moment to moment as novel actualizations of what were previously only possibilities come into being. Not only *could* God change, God *must* exhibit eminent change in order to be the greatest conceivable being. When a being that previously did not suffer starts to suffer, the best being, the *most and best* moved mover, would re-spond to such creaturely suffering. The greatest conceivable being *always changes*, with emphasis needed on both words. There simply is no logical contradiction.

Whitehead's God is not a perfect being, on Stengers' interpretation, despite the fact that Whitehead says that in "purified religion" God's goodness should be imitated and that God's power consists in the ideal standard provided by the divine nature itself (*RM* 41, 156). And Whitehead's God encourages no "mystical élan," on her interpretation, despite the fact that Whitehead held on the last page of his last book that the purpose of philosophy is to rationalize mysticism (*MT* 174). It is to Stengers' credit, however, that she engages directly Hartshorne's view of God, and his critique of Whitehead's view of God, on at least one significant point that tends to divide process theists. She defends the concept of God as a single, atemporal actual *entity*, an idea that is clearly in *PR*, even if there are debates regarding the extent to which this indicates Whitehead's overall view, whether in *PR* or elsewhere. This concept of God is in tension with Hartshorne's concept of God, which tries to ameliorate the difficulties in Whitehead's concept of God, and especially in the classical theistic concept of God, by defending the idea that God is a temporal series of actual *occasions*, with the everlastingness of this series constituting divine permanence.

As far as I can tell, Stengers has four criticisms of Hartshorne's view on this point. The first is that, on Hartshorne's view, God is a lineage of occasions that inherit from themselves and from the world what has been decided in previous occasions, which would indicate that divine feeling at any particular moment would constitute "a 'true' definition of the world." Although this is an odd way to put the point, in that it is hard for me to understand how a feeling could be a *definition*, I think I understand Stengers' point, which is that Hartshorne's philosophy pushes us toward a view of truth wherein pragmatic criteria, although part of the story, must be supplemented by correspondence criteria when it is considered that Hartshorne's God has ideal knowledge of all that has happened to date. I doubt if this is as big a problem as Stengers alleges. Indeed, I think that it is a benefit to keep correspondence considerations on the table, especially when there are two competing theories that have the same pragmatic worth but that are at odds with each other conceptually. Stengers often reads like Richard Rorty in her indifference to, or antipathy toward, any discourse regarding *the* truth. This leads one to wonder whether Stengers, along with Rorty, is a relativist, although presumably both of these thinkers would respond in terms of a desire to get beyond the Platonic tradition that opposes objective truth and relativism. It should be noted, however, that the price one pays for this view is not only an inability to say what is true but also an inability to falsify with assurance, as Karl Popper has argued (Popper 1972, chap. 9). This is why I previously noted that Stengers' attachment to Popperian falsification is peculiar (Stengers 2011, 261, 405, 452–458).

The second criticism calls into question the compatibility between Hartshorne's view of God and skepticism regarding simultaneity in contemporary physics. I admit that there is probably more to this criticism than I am able to understand, but Hartshorne is, at the very least, quite clear that he is aware of the problem. God-here-now prehends previous occasions in the divine life in a temporal sequence, hence avoiding simultaneity. But what about divine prehensions of activities in distant galaxies if these are also animated by God as the soul for the body of the whole world? On the analogy of a pain in my toe taking a finite amount of time to be experienced by me as a whole and as a source of a headache, simultaneity is not necessary to understand the divine individual. As Hartshorne puts the point, "I strongly suspect that there should not . . . and indeed could not be absolute simultaneity" (Hartshorne 1970, 124; cf. Stump and Kretzmann) if God animates distant parts of the universe as well as those close at hand.

The third criticism involves the idea that Hartshorne's God exhibits not only *continuity* from one occasion in the divine life to the next but also *conformity* between divine occasions and the nondivine occasions in the world. The problem here, if I understand correctly, is that this feature of the divine life makes God sound like the God of religion. Of course, this begs the question as to whether there is anything necessarily wrong with a God of religion, even if it is true that the classical theistic God of religion is problematic. Stengers' response seems to be that if conformity is a defining characteristic of God, it will be a dangerous characteristic that is hard to stop once it gets going such that one would be able "to *deduce* from him [God] the divine projects for the world" (Stengers 2011, 457; emphasis added). This seems to piggyback on Stengers' earlier claim that Hartshorne tries to base theism on rational arguments alone. The fourth criticism is related to the third: if one says that God is *necessarily* good, then one cannot adequately respond to Job (Stengers 2011, 457).

I would like to respond to the criticism regarding Job's query first. Stengers assumes (incorrectly, I think) that necessary omnibenevolence is the problem. But for neoclassical or process theists, omnibenevolence is the least problematic of the classical theistic divine attributes. Omnipotence is the real culprit (Hartshorne 1984c; Dombrowski 2005, chap. 2), as we have seen, but omniscience in the sense of claiming that God knows with absolute assurance and in minute detail what will happen in the future is also deeply problematic (see Shields and Viney). That is, the combination of divine omnipotence and classical theistic omniscience *does* make an adequate response to Job impossible. To locate the theodicy problem with necessary omnibenevolence, however, in the absence of a critique of neoclassical or process theodicy (e.g., Griffin 1976, 1991), leads one to wonder if Stengers is even aware of the neoclassical or process theistic account. One wonders if the "cosmic reconciliation" asked for by Stengers (Stengers 2011, 491) once again indicates that she assumes that theism is supposed to deliver all of the things listed on the classical theist's promissory note. Life, even divine life, is tragic, for Whitehead, and Hartshorne's critique of omnipotence and classical theistic omniscience makes us especially aware of this fact.

The problem with the third criticism is that Stengers does not carefully enough distinguish between the necessary and the contingent in Hartshorne. Necessary truths (including the necessary truth found in the conclusion of the ontological argument) have gotten a bad name due to the assumption that they concern a classical theistic God who is an eternal reality outside of time altogether, rather than an everlasting reality that endures through all of time. The "eternal" is so abstract that it cannot really have internal relations with that which becomes contingently. Another mistake that has given necessary truth a bad name concerns confusion between the necessity of a proposition and our knowledge of it. Our knowledge of a necessary truth (e.g., knowledge of the conclusion of the ontological argument), if we have such, is not itself necessary. Or again, Stengers seems to work on the mistaken idea that if one knows a necessary truth one can then deduce contingent truths from the necessary one (see Hartshorne 1941b, 531). But this would end not only creaturely creativity but process itself. Even with knowledge of necessary truth under one's belt (e.g., regarding the *existence* of God) one would still have to await the outcome of contingent decisions (regarding creatures or even regarding the concrete *actuality* of God from moment to moment). A God who is necessary in existence and contingent in actuality escapes Stengers' third criticism. It is one thing to know *that* a decision has to be made, another to know *which* decision.

Stengers clearly thinks that it is a problem to view God as a preeminent being who exists through an everlasting series of occasions because this is to "atomize" God, but she does not indicate *why* this atomization of God is a problem if such atomization is part of an everlasting series. One advantage of Hartshorne's view is that it enables us to understand divine experience as *social* (which would otherwise be a plus, for Stengers) in that the divine nature itself is a social relation among divine occasions of experience. Whitehead's occasional language regarding "perpetual perishing" does not help here in that it gives the mistaken sense that what has happened has been utterly lost. But for both Whitehead and Hartshorne, and for Wordsworth as well, what having been will ever be in the divine memory (Stengers 2011, 469, 472).

In order to understand Hartshorne's view of God, and the similarities it has to Whitehead's view, it makes sense to admit that the
primordial nature of God refers to God's being infinite, immutable,
and independent *in existence*. But the primordial nature is an abstraction away from the fullness of divine reality, a fullness that requires
the consequent nature, which deals with divine *actuality* or *how* God
exists from moment to moment in contrast to the fact *that* God exists
everlastingly. In the consequent nature God receives particular content
from the world and prehends the world in a preeminent, loving feeling of feeling. This aspect of God is preserved in the famous moniker
"the fellow-sufferer who understands" (*PR* 351). That is, the consequent
nature follows logically from the requirements of *PR*, and, in contrast
to Stengers, is not a mere concession to either religious feeling or to the
alleged intellectual inadequacies of those who do not really understand
what Whitehead is doing (see Hartshorne 2011, 7).

If it is true that it is the religious aspect of the changing world
that haunts many readers of Whitehead's books, this is because they
wonder at the endless succession of drops of time passing into everlastingness without being entirely lost. The eros toward perfection and
against transiency is lost on Stengers. And if eros is lost, life is lost. It
is Whitehead's very philosophy of *organism* that eludes Stengers (see
Bixler 489, 496, 504).

IMPLICATIONS REGARDING FTP

My purpose in this chapter has not been to resolve any of the major
issues in neoclassical or process theism. Rather, it has been to indicate
points of contact, indeed points of tension, between neoclassical or
process theism and a major voice in contemporary process thought.
Stengers says a great deal not only about Whitehead but also about
Whitehead's view of God. As I see things, her criticisms of classical
theism are on the mark, but the fact that she does not *argue* against
theism in general, rather she assumes agnosticism, is a problem. This
problem negatively affects her reading of Whitehead in that she ends
up inconsistently defending Whitehead's God, but without theism.
This effort involves an illegitimate, or at least premature, transfer of
her own agnosticism to Whitehead. I have also tried to indicate why
a more careful engagement with Hartshorne's dipolar theism, wherein

the *necessary existence* of God is not to be confused with the *contingent actuality* of God, might provide the resources to avoid the conclusion that there is a logical contradiction between the primordial and consequent natures of God in Whitehead.

Stengers contributes in the effort to understand and criticize the "F" in FTP in terms of her legitimate objections to classical theism. But her unargued-for agnosticism does not help much in the effort to better understand the "P" in FTP, specifically in terms of Whitehead's Platonic belief that God persuades the world toward as much order and beauty as are possible given the multiple spontaneous powers that exist in the world. She does notice the link between power and adventure in Whitehead, but not the Platonic claim adopted by Whitehead and Hartshorne that being *is* power. This omission makes it easier for her to claim (again, without argument) that Whitehead's concept of power is like that of Michel Foucault. Her use of Foucault here alerts us to the fact that her interpretation of Whitehead is not well suited to appreciate the concept of persuasion. She even sees Whitehead as a Marxist without realizing it (!), for whom the concept of political autonomy is obsolete, despite Whitehead's own political liberalism (see Morris), and she thinks that one never *has* a right, rather one *takes* a right by force (see Stengers 2011, 136, 159–160, 240).

Given the hardnosed concept of political power that seems to be at work in Stengers, it seems that she supports not the transition from FTP but rather a transition from belief in divine omnipotent force to human force. Indeed, at several points she notes Whitehead's interest in Quaker "concern," but it is not easy to determine what her point is in these citations; she does not seem to see such a concern as a clue to the meaning of prehension (e.g., Stengers 2011, 446). She is decidedly against the interpretation of Whitehead that would suggest he is calling for greater toleration (Stengers 2011, 513).

She thinks that there is no room whatsoever for expression of religious conviction in the public square. In fact, she claims that this view is self-evident in Europe. This issue is notoriously difficult (see Dombrowski 2001a, 2011), such that if Stengers is correct about the need for complete privatization of religion, this view is by no means self-evident. Consider the Rawlsian proviso wherein one *is* allowed to bring religious conviction to bear in the public square *as long as* the terms of such conviction can be translated in a way that any reasonable person could understand and plausibly accept. For example, when

Martin Luther King dreamed out loud about a time when all of *God's* children would walk together hand-in-hand in a discrimination-free society, reasonable agnostics and atheists knew exactly what he was getting at: the dignity of persons regardless of race. King is now a world historical figure precisely because he was able to *persuade* the majority of the correctness of his views.

With regard to both MTO and FTP I think we would be better served by following Griffin's lead rather than Stengers'. In the following section, however, I will indicate why I think that Stengers' view is nonetheless noteworthy. In order to transition into the importance of her critique, it should be noted that she is surely on the right track in welcoming a return of final causes into the study of organisms, albeit a processual final causality that is stripped of Aristotle's metaphysics of substance. An actual occasion does not so much try to achieve a pre-destined end state as it inwardly *experiences* the need to make decisions regarding the future. That is, Stengers is to be thanked for militating against what she calls the "holy war" against final causes (Stengers 2011, 126).

THE IMPORTANCE OF STENGERS' CRITIQUE

In this final section of the chapter I would like to emphasize the fact that, despite my criticisms of Stengers' view, her stance is an important one for several reasons. She is surely correct that for many or most intellectuals, and for many people in the general population, "God" has become an empty word, such that it makes sense to either drop the word—Nietzsche's or Stengers' response—or to rethink the concept of God so as to give it revitalized meaning—Whitehead's, Hartshorne's, Griffin's, and Cobb's response (see Cobb 2007, xvi–xvii).

Stengers is also astute to emphasize the fact that in Whitehead's first explicit treatment of the concept of God in *SM* he brings in God as a result of a philosophical need for a principle of limitation, with little reference to religious experience, as Cobb also emphasizes. (Because of his introduction of the concept of God in *SM*, Whitehead was never forgiven by *both* his atheist friends, who were shocked by his discovery of theism, *and* his classical theistic friends, who were shocked by his innovation—see Cobb 2007, 139.) I have nonetheless noted earlier that this relative paucity of appeal to religious experience in *SM* is mitigated by Whitehead's claim that the God of which he speaks is the one who has inspired worship throughout the ages (*SM* 257, 275–276).

It is unfortunate for several reasons that Stengers *identifies* God as a principle of limitation: God is at once a principle of abstraction, of possibility, as well as a principle of limitation, of limited realization of possibility, God is not merely a principle or a set of principles in Whitehead in that God is a concrete actual entity of universal significance, and God is not only an agent in Whitehead but the supreme agent (see Hartshorne 1941b, 550). Stengers' attenuated list of divine functions is misleading in the extreme.

It is also unfortunate that Stengers almost entirely ignores *RM*, where Whitehead makes much more extensive use of religious experience, a use that makes us very much aware of the complexity of the issue regarding whether or not Whitehead's God is personal. Whereas Stengers courageously lands entirely on the side that says that Whitehead's God is not personal, a more judicious approach might mediate between two tendencies in Whitehead (both in *RM* and toward the end of *PR*) that are in tension. On the one hand, God is deeply personal in that God shapes human (and other) experience moment to moment by providing initial aim for each drop of experience, and God cares for what happens to those who experience in terms of God's status as the fellow sufferer who understands. On the other hand, God works in the same way everywhere and at all times; hence, God impersonally plays no favorites. Once God is no longer merely a *principle* of limitation but is viewed in *RM* and *PR* as *actual*, Whitehead's personal God becomes a bit more intelligible. Although it is unclear in *RM* what the relationship is between religious experience and a personal God, it is clear that he is willing in this book to describe God in personal terms like "wise" and "loving."

Stengers is also to be thanked for pushing hard on the distinction in *PR* between God as primordial and God as consequent, but I think she would have been well served to note that the Gifford Lectures on which *PR* was based were devoted to the very theme of natural theology. The primordial nature is rightly seen by Stengers as a reiteration of the *SM* God as a principle of limitation. However, one wishes that she would have put greater emphasis on the idea that Whitehead's intent here was to avoid the theological determinism implicit in the omnipotence and omniscience (even with respect to what are, from a human point of view, future contingencies) of the classical theistic God. Whitehead's

God "limits" in the honorific ancient Greek sense of *peras*: God gives order to possibilities that would otherwise be a formless (*apeiron*), chaotic mess but not to the point where any particular result is pre-ordained, even if the God of *PR* does lure us toward the realization of possibilities that are optimal in terms of our particular value intensity.

Whereas Stengers' remarks on God as primordial need to be adjusted somewhat, her comments regarding God as consequent are deeply troubling. This is because she severs altogether the relationship between the religious *and philosophical* concerns that lie behind God as consequent. That is, she assumes that there are no philosophical reasons in favor of the introduction of God as consequent. But there are such reasons. In order for God to have real relations to the world (in contrast to the classical theistic view of God as an unmoved mover who is not really related to the world), and to be really influenced by the world, the consequent nature is needed, and in order for God to avoid being an exception to metaphysical principles, the consequent nature is required, in that without the consequent nature God would influence but not be influenced, contra all other dynamic centers of power in the world (*PR* 343). It is also helpful to note Cobb's claim that, although there is little talk of God in *AI*, it is in a way (via divine eros) Whitehead's most religious book (Cobb 2007, 106).

Finally, Stengers is to be thanked for pointing out certain problems in Whitehead's concept of God, problems that I think are resolved decisively by Hartshorne, as previously noted. Admittedly, Stengers is correct that God is not as central to Whitehead's project as it is in Hartshorne's God-intoxicated philosophy. But Cobb is also correct in noting that this legitimate point can be overemphasized: "In retrospect we can see that this whole enterprise of understanding and of life [i.e., Whitehead's entire corpus] is suffused and sustained by the dim apprehension of the beyond. In this sense Whitehead's vision is religious through and through" (Cobb 2007, 145).

The question is: What sort of concept of God can give vitality to "God"? Whitehead's vision of God as a nontemporal (yet, as Stengers rightly notes, curiously processual) actual entity is a good first approximation toward such a goal. Hartshorne's view is a closer approximation to a defensible view of God at least in part because, if an event can influence others only when the event reaches satisfaction (as Whitehead admits), then Whitehead's nontemporal God as a single actual entity resembles Boethian eternity too much and might never have such influence. Hence, the appeal of Hartshorne's view, which has influenced most Whitehead*ian* theists, including Griffin and Cobb: God is an everlasting series of finite actual occasions of experience.

My thesis in this chapter was anticipated by Whitehead himself when he said the following: "The chequered history of religion and morality is the main reason for the widespread desire to put them aside in favour of the more stable generalities of science. Unfortunately for this smug endeavor . . . the impact of aesthetic, religious and moral notions is inescapable" (*MT* 19).

THREE

Rawlsian Political Liberalism and Process Thought

CONVIVIALITY

It is precisely the *inescapability* of religious, aesthetic, moral (and hence political) questions, mentioned in the quotation from Whitehead at the end of the previous chapter, that provides the transition to the present chapter. How can people live together in a free yet peaceful manner in a condition of pervasive pluralism of religious and moral comprehensive doctrines? It is precisely this question that is the focus of the present chapter. However, the purpose of this chapter is not to develop an entire political philosophy on the basis of process theism, which would be an enormous undertaking. Rather, my goal is to indicate the ramifications of *a* version of political theory based on process theism for one of the themes of the present book: FTP. This theme is closely related to conviviality or living together in a peaceful and fair way with both those who share one's own religious beliefs (or lack thereof) as well as those who do not share them. Although it would be hubristic to claim to have *the* process view of politics, the politically liberal stance I will defend nonetheless deserves serious consideration if only because the two greatest figures in process theism—Whitehead and Hartshorne—were themselves "political liberals," as I will define this term. In fact, the theme of FTP lies precisely in the area where political liberalism has achieved its greatest success: in ending both theoretically and practically the wars of religion that plagued Europe in the early modern period.

The hope is that politically liberal conviviality will continue to spread across the globe in peaceful ways as a result of a willingness of citizens of various states in a condition of pervasive pluralism to show respect for fellow citizens, no matter what their religious beliefs (or lack thereof), so long as they are "reasonable," as this semi-technical term will be defined. Throughout the chapter I will be arguing for a conception of political liberalism very similar to that found in Rawls, whose views help to illuminate the political liberalisms of Whitehead and Hartshorne. I will also indicate how Whitehead and Hartshorne can offer metaphysical support for political liberalism. To be clear, process philosophy is but one among many comprehensive doctrines that are compatible with politically liberal justice. It has the advantage of being not only compatible with political liberalism but actually facilitates the goals of political liberalism in a manner that is superior to rival comprehensive doctrines that are theistic. Imitation of the omnipotent tyrant found in classical theism, often criticized by Whitehead, is ill-suited to the development of democratic virtues. Imitation of the persuasive God of neoclassical or process theism, by contrast, *is* conducive to such development.

BEFORE LIBERALISM

Pre-liberal political philosophy or political theology concentrated on two major tasks: (a) to figure out the characteristics of *the* good (the definite article is crucial here), and (b) to figure out how to get those who understood the good into power and to make sure that they were succeeded by rulers who were equally knowledgeable. This characterization of pre-liberal political thought applies equally to thinkers who are otherwise quite different: Plato, Aristotle, St. Augustine, St. Thomas Aquinas, Luther, Calvin, among others. They may have differed in their accounts of the good, but they agreed that one of the main tasks of political thought was to come to grips with it intellectually. And they may have differed regarding how many individuals were equipped to understand the good, how difficult it would be to get them into power, and how best to solve the problem of succession, but they agreed that the overall goal was to get those who understood the good into power and to keep them there.

One very interesting feature of pre-liberal political thought was that in these views toleration was not seen as a virtue. Indeed, it was a vice. The reason why pre-liberal political theorists wanted those who understood the good to be in power was to guard against those who did not understand it. To cite just three examples, think of Plato's expulsion of the poets from the ideal city (e.g., *Republic* 605b), St. Thomas Aquinas' willingness to have recalcitrant heretics put to death (*Summa Theologiae* 2a2ae. q. 11. a. 3), and Calvin's willingness to kill Servetus, which was noticed more than once by Hartshorne (see Dombrowski 2001a, chap. 1; Hartshorne 1997, 70, 79). An admirable ruler, in pre-liberal political thought, guarded the populace against heresy or against anything else that would lead them away from the good. In fact, not to do so would be to fail to do one's duty as a just ruler in that their very success as rulers was measured in terms of the degree to which they could lead the populace toward an approximation of the good. In sum, pre-liberal political thought was characterized more by force than by persuasion.

LIBERAL POLITICAL THEORY

In the early modern period in Europe something of a crisis occurred in political theory. (Outside of Europe there were historically pockets of religious toleration, as in Asoka's leadership in India, even if such commendable toleration did not receive much by way of theoretical justification.) What are we to do when two competing conceptions of the good (in Rawlsian terms, competing comprehensive doctrines) each claim to have *the* truth (once again, the definite article is crucial here) on their side and each claim absolute political authority, such that as a result society is ripped apart in religious warfare? John Locke's rightly famous "A Letter Concerning Toleration" is an initial attempt to deal with this crisis. *Either* one could wait until one of the competing comprehensive doctrines eventually got the upper hand and dominated the other *or* one could develop a political theory that would allow adherents to competing comprehensive doctrines to coexist in peace. Political liberalism is the disciplined effort to think through carefully and to justify the latter approach. In contrast to pre-liberal political thinkers, political liberals see toleration not as a vice but as a virtue. Indeed, it is seen by political liberals as the key virtue that is necessary for people to not only survive but to flourish in a state with a plurality of comprehensive doctrines. In other words, in order for politically liberal states to flourish, there has to be a certain victory of persuasion over force.

In order to bring about justice in a condition of a plurality of competing comprehensive doctrines, however, questions regarding the good have to be largely taken off the table *in politics*, although it makes sense to debate them elsewhere. That is, politics is not the place to debate *ultimate* questions regarding the purpose of human life, the meaning of death, the existence of God, or the theodicy problem. Rather, political questions are *penultimate* and concern the conditions under which defenders of different comprehensive doctrines can nonetheless get along with each other in a peaceful and fair manner. In short, political liberals concentrate in politics on justice or fairness in contrast to *the* good or *the* truth of any comprehensive doctrine, whether religious or nonreligious.

It must be admitted that, according to Whitehead, despite the contributions of liberal democracies to the humanitarian ideal, the long-term prospects are not good *if* political liberalism entails a loss of intellectual justification (*AI* 36). (I have Franklin Gamwell to thank for this important reference.) But to rightly claim that political liberalism requires *some* sort of intellectual justification is not to claim that there is only one such justification. The Rawlsian view I defend is that such a justification could be provided by a defender of any reasonable comprehensive doctrine. For example, it makes sense to assume that there is a rather formidable overlapping consensus among theistic defenses of political liberalism and secular defenses of the same. All that is needed is sufficient overlap on the assumptions that human beings are free, equal, reasonable, rational, and that they are not means only. The fact that there are many ways to do this is indicative of the fact that we can meet Whitehead's (and Gamwell's) understandable concern for intellectual justification in terms of many different, yet in some respects compatible, intellectual justifications. That is, political liberalism is a module that in different ways fits into, and can be supported by, various reasonable comprehensive doctrines (see Rawls 1996, 144–145; also Gamwell 2005).

TWO KINDS OF CONVIVIALITY

At this point in my argument it is possible to distinguish between two sorts of conviviality: conviviality-L and conviviality-C. The former, liberal conviviality, refers to literal con-viviality or "living with" others who are committed to comprehensive doctrines different from one's own, sometimes uncompromisingly so. Conviviality-L is found when citizens in a democracy get along with each other in a peaceful and fair manner despite the fact of religious pluralism, indeed despite the fact that many citizens in liberal democracies defend nonreligious comprehensive doctrines. In this regard political liberalism should be seen as one of the great achievements of human civilization! No longer do we believe in principle that everyone has to share the same comprehensive beliefs about what is important in life in order to get along in a peaceful and fair manner.

Conviviality-C, or communitarian conviviality, generally refers to the more intimate sort of conviviality present when one banquets with those who share one's own comprehensive doctrine. Think of the Christian Eucharist, the Jewish Passover, or the Muslim post-Ramadan feast. Or again, think of a Thanksgiving meal with family members or sharing beers after a game with one's intramural basketball teammates.

SOME OBJECTIONS

The warmth associated with conviviality-C leads some to speak disparagingly about the "mere toleration" associated with conviviality-L, but political liberals think that this indicates a misunderstanding of conviviality-L. That is, the two sorts of conviviality are perfectly compatible with each other in that in the context of liberal pluralism conviviality-L is the generic sort of conviviality that can include many different types of conviviality-C. The politically liberal hope is that one would have both convivial-L relations with all reasonable persons in a democratic state and convivial-C relations with those with whom one shares comprehensive beliefs, family ties, or joyful activities. To be precise, to expect that we would have convivial-C relations with *everyone* in the state is both unrealistic (given the fact of pervasive pluralism) and dangerous (in that it runs the risk of encouraging some enthusiastic defenders of certain comprehensive doctrines to ram their views down the throats of those who do not share these comprehensive doctrines or at least to proselytize others in disrespectful ways).

In addition to the allegation that conviviality-L is too tepid, it is also common to hear something like the following criticism: The price one has to pay for conviviality-L is too costly in that one must "privatize" one's religious beliefs. According to those who offer this criticism, it is unfair to demand that one sequester that which is most dear. One is forced, it is alleged, to segment one's life in conviviality-L between the religious and the political, thus violating the whole cloth of what should be an integrated life.

To be honest, I think that this criticism is telling against some political liberalisms, but not all. The issue is quite complicated and has elicited an internecine dispute among political liberals themselves. Some political liberals like Richard Rorty think that in a liberal democracy religious beliefs do in fact have to be privatized in order to maintain an approximation to justice or even to maintain public order. At the other extreme from a pure exclusivist view like Rorty's is a pure inclusivist stance that suggests that one should be able to include one's comprehensive (religious or nonreligious) beliefs into what one says and does in the public square because to prohibit them would be to violate citizens' rights in a democracy. Pure inclusivists are thus not to be confused with pre-liberal political theorists whose commitment was to the good more than it was to justice in a condition of pluralism in the midst of competing conceptions of the good. That is, the pure exclusivism–pure inclusivism debate occurs within political liberalism itself. It should also be noted that among the pure inclusivists can be found both conservative-leaning liberals like Nicholas Wolterstorff and progressive liberals like Gamwell, who is also a process theist.

My own view on this matter is, I contend, a moderate one between these two positions. I think that one can legitimately bring one's comprehensive doctrine into the public square *as long as* one is willing to translate it into terms that any reasonable citizen could understand and possibly accept. Not being willing to engage in such translation efforts (a la pure inclusivism) could be seen as disrespectful of fellow citizens who are not committed to one's comprehensive doctrine, or who might not even understand the terms of that doctrine, and not being willing to have *any* introduction of comprehensive doctrine into the public square (a la pure exclusivism) does in fact violate the basic (First Amendment) right of a citizen to free exercise of religion. I am proposing this Rawlsian translation proviso as a moral, if not constitutional, essential in a just state.

Once again, think of the success Martin Luther King had in translating his explicitly Christian view into the terms of public reason, the latter of which became codified in United States law. Even atheists and agnostics who were reasonable agreed wholeheartedly with him. By "reasonable" I mean a willingness to abide by fair terms of agreement, in partial contrast to being "rational" in terms of the abilities to follow a logical argument, weigh evidence, and so forth. To put the point in Rawlsian terms, it takes a *reasonable* person to be willing to enter the original position, but it takes a *rational* person to deliberate there. Full moral agency requires both reasonableness and rationality, even if moral patiency status is far less demanding and requires only sentiency, as we will see in a later chapter.

NOT COMPREHENSIVE LIBERALISM

The upshot of my responses to the previous two criticisms is that, first, various convivialities-C can flourish in a convivial-L state, and second, reasonable religious believers (along with reasonable religious skeptics) can bring their comprehensive doctrines to bear in the public square as long as they do so in terms of the translation proviso, which is meant to show convivial-L respect for persons who do not share one's own comprehensive doctrine.

These responses are part of *political* liberalism, not *comprehensive* liberalism. The latter is the view (exemplified by John Stuart Mill and John Dewey) that, as a consequence of the Enlightenment, as people converted to reason they would and should leave behind the religious ages and move toward liberalism interpreted in terms of agnosticism or atheism or merely pragmatic theism. The problem is that this view is just one more comprehensive doctrine that has to compete with others in the pluralist world in which we live. It makes sense to see politically liberal democracies as not so much postreligious as postsecular, with "secular" here referring to the hubristic hopes of comprehensive liberals. (I have benefited greatly from Thomas Schmidt regarding the concept of liberalism as postsecular.) Political liberalism does not privilege comprehensive liberalism in that it is now clear both that religion is not going away and that reasonable religious believers can and should be brought within the sphere of conviviality-L. Presumably, religious believers always engaged in convivial-C relations, but now they can and should be seen as full-fledged members of the convivial-L society. John Courtney Murray is one of several theologians who have carefully examined the consequences of this view. That is, one's convivial-C relations with coreligionists can coexist with one's convivial-L relations with everyone else in the state who is reasonable. In stronger terms, in order to insure the long-term flourishing of convivial-C relations with likeminded people, it is crucial for all of us to foster convivial-L relations.

In the remaining sections of this chapter I would like to explore the political liberalisms of Whitehead and Hartshorne so as to benefit from the light they shed on these two sorts of conviviality. Their contributions to political theory lie primarily in the metaphysical background they supply for both types of conviviality. Political liberalism and toleration can be seen as parts of what Whitehead refers to as the transition from force to persuasion, that is, FTP. This transition, in turn, is part of the upward adventure of the cosmos itself; indeed, the very meaning of life *is* adventure. Or, in Hartshornian terms, the best hope for politically liberal democracies is if religions themselves grow up and accentuate worship of Love (*Deus est caritas*) or of a God who omnibenevolently cooperates with others (see *AI*, 50, 69–86; *DW*, 254; Hartshorne 1997, 72–73).

METAPHYSICAL BACKGROUND

Although neither Whitehead nor Hartshorne developed a systematic political theory, they did explicitly identify themselves as liberals in politics. Whitehead worked tirelessly on the issues of egalitarian educational reform and women's suffrage, causes that led him to be pelted with rotten eggs and oranges. His overall sympathies were with the Labour Party in England. And Hartshorne was one of the founders of the Liberal Club at Harvard, although we will see a certain tension in his political thought: His idealism pushed him toward socialism and his defense of freedom pushed him toward some version of free enterprise. Further, his social background (this is probably true of Whitehead as well) gave him a certain sense of noblesse oblige (e.g., *AN* 13;

ES 13; *DW* 358; Hartshorne 1935; 1990, 69–70, 155, 168). By "liberalism" here I do not mean the laissez-faire version of liberalism popular
in the nineteenth century, which Whitehead thought had given to us
a remarkably unconvivial industrial slavery at the base of the state (*AI*
34). This type of classical liberalism relies on a view of human persons
as independent substances that are unrelated to the rest of nature and
to each other, a view that is opposed to Whitehead's and Hartshorne's
metaphysical commitments to events (rather than substances) as the
res verae and to a relational worldview (rather than to a worldview that
emphasizes independent existents). So although Whitehead and Hartshorne were political liberals at least in part due to their theism (as in
Whitehead's religious beliefs as they developed from the 1920s on), they
were not classical liberals if this means a commitment to laissez-faire
economics. In Whitehead's case, at least, his own label for his overall
view, philosophy of organism, applies not only to his view of nature but
also *in a way* to his view of the state as quasi-organic and relational.

We have seen that for Whitehead and Hartshorne, to be is to have
the dynamic power to be affected by others and the dynamic power to
affect others, in however slight a degree (see Dombrowski 2005, chap.
2). In different terms, to be is to be causally implicated in the lives of
others. One result of this view is that, although it enshrines freedom or
creativity in every event, it is also at odds with the laissez-faire fetish for
absolute freedom or independence. The past actual world both supplies
the possibilities for creative advance *and* limits the degree to which
this freedom can be exercised. Freedom is always canalized and social.
By metaphysically excluding both absolute determinism and absolute
freedom, Whitehead and Hartshorne provide the context within which
we can better understand the conviviality-L that characterizes social
relations with others in a democratic state. Or again, Whitehead and
Hartshorne share an aesthetic theory wherein both the uniformity and
monotony of collectivist states, on the one hand, and the diversity bor-
dering on chaos in laissez-faire states, on the other, are deviations from
beauty that are extreme. It is the intensity of the experience of unity in
the midst of diversity that is the ideal (see Dombrowski 2004a, chap. 2;
Hartshorne 1970, 97).

Hartshorne agrees with Whitehead that if one were to alter the
data from the past that are prehended by a present event, then one
would alter the subject of the experience. Thus, both thinkers subscribe
to a view that could be described as either partial freedom or partial

determinism. In this view God establishes optimal limits within which this partial freedom (and conviviality-L) can be exercised, although political rulers are nonetheless needed to protect this freedom when it is threatened. Both thinkers reject the idea of a God as a tyrant who decides on all of the details. In fact, political power should ideally be modeled after divine power in being persuasive and convivial-L rather than coercive, although less than ideal circumstances sometimes threaten to overwhelm this ideal. Too little government control (as in the minimal laissez-faire state) flirts with anarchy, whereas too much government control dampens creativity. The optimal limits for the exercise of partial freedom in human beings that are set by God insure that political arrangements are local exemplifications of cosmic variables (see Loomer 2013). In different terms, as Whitehead sees things, "morality of outlook is inseparably conjoined with generality of outlook" (*PR* 15).

Although both Whitehead and Hartshorne abhorred the mechanistic view of the state, they nonetheless thought that connectedness was in the order of things, specifically the internal relations between a present event and its past causal influences. Both saw time as asymmetrical in that a present event is *not* internally related to "its" future (if there be such) in that until future determinables are rendered determinate by some decision, they cannot be prehended and hence they cannot be internalized. The state is the result of several present lines of inheritance being shaped by the same or by significantly overlapping causal influences from the past.

We have seen that neither Whitehead nor Hartshorne developed a systematic political philosophy. Although they are more famous for their cosmological or metaphysical views, it should not escape our notice that the most important function of metaphysics, on Hartshorne's view, is to help in any way possible to enlighten us and to encourage us in our agonizing struggles in religion *and politics*. In the mid-decades of the twentieth century this meant that the tenuous status of the state as a quasi-organism, as found in Whitehead and to a lesser extent in Hartshorne, to be discussed momentarily, made both communism and fascism as metaphysically indefensible as the near absolute freedom that is required for the laissez-faire state. A metaphysics that makes intelligible the claim *Deus est caritas* (God is love) is efficacious in relieving this agony, a relief that is not given in the classical view of God as strictly permanent and immune to human and other influence. Neoclassical or process metaphysics has us take very seriously the historical struggles of creatures as well as the history of divine reception/response to these struggles. In fact, because of scientific and metaphysical problems with simultaneity, even perception is historical in the sense that it takes a finite amount of time to receive the information that we see and hear in everyday perceptions, as becomes clear to us when we perceive really distant events, as in the epistemically present perception of a star that burned out light years ago. In effect, history should be our cognitive paradigm, not mathematics (Hartshorne 1970, 55–56, 119).

The ultimate roots of political freedom can be seen as lying in the very nature of things, on the process view; hence, it is important in both religion and politics to develop institutions that are compatible with this fact. As before, the freedom in question does not refer to the absence of influence from others. Although Hartshorne admits that, as a result of entangling influences, political questions are much harder than metaphysical ones, he is nonetheless convinced that mistakes at the metaphysical level insure that political disasters will follow (Hartshorne 2011, chap. 13; 2001, 93).

DIFFERENT EMPHASES?

It must be admitted that there are differences in emphasis in the political liberalisms of Whitehead and Hartshorne and that these differences could have an effect on how we might interpret FTP and conviviality-L. Whitehead is more likely than Hartshorne to subscribe to the view of the state as a quasi-organic whole. Although Hartshorne has a view of organic wholes that is similar to Whitehead's (in that both see them as being compounded out of organic, feeling microconstituents, in contrast to a mere aggregate of microscopic feeling as found in a plant or a rock), he is reticent to talk of states as organic wholes. For Hartshorne, political democracies (and other forms of government) are also metaphysical democracies in that they lack a presiding actual occasion that would make them metaphysical monarchies or true "ones." A cell is a true one or a center of experience, an animal with a central nervous system is a true one or a center of experience, and God as the soul for the whole body of the world is a true one (the Truest One) or a center of experience; hence, all of these are metaphysical "monarchies." But a state is a metaphysical "democracy," no matter what form of government is in place and despite the fact that such a state is composed of various metaphysical monarchies. Although we whimsically personify the state in the United States in terms of "Uncle Sam," there really is no organic center of experience in this state. It is a collection of parts, some of which are metaphysical monarchies and some of which are metaphysical democracies. It must be admitted, however, that Whitehead was aware of the fact that a national hero like George Washington could become a symbol that could metaphorically animate the activities of the state (*SY* 77). To put the point in terms of political theory, Hartshorne could be seen as having a bit more in common with classical liberals than Whitehead does. Whitehead could be seen as leaning more in the direction of a modern liberal view, as Randall Morris insightfully argues.

The differences between the two can be easily overstated, however. This is due in part to the fact that even in Whitehead the state is only a quasi-organic whole and is not to be literally identified as a super-organism like "Mother Russia" or the "Fatherland." That is, in both Whitehead and Hartshorne there is opposition not only to anarchic and substantialist individualism but also to collectivism. These oppositions lead us to realize that political moderation is metaphysically grounded. Both Whitehead and Hartshorne were very familiar with (having lived and suffered through the early and mid-decades of the twentieth century), and both were decidedly opposed to, the remarkably unconvivial relations among people found in those states, both communist and fascist, that had totalitarian aspirations based on their aggressively organic view of the state. Although both had severe criticisms of fascism, Whitehead thought that the Soviet system might have been a slight improvement over political relations in Russia under the czars, and Hartshorne was thankful for the role the Soviet Union played in making an asymptotic approach to the political ideal possible by defeating the Nazis, even if the Soviet Union itself did not closely approximate the ideal: the synthesis of order *and* freedom (*DW* 128, 220, 294; Hartshorne 1948, xvi, 150; 1987, 44–47; 2011, 143).

However, the differences between the two can also be easily overstated at Hartshorne's end. His greater reticence to view the state as an organism in its own right could be interpreted, as Morris does, as a tip of the hat to the grain of truth (if the mixed metaphor be permitted) found in defenders of free enterprise. But it could also be interpreted as further evidence of his theocentrism, which is by all accounts somewhat more pronounced than Whitehead's. Hartshorne is a bit more insistent than Whitehead (although the point may well be implicit in Whitehead, too) that we are more citizens of the cosmos than we are citizens of any quasi-organic (at best) state. Once again, the cosmos as a whole is an organism, according to Hartshorne, that is animated by a panentheistic God. In addition to the two aforementioned convivialities, Hartshorne points us toward conviviality-W, world-inclusive conviviality, where the FTP transition has relevance for our current environmental crisis, as we will see.

In effect, Whitehead sometimes tempts us in a communitarian way to have convivial-C values seep into our appreciation for conviviality-L, whereas there is less of a temptation to do this in Hartshorne. On my own Hartshornian view, conviviality-L should remain somewhat abstract due not only to the desire to be fair to others in a condition of pervasive pluralism of comprehensive doctrines but also to remind us of the more concrete sorts of organic reality found in conviviality-C and conviviality-W. Nonetheless, Hartshorne is as much a political liberal as Whitehead, with a "liberal" being defined as one who knows he or she is not God (Hartshorne 1984a, 9). Further, Hartshorne is insightful in pointing out that most political incompatibilities involve a conflict of good with good; it is the mark of unconvivial dogmatism to think that the major source of discord is the conflict between good and evil (Hartshorne 1953b, 99). The noticeable unconviviality evidenced in recent United States politics seems to be due to a failure to acknowledge Hartshorne's point here. The problem, as political liberals have long noticed, is the unmitigated intensity with which religious and political beliefs are often held. Hartshorne tellingly admires Jews and Christians who are friends without the (especially Christian) temptation to convert the other (Hartshorne 1997, 67, 77).

In both thinkers there is, on the one hand, an affirmation of the partial freedom of the *individual* and, on the other, an affirmation of what Hartshorne calls reality as *social* process. And in both thinkers there is an admiration for a mixed economy that includes both individual initiative and socialized industry and projects. Like Whitehead, Hartshorne saw contemporary capitalism as ugly. The mixed economy need not be seen as a lukewarm compromise but could be seen as a use of bold contrasts in an overall aesthetic harmony (e.g., Hartshorne 1953b, 47). For both Whitehead and Hartshorne there is an attempt to avoid the twin evils of abstract individualism and abstract or mythically organic collectivism. There is never a vacuum of power in that when the gods leave, the half-gods arrive. Among these half-gods are state worship, Nazi power worship, Lenin worship, but also self-worship or despair (Hartshorne 1948, 148; 1953b, 68).

The differences in emphasis in the two thinkers are thus not as striking as their similarities, on my view. No mere state is a subject because it does not experience. (Nor do corporations experience; hence, they ought not to be seen as persons.) To say that a state *does* experience is shorthand for saying that the state's members do. Likewise, states are real and important because their members are real and important. The intrinsic value in the world is to be found in experiencing individuals (i.e., metaphysical monarchies) in that only they enjoy or suffer. If Whitehead and Hartshorne are panpsychists, as I think they are, this is not to be taken to mean that literally *everything* feels or experiences. To be a panpsychist is to hold that all concrete singulars feel or experience, but not abstractions or abstract aggregates of concrete singulars. Animals (including human ones) are distinctive in the ways that they can take the feelings of concrete singulars like cells and then gather them together and transmute them at the multicellular level such that, as Hartshorne emphasizes, if you hurt my cells you can hurt *me*. But states are only metaphorically sentient. Any whole that has less unity than its most unified parts is not a sentient organism in any morally relevant sense (Hartshorne 1970, 111, 141; 1962, 192).

Hartshorne bridges whatever gap there might be between his view and Whitehead's when he devotes an entire chapter to the elements of truth in the group mind concept. The key idea here is that the characters of individuals vary in light of the characters of groups they belong to (Hartshorne 1953b, chap. 3). But a state cannot love us, as God can. Hence, extreme organicism should be avoided. We need to resist the absolutization and personification of the state or the party, just as we should resist the selfishness that is permitted (despite Adam Smith's distinction between rational self-interest and selfishness) in capitalist countries (Hartshorne 1937, 33–34). The process metaphysics of democracy, for both Whitehead and Hartshorne, also involves a critique of the classical theistic God, who functions as a despot and who provides a model for various political dictators. That is, the worship of sheer omnipotence is not unconnected to a hierarchical and undemocratic view of ecclesial or other polity. By contrast, the model provided by the neoclassical, process God is that of a divinity who is not only influenced by the creatures but who is omnibenevolently *most* influenced by them. It is a poor ruler (or dialectical partner) who only speaks and does not listen (Hartshorne 1948, 50–51, 111; 1953a, 20; 1970, 232).

It should be noted that strictly speaking in process thought the most concrete realities are neither states *nor individuals* but sequences of events that are characterized by a high level of symbolic functioning and a certain degree of creative freedom. Both Whitehead and Hartshorne militate against the dominant Western tradition of taking individualism as ultimate. This tradition prevented many people in the West during the Cold War from seeing the ignoble side of individualism in addition to the noble (human rights) side. This failure is not unrelated to metaphysical confusion regarding the relation of events to enduring things (which are called "societies" by Whitehead and Hartshorne). Event pluralism "cuts the nerve" of even subtle forms of self-interest theory in politics (Hartshorne 1970, 190–191, 198; 1997, chap. 12, titled "Beyond Enlightened Self-Interest: The Illusions of Egoism"). Process thought involves a social conception of the universe that Hartshorne even calls "societism." The divine attributes themselves are types of social relationship (e.g., being affected by the object known or the person loved). And our own feeling is really a feeling *of* feeling at the cellular level; hence, human experience itself is inherently social: The individual freedom of action found in an event is conditioned by its passivity to the influence of preceding others. We have seen that this power to receive influence from others and to creatively respond to it is spread throughout the universe on the process view (Hartshorne 1934, 193–195; 1948, 134, 156; 1953b, 24).

NEED FOR IDEOLOGY CRITIQUE?

Hartshorne has argued that there are metaphysical reasons for optimism. On the basis of traditional metaphysics, causes were seen as more exalted than effects, such that the transition from one to the other meant a descent from better to worse. This etiolatry (worship of causes) makes pessimism a metaphysical axiom. On the neoclassical or process view, however, God both causally influences all *and* is influenced by all, so it is just as true to say that God is first effect as it is to say that God is first cause. In fact, effects are more inclusive than causes in that effects both assimilate the influence from causes and creatively advance beyond them (Hartshorne 1970, 108, 127, 157).

The inherent optimism of the process view is in contrast, say, to Heidegger's version of romanticism, which is inherently pessimistic in that if philosophy and hence culture have been deteriorating even since the time of the pre-Socratics, our best or perhaps only hope comes from recovering or unearthing something from the past. Whitehead goes so far as to claim that "the pure conservative is fighting against the essence of the universe" (*AI* 274). And Hartshorne thinks that unmitigated conservativism is doomed (Hartshorne 1953b, 51). Despite the dominant progressive tendency in both Whitehead and Hartshorne, their politics is ironically just as likely to be criticized from the left as from the right. This is odd when it is considered that Hartshorne thought that politics requires *mutual* sympathy and that he commended a book by Martin Weitzman with the title *The Share Economy*; this citation provides a counterbalance to his treatment of the Chicago economist Henry Simons (Hartshorne 1997, 20, 69; also 1935).

For example, Morris thinks that the political thought of Whitehead and especially Hartshorne is in dire need of ideology critique because it is alleged that their cosmological or metaphysical positions are masks for underlying bourgeois ideals like "freedom" and "individuality" (Morris 1991, 221). Because Morris has offered one of the most insightful commentaries on the political thought of Whitehead and Hartshorne to date (and whom Hartshorne thought surely got some things right regarding process political philosophy—see Hartshorne 2001, 92), his position here deserves criticism on at least two points, both of which are related to the theme of conviviality and the FTP transition.

First, even in Hartshorne, and especially in Whitehead, there is not only familiarity with, but also agreement with, the traditional Marxist criticism that liberal freedoms *as found in* laissez-faire arrangements are merely formal. That is, convivial-L freedoms of religion or the press do not amount to much for people who are starving or who do not have the material basis on which to exercise such freedoms. Consider Hartshorne's comment that "without a substantial measure of economic equality genuine political equality cannot be achieved" (Hartshorne 1984a, 235). The fact that the measure of economic equality called for is "substantial" gives Hartshorne's view a family resemblance to the Rawlsian view, with its three principles of justice (the first principle—the equal liberty principle—plus the two parts of the second principle—the equality of opportunity principle and the difference principle). If this politically liberal, rather than libertarian, view were enacted in practice, it would lead to a state that was more egalitarian than any existing one, including the Scandinavian social welfare states (see Daniels). My claim here is that if we unmask process metaphysics, what we find underneath is not something concerning which we should be ashamed but, by contrast, a nuanced and defensible view of what a just state would look like with all three convialities flourishing: L, C, and W (regarding conviviality-W, see Hartshorne 1937, 238–239).

Second, "freedom" and "individual," as these terms are used in Whitehead and Hartshorne, strike me as quite unlike the bourgeois uses of these terms that Morris rightly disparages. We have seen earlier that in process thought freedom is always canalized by historical circumstances (and hence is opposed to classical liberalism's myth regarding absolute freedom) and is inherently social and relational (and hence is opposed to classical liberalism's and modern philosophy's myth regarding nonrelational independent substances). Thus, the uses of "freedom" in Whitehead and Hartshorne are thoroughly consistent with, and actually foster, all three aforementioned sorts of conviviality.

Likewise, "individuals" in process thought are identified in terms of their ability to be centers of feeling. Reasonable people can disagree, for example, regarding whether or not plants can feel as "ones" in addition to the feelings that occur in the cellular parts of plants. Whitehead and Hartshorne think that they cannot; hence, plants are metaphysical democracies, on their view. Or again, neither Whitehead nor (especially) Hartshorne think that contemporary political states are really metaphysical "ones," but this does not commit them to individualism as construed by defenders of laissez-faire. Human individuals have only partial freedom and are subject to all of the constraints present in a relational, event-pluralist worldview as such is defended by Whitehead and Hartshorne. The quite different types of real conviviality, I allege, are to be found within such constraints. Granted, some human rights claims are argued *against* the state (as in the right not to be lied to or tortured by the government), but others are argued *through* the state (Hartshorne 1937, 32).

Although their contributions to political theory lie primarily in the metaphysical backing they provide for Rawlsian politically liberal attitudes and institutions, at times Whitehead and Hartshorne can be quite perceptive about very particular social realities. For example,

Whitehead argues that because of the relative paucity of class barriers in the United States, those who have, through talent or luck or both, risen through economic strata have tended to leave behind those with whom they were previously connected; deracination is the rule. By contrast, the thicker class barriers in England have encouraged talented people from the lower classes to stick with their class, as in the historically energetic labor movement in that country that cannot be ignored by those who are in power. The result, Whitehead insightfully observes, is that in England the aristocracy is being forced to bring into existence a more genuine sort of democracy than in the United States, and in the latter country there is a real danger that democracy could evolve into an economic aristocracy (*DW* 44, 86). Whether Whitehead is correct in this nuanced observation is less important than the fact that he provides ample evidence that he is anything but naïve about political and economic realities. The political beliefs of Whitehead and Hartshorne are in the open and available for criticism; there is no need to unmask them or to disentangle them from metaphysical abstractions.

Process thinkers can agree not merely with the idea *that* there is a need to have sufficient material goods in order for formal rights to have any meaning but also with the idea that highlights *how* people meet their needs for food, shelter, health care, and so forth, which can affect religious, philosophical, and political beliefs. But process thinkers are, like Rawls, typically skittish about the claim that this material underpinning to ideation is all-determining or absolute. In different terms, it is one thing to admit that people tend to think positively about the political system under which they live as long as it provides a satisfying life, but it is another to push beyond this to claim, as Morris does, that process metaphysics is a mask for Whiteheadian or Hartshornian material contentedness. For example, there are independent reasons to agree with Hartshorne in his critique of the Soviet system, where "orders are not given gently or rarely" (Hartshorne 1983, 220). It now seems that the tyranny and cruelty that Hartshorne noticed in the Soviet Union were even worse than they seemed (see Snyder; also Hartshorne 1987, 139; and Dikotter). Hartshorne readily granted that the relatively mixed economy of the United States had been good to him, but this is not sufficient warrant for the idea that we should adopt a hermeneutics of suspicion with respect to either his political or metaphysical views.

"Our vast inequalities in economic status are no cause for complacency insofar as they mean near helplessness for many to achieve decent, healthy, and intelligent participation in social and political life" (Hartshorne 1983, 222). With these words we realize why Hartshorne, like Whitehead, opposed the unconvivial character of laissez-faire economics, or, if he did sometimes speak favorably of the laissez-faire idea, it was an odd version of the idea that included consumer cooperatives, limitations on advertising, and measures that would be conducive to all three ideals of the French Revolution: not merely liberty but also equality (as long as it is not absolutized) and fraternity/sorority. In this regard, process thinkers are like Rawls in moving beyond libertarian fascination with only the first of these three ideals. Pervasive belief in the brotherhood/sisterhood of all human beings is especially conducive to conviviality-L as well as to various convivialities-C (Hartshorne 1983, 226–227; 1970, 221; 1997, 67 as well as chap. 14; Rawls 1999b, 90–91).

PROCESS LIBERALISM

As Thomas Nagel emphasizes, the term "liberal" can mean many different things to many different people (Nagel 2003, 62). In Europe and Latin America, it tends to be used (along with "neoliberal") by those on the left to castigate the right, whereas in the United States it tends to be used by those on the right to castigate the left. It is therefore just as important to be clear regarding what one does not mean by "liberalism" as by what one means. Four points should be made.

First, I am not defending, nor were Whitehead or Hartshorne or Rawls defending, comprehensive liberalism as a nonreligious worldview meant to replace the one that dominated in the religious ages. My goal (as well as Whitehead's and Hartshorne's and Rawls' goal) is the more modest one of defending political liberalism, which in Whitehead and Hartshorne involves the search for metaphysical principles that facilitate the articulation of principles of justice whereby citizens who adhere to quite different comprehensive doctrines can nonetheless live together in a peaceful and fair manner. I do not detect even the slightest bit of evidence in Whitehead or Hartshorne in favor of the view that one would have to be "converted" to a process worldview or to theism in order to be a full-fledged and equal member of a democratic state. In this regard Whitehead and Hartshorne contribute to conviviality-L by encouraging religious believers to emulate the neoclassical God as persuasive rather than the traditional God as coercive, indeed as omnipotent tyrant, who is even compared by Whitehead to Adolf Hitler (*DW* 176)!

Second, I am not defending what can variously be called classical liberalism or neoliberalism or libertarianism or a laissez-faire state. In fact, the Rawlsian view of liberalism I defend is at odds with these views, as the sharp debate between the libertarian Robert Nozick and Rawlsians indicates (see Nozick, chap. 7). Whitehead clearly saw problems with laissez-faire versions of liberalism, as is indicated in his aforementioned nasty language regarding industrial slavery and the ugliness of contemporary capitalism. Further, I would like to emphasize that even Hartshorne, who admittedly has an attitude toward markets and economic competition that is a bit friendlier than Whitehead's, defends a stance "between present-day capitalism and socialism," in which "the ideal of complete socialization is illiberal," yet also in which the notion that private agencies could manage all business is "calamitous." That is, Hartshorne is well aware of the facts, as we all should be, that both unbridled competition and unchecked government bureaucracy (as ridiculed by Franz Kafka) can be unconvivial. In fact, they can be unjust to individuals. Neither of these are foolproof and neither should be fetishized (Hartshorne 1935; 2001, 14).

Hartshorne is also clear that unthinking attachment to Smith's invisible hand unwittingly commits one to a sort of Stoic determinism. (In fact, Smith borrowed the invisible hand metaphor from the Stoics.) But this implied determinism is at odds with process metaphysics, wherein each concrete singular exhibits at least *some* degree of creative response to what it has received. In different terms, all determinists are theologians in the sense that they are positing, whether explicitly or implicitly, the sort of knowledge of the future, with absolute assurance and in minute detail, that was claimed for the classical theistic God. But this is to turn the indeterminateness of the future into the determinateness of the past, and it is to trivialize the power of creative agents to render future determinables determinate in the clutch of vivid immediacy in the present. Further, as we have seen, neither selfishness nor an ethics based on self-interest make sense metaphysically if, as process theists maintain, one's purpose is not merely to serve oneself but to serve others and to serve God, who is here seen as an analogy between a thinking animal and the cosmos conceived as animate. As before, the political consequences of metaphysical blunders can be catastrophic, it seems (Hartshorne 1937, 151; 1948, 133; 1953b, 108; 1970, 220).

Third, just as conviviality-L acts as an umbrella for various convivialities-C, analogously conviviality-W shelters various convivialities-L and *a fortiori* convivialities-C. Whitehead's way of articulating conviviality-W is in terms of his triadic theory of value, wherein intrinsic (i.e., not merely instrumental) value is found in sentient individuals, others, *and the whole* or God (e.g., *MT* 117; also see Henning 2005) and in terms of what he calls the "solidarity of the universe" (*PR* 56). And Hartshorne's way of understanding conviviality-W is in terms of his belief that God is the mind or soul who animates not this or that particular body but the whole embodied cosmos (see Dombrowski 2005, chap. 1). It is no accident that the very first philosophical dissertation in environmental ethics was written from the point of view of process thought (Armstrong) and that environmentalism has flourished in process circles in various publications. The reticulative vision encouraged by Whitehead and Hartshorne facilitates not only environmental justice but also liberal international justice. The problems here are largely conceptual: Crises in international justice and environmental justice are very often the result of a failure to even imagine, much less to explicate and defend, an organic reality greater than the state.

And fourth, it is no accident that both Whitehead and Hartshorne were political liberals in that the overall method that is operative in political liberalism (reflective equilibrium) is itself thoroughly processual and fallibilist. The Rawlsian method of reflective equilibrium is an attempt to move away from the proof paradigm in political philosophy, wherein the goal is to search for absolutely certain starting points and then to deduce secure political conclusions from them. By contrast, reflective equilibrium is similar to Aristotelian dialectic, wherein one starts from intuition or habit or prevailing opinion, but then these starting points are put to the test by theory and empirical investigation and counterexamples (see Rawls 1999b, 45). If disequilibrium occurs between, say, intuition and theory, then further inquiry is required in order to more closely approximate equilibrium between the two. Nothing is held to be fixed in advance in that intuition or public opinion may change and theory may be criticized in the *ongoing process* of dialectical exchange. That is, the method of reflective equilibrium is a self-correcting procedure in the continuing effort to live together in a peaceful and fair manner in a convivial-L state (see Dombrowski 2011, chap. 1; also see Malone-France 2012, chap. 6). When FTP or conviviality-L breaks down, the tendency of political liberals like Whitehead, Hartshorne, Rawls, and me is to urge that further civil discourse and rational inquiry are required. From a methodological point of view, political liberalism is not so much a political program as it is a *process* for both adjudication of disputes and facilitation of convivialities when and where these exist.

FOUR

Hartshorne, the Process Concept of God, and Pacifism

DIPOLAR THEISM

Process thinkers are likely to claim that Whitehead and Hartshorne should be ranked toward the top of the list, or perhaps even at the very top, of twentieth-century philosophers (see Latour ix). Most of the enormous attention their work has received has concerned their metaphysics, their views of science and religion, and so forth, and rightfully so. Yet this should not hide their contributions as ethicists. In this chapter I will concentrate on the relationship between their dipolar theory of God and pacifism, which has not yet received sufficient scholarly analysis.

My thesis is that Whitehead and Hartshorne have offered the richest criticisms of pacifism to date in metaphysics, which is saying quite a bit when it is considered that they have competition from the likes of G. E. M. Anscombe. However, I will also claim that Whitehead's and Hartshorne's criticisms of pacifism are often inadequate. My procedure will be to start with Hartshorne and then move to Whitehead in something like a sonata form, where my own view becomes apparent regarding the common theme of the chapter—FTP—as it is repeated by these two great figures in the history of process thought.

Hartshorne's neoclassical or process theism is based on a distinction between invidious and noninvidious contrasts. The contrast excellent-inferior is the truly invidious contrast when applied to God. If to be invidious is to be injurious, then this contrast is the most invidious one of all when applied (both terms) to God because God is only excellent. God is inferior in no way. Period. To suggest that God is in some way inferior to some other being is to no longer speak about God but about some being that is not supremely excellent, all-worshipful, or the greatest conceivable. Hartshorne's major criticism of classical theism is that it has assumed that all contrasts, or most of them, when applied to God are invidious.

Let us assume from now on that God exists. What attributes does God possess? Consider the following two columns of attributes in polar contrast to each other:

one	many
being	becoming
active	passive
permanent	changing
necessary	contingent
self-sufficient	dependent
actual	potential
absolute	relative
abstract	concrete

Classical theism tends toward oversimplification. It is comparatively easy to say "God is strong rather than weak, so in all relations God is active, not passive." In each case, the classical theist decides which member of the contrasting pair is good (on the left), then attributes it to God, while wholly denying the contrasting term (on the right). Hence, God is one but not many, permanent but not changing, and so forth. This leads to what Hartshorne calls the monopolar prejudice. Monopolarity is common to both classical theism and pantheism: The major difference between the two is the fact that classical theism admits the reality of plurality, potentiality, and becoming as a secondary form of existence "outside" God (on the right), whereas in pantheism God includes all reality within itself. Common to both classical theism and pantheism is the belief that the preceding categorical contrasts are invidious. The dilemma these two positions face is that either the deity is only one constituent of the whole (classical theism) or else the alleged inferior pole in each contrast (on the right) is illusory (pantheism).

For Hartshorne this dilemma is artificial. It is produced by the assumption that excellence is found by separating and purifying one pole (on the left) and denigrating the other (on the right). That this is not the case can be seen by analyzing some of the attributes on the right side. At least since St. Augustine classical theists have been convinced that God's eternity meant not that God endured through all time, but that God was outside of time altogether and did not, could not, be receptive to temporal change or to the suffering of temporal beings. St. Thomas Aquinas identified God, following Aristotle, who was the greatest predecessor to classical theism, as unmoved. Yet both activity and passivity can be either good or bad. Good passivity is likely to be called sensitivity, responsiveness, adaptability, sympathy, and the like. Insufficiently subtle or defective passivity is called wooden inflexibility, mulish stubbornness, inadaptability, unresponsiveness, and the like. Passivity per se refers to the way in which an individual's activity takes account of, and renders itself appropriate to, the activities of others. To deny God passivity altogether is to deny God those aspects of passivity that are excellences. Or again, to altogether deny God the ability to change does avoid fickleness but does so at the expense of the ability to lovingly react to the sufferings of others. These defects are not unrelated to classical theism's easy acceptance of the use of violence, as I will show.

I should note at this point that recent defenses of "free will theism" or "open theism" partially escape my criticisms of classical theism in that defenders of these views see God as relational and they do not allege that God knows with absolute assurance and in minute detail what will happen in the future. However, defenders of these views nonetheless think that even if God does not exert unilateral power, God *could* do so, which seems to indicate an oblique attachment to divine omnipotence on their part. If being *is* power, as Hartshorne and Whitehead think, then no being, not even a divine one, could be claimed to have *all* power, even if a divine being could influence or have persuasive power over everything else.

The terms on the left side have both good and bad aspects as well. Oneness can mean wholeness, but it can also mean monotony or triviality. Actuality can mean definiteness, or it can mean nonrelatedness to others. What happens to divine love when God, according to St.

Thomas, is claimed to be pure actuality? God ends up loving the world but is not intrinsically related to it, whatever sort of love that may be. Self-sufficiency can, at times, be selfishness.

When thinking of God, the task for Hartshorne is to attribute to God all excellences (left and right sides)—hence, Hartshorne calls his position "dual transcendence"—and not to attribute to God any inferiorities (right and left sides). In short, excellent-inferior, knowledge-ignorance, or good-evil are invidious contrasts, but one-many, being-becoming, among others, are noninvidious contrasts. Unlike classical theism and pantheism, Hartshorne's theism is dipolar. To be specific, within each pole of a noninvidious contrast (e.g., permanence-change), there are invidious elements (inferior permanence or inferior change) but also noninvidious, good elements (excellent permanence or excellent change).

For Hartshorne, God is, in one aspect of God, lovingly related to the world. In fact, in this aspect God is the integral totality of all ordinary causes and effects, but in another aspect, God's essence, God is conceivable in abstraction from contingent beings. It is only the latter aspect of God (the left side) that St. Thomas and the medievals came close to describing, yet they erred even here, according to both Hartshorne and Whitehead, as we have seen, by making God a tyrant, a despot, who was immune to influence by others. By contrast, dipolar theism not only distinguishes God from the "all," it also makes God, in a way, include and hence be influenced by the "all" (see Hartshorne 1941a, 348; 1953a, 1–25).

DIPOLAR THEISM AND PACIFISM

Hartshorne explicitly establishes a connection between pacifism and his theory of God in *Beyond Humanism*. As he sees it, the notion of a tyrannical God, albeit a supposedly benevolent one, cannot be logically defended. He spent a good deal of his career elaborating this thesis. He thinks it follows, then, that human beings should not emulate the classical God as tyrant by developing a fetish for force or coercive power. On the other hand, he also opposes "absolute pacifism," which lies at the other end of the spectrum and tries to settle all human affairs by love, without resort to force. He even goes so far as to say that both positions—militarism and pacifism—are "contrary to theism," thereby suggesting not only that he is opposed to pacifism but also that pacifism is not a position that he would even acknowledge as a logically possible one for other theists to hold. Very few theists would go this far, fewer still on logical grounds (Hartshorne 1937, 26–27).

How does Hartshorne support his view? He suggests that "only God possesses the degree of love which renders superfluous the nonsympathetic forms of power." That is, pacifism is a type of hubris exhibited by those who think they can rival the "power" of God's love. For Hartshorne, we are "bound" to coerce one another "more or less unsympathetically," although he admits that some (he seems to have Hitler in mind—Hartshorne 1937, 26–27; 1970, 308, 320) do so in an "egregious and intolerable fashion." Tyrants "feed upon the pacifist delusion," we are told, almost as much as they do "upon the delusion that unsympathetic power is divine." Only a sentimental theism, not a rationally metaphysical one, leads to these erroneous conclusions: (1) militarism as an imitation of the transcendent tyrant of monopolar classical theism and (2) pacifism as a syrupy or hubristic imitation of the God of love.

In a chapter on "God and Righteousness" in *Man's Vision of God*, Hartshorne again suggests that pacifism fails to "imitate the divine awareness" by exhibiting, surprisingly, a *deficiency* of social awareness (Hartshorne 1941a, 166–173). To fail to veto the desires of a tyrant leads to a net deficiency of desires for all, whereas God seeks the lesser sacrifice, even if it means using coercive force. The following remark is crucial:

> Dogmatic pacifism is often the expression of a preference for a certain enjoyable sentiment as against facing the tragedy of existence, which even God does not escape, and which we must all share together. To decide to shorten a man's life (we all die) is not *ipso facto* to lack sympathy with his life as it really is, that is, to lack love for him. (Hartshorne 1941a, 168)

What remains to be seen is why and how the pacifist fails to face the tragedy of existence and how killing a person can be an act of love.

Pacifists do provide a service, however, in that they "can remain more aware of *some* of the social realities" while the soldier fights. "Only God can entirely avoid specialization of sympathy without falling into utter superficiality." But "proud, willful, uncooperative men" (the militarists who find unsympathetic power divine) will never understand the gentle passivity of God. So also, "weak and flabby men" (sentimental pacifists) will never understand the energy of God's resistance to the excesses of creaturely will at the point where these excesses threaten the destruction of creaturely vitality. Like Plato's child crying for both (*Sophist* 249d), Hartshorne wants to have the virtues and avoid the vices of these two positions, as God does in a "cosmic way," setting "limits by constraint to the destruction of mutuality" (Hartshorne 1941a, 166–173).

"A Philosophy of Democratic Defense," although a little-known essay, exhibits Hartshorne's theory at a deeper level still (see Hartshorne 1942). He defines love as taking the interests of others into one's own sphere of interest. If there are discords among human interests, as Hartshorne thinks there must be (we are "bound" to coerce one another "more or less unsympathetically"), then "such discords will, through love, become discords within the loving Being." Perhaps this is the tragedy that the pacifist fails to face, by thinking that tragedy contradicts the perfection of God. But Hartshorne says:

> A love static-and-dynamic in its perfection could include within its own content such conflicts of interest as render war sometimes the lesser evil than refusal or failure of the wronged party to resist by force of arms. This completes our critique of pacifism, which seems to evade rather than face the tragedy of existence. (Hartshorne 1942, 159, 162)

The critique is only temporarily ended, however, and is resumed again in *The Divine Relativity* (Hartshorne 1948, 149, 154–155). Hartshorne directs his attention to classical theism and to monopolar medieval theology, with its "abject power worship, tinged with cowardice." This theory claims that God is good because active while, "in relation to him, all else can be only passive." It did not dawn on the medieval theorists, and their epigoni, that "the ultimate power is the power of sensitivity." Pacifism is the almost contrary error, he thinks, in that the pacifist engages in "magical politics" if he or she thinks that *human* sensitivity is enough. To be clear, whereas free will theists and open theists grant that God allows human freedom, even if such freedom is misused, God *could* overrule human freedom; by contrast, Hartshorne's view is that it is not within God's power to unilaterally coerce the freedom of any creature because God's power is inherently persuasive and relational, not coercive and unilateral. This is the result of both meta-physical reasons (if being *is* dynamic power, all concrete singulars have *some* power of their own) and moral ones (in that unilateral power is at odds with omnibenevolent relationality).

"All power is sensitivity," for Hartshorne, but there are direct and indirect uses of power. "God acts on all things directly," but "one man's purpose influences another man, telepathy apart, only by first modify-ing the man's bodily parts." For this and other reasons, human power of sensitivity is indirect. "Brute power" is also an indirect relation, "never a direct one," even if it is efficacious. We will see why this is the case later. Commenting on this brute power, Hartshorne says: "The one thing we need not and ought not to do," and here the pacifist would agree with Hartshorne, "is—to worship it!" (Hartshorne 1948, 149, 154–155).

PACIFISM AND PRACTICALITY

Although Hartshorne's disdain for pacifism largely seems to emanate from his dipolar theory of God, its source may also be a theory regard-ing pacifism's impracticality. We have seen that Hartshorne believes that we are "bound" to coerce one another "more or less unsympatheti-cally," and tyrants "feed upon the pacifist delusion." Seeing pacifism as a type of inertia, rather than as a type of nonviolent *resistance* to evil, he also states that "the pacifist must be ready to *cooperate with anyone who sets out to take advantage of him*" (my emphasis—see Hartshorne 1941a, 171). Or again, pacifists are "unheroic," "weak and flabby men" (Hartshorne 1941a, 173). Hartshorne quickly disposes of Gandhi as a "partisan." Presumably, Gandhi's pacifism would be, for Hartshorne, contrary to theism (see Hartshorne 1941a, 171; 1962, 298–299). The important thing to notice is that it is *only if* these practical or factual claims are true that the pacifist produces a deficiency of social aware-ness, and hence provides an untrue likeness of the divine life and love, even to the point where the pacifist can be claimed to be "contrary to theism." And *only if* these practical or factual claims are true does the pacifist, by failing to admit pacifism's deficiency of social awareness, also fail to face the tragedy of existence, even divine existence. For these reasons the issue of practicality must be considered in order to under-stand the relationship between dipolar theism and pacifism and hence to understand FTP.

In order to show that the supposed impracticality of pacifism cannot be established, I will not treat a straw person, but what most would regard as the most difficult case of all for the pacifist, and the one Hartshorne (as well as Whitehead, as we will see) almost always has in mind when he criticizes pacifism: Hitler. Many accept Hartshorne's view as a truism that pacifism would not "work" with Hitler, yet at the end of his well-known book *The Origins of the Second World War*, A. J. P. Taylor makes the following crucial points regarding World War Two:

> Men will long debate whether this renewed war could have been averted by greater firmness or by greater conciliation; and no answer will be found to these hypothetical speculations. Maybe either would have succeeded, if consistently followed; the mixture of the two, practiced by the British government, was the most likely to fail. (Taylor 1962, 278)

"Greater firmness" would have been Winston Churchill's, and presumably Hartshorne's (and to a lesser extent, Whitehead's), approach. But Neville Chamberlain's approach, the one that failed, does not exhaust the possibilities. Appeasement is not the same as pacifism. The former is the "mixture" alluded to above, which in effect drew lines in the sand at Versailles and threatened Germany with retribution if it crossed those lines—and when Hitler crossed one line and nothing happened, then another. . . . But a pacifist, if interpreted not only as an opponent to violence as a means of settling disputes but also as an opponent to threats of violence, would never have been party to the treaty at Versailles in the first place. As Taylor suggests, pacifism or "greater conciliation" may have succeeded as well as "greater firmness."

Of course, we will never know if pacifism would have succeeded against Hitler, but the point is that Hartshorne cannot claim to know that it would not have succeeded. Hartshorne himself admits that the reparations and guilt-admissions sections of the Versailles treaty showed a lack of "even handed sympathy," as did America's tariff policy toward Germany (Hartshorne 1941a, 167). Thus, it seems unfair to blame the pacifist for the consequences of these policies and the threats that stood behind them. Violence (and threats of violence) breeds more violence. An absence of these sorts of threats and a conciliatory economic policy (as recommended by John Maynard Keynes) might have taken away the breeding ground for the Nazis and Hitler. But even if

Hitler would still have come to power, it may have been possible to nip him in the bud in the early 1930s or at any other time through Gandhi-like, nonviolent resistance from massive numbers of religious pacifists. The various religious groups in Germany, however, failed to promote pacifism not because they were skeptical of its efficacy but rather because they were not necessarily opposed to Hitler. In fact, as is well known, many religious leaders greeted Hitler with open arms and even made agreements with him. Unfortunately, we do not know if nonviolent resistance in Germany would have stopped Hitler, not because it was tried and failed, but because Hitler received very little resistance in Germany, violent or otherwise.

The problem is that Hartshorne seems to equate pacifism, appeasement, and passivity when he says that at one point (the late 1930s?) "all the world was being passive to the Nazis" (Hartshorne 1948, 154). Perhaps so, but those who were passive were seldom pacifists or nonviolent *resisters* to evil. It should also be noted that, counterintuitively, the few examples of nonviolent resistance to Hitler *did* work (see Dombrowski 2011, chap. 2).

In short, Hartshorne has not shown (as he thinks he has) that pacifism could not work either against or in Germany, nor has he shown that pacifism is a vain attempt to rival God's love. On the contrary, the pacifist might claim that both "greater firmness" and appeasement are consequences of a too feeble attempt at such rivaling, without thereby suggesting, as in Hartshorne, that those who think otherwise are contrary to theism. Pacifists are well aware of the tragic fact that we will die, often too early, but they gain some small solace in knowing that they will not kill. And pacifists who are dipolar theists are aware of the fact that the tragedy of our existence, when incorporated into the divine life through love, makes God tragic too.

PRELIMINARY CONCLUSION

Hartshorne has often remarked that St. Anselm's ontological argument was a great discovery, but its author never fully appreciated his own genius because he assumed that the God whose existence he proved was the monopolar God of classical theism (see Hartshorne 1953a, 96–98, 103–106). Might not something analogous be said about Hartshorne? Similar unwitting discoveries are common in the history of ideas, such as when Antoine Lavoisier discovered oxygen even though he thought he discovered dephlogisticated air.

Hartshorne's dipolar theism has convinced many scholars that the traditional monopolar conception of God as an active not passive, unmoved tyrant is inadequate. The God of the classical theists cannot be a God of peace but is at best an anesthetically abstract God because this God cannot receive, only act. The classical theist's God cannot experience the tragic suffering of war. And this God cannot persuade the warlike world toward a more perfect state because this God does not persuade but orders. Much less can such a God be persuaded. Hartshorne's God *can* do all of these things, without mediation. In fact, Hartshorne may have unwittingly discovered that a pursuit of peace without the mediation of violence is a more fitting type of worship to give a dipolar God than brute power.

That is, the very abstract problems with classical theism found in its concepts of omnipotence and creation *ex nihilo* have a negative impact on the transition from FTP in that on a classical theistic basis there just is no transition. On the basis of Hartshorne's neoclassical theism, however, the case for such a transition is enormously facilitated, as Colin Gunton implies (see Gunton 45–46). Quincy Wright is another scholar who is convinced that what is most noteworthy about Hartshorne's thought is its ability to reconcile at every turn: science and theology, naturalism and spiritual fulfillment, and so forth (Wright 370, 404–405).

The preliminary conclusion here is that although Hartshorne was not a pacifist, several commentators (Gunton, Wright, Brightman, myself) seem to think that he should have been one. For example, there was extended correspondence between Hartshorne and Edgar Brightman between the eventful years of 1933 and 1944. Brightman is correct to notice that Hartshorne (like Whitehead) did not take into consideration adequately the long-term consequences of a "consistently pacifist approach." Instead, Hartshorne thought it necessary to "amputate" Hitler and the Nazis. From Brightman's point of view, this approach flies in the face of personalism and the belief that human persons are ends-in-themselves. It is significant that one of Brightman's students, Martin Luther King, makes us aware of the positive practical results that are possible on a consistently pacifist approach to evil. It is also significant that Solidarity and other nonviolent resistance movements in Eastern Europe in the 1980s provide a monumental example of dictatorial power being overthrown without a shot being fired (see Auxier and Davies 121–131, 154).

NUCLEAR WEAPONS

In 1953 Hartshorne implied that his criticisms of pacifism applied to so-called nuclear pacifism as well (Hartshorne 1953b, 213–219). Later he refined his position regarding these weapons. As Kant foresaw, technological progress has made war increasingly destructive, and the rational ideal would require us to "find other ways to deal with group conflicts." Hartshorne relates this insight to his denigration of the monopolar, tyrannical God of classical theism: We need not fear God, but ourselves and our fellows, as even Douglas MacArthur realized when he noted in his 1951 address to the United States Congress that the problem is basically theological. We have built the foundations of hell on earth; hence, we no longer need hell to frighten us. Hartshorne thinks this is the lesson of Hiroshima, both that in comparison to nuclear warfare talk of a supernatural hell "seems childish folly," and that if we were more civilized we would not only have avoided using nuclear weapons twice ourselves but we would have realized that divine power is "to creatively foster and above all appreciate and love a vast variety of creatures." The irony is that Hartshorne's own views, treated earlier, are indicative of the poor foresight that he sees in others regarding the fact that advanced technologies "turn war into mass genocide if not race suicide" (Hartshorne 1981, 181; 1983, 183–184, 220–221, 223, 225, 228–229, 240, 244, 261, 321, 335–336; 1984c, 24, 86, 110, 131–133). But there is an aperture of hope: "Perhaps the threat of nuclear warfare, as close to absolute absurdity as one can fear to think of, will lead us to trust less to our individual and collective rages and greeds and more to our sympathies and admirations toward fellow creatures" (Hartshorne 1983, 336). That is, there is some small hope that there would be an end to "the many centuries spent in worshipping power more than love (and being more than creative becoming)." For example, a straightforward interpretation of God as eminent love was beyond Abraham Lincoln, who believed that the Civil War would last as long as God willed it to last. Like many theologians, Hartshorne thinks, Lincoln was more willing to confess his "ignorance of God's goodness than of his power" (Hartshorne 1984c, 24).

The question is: Did two world wars and the development of perhaps the subtlest view of God in contemporary philosophy move Hartshorne in his later writings far enough away from Lincoln's view? He still assumed in his later writings that militarism and appeasement were the only two options to deal with a Hitler or some other violent threat, and he still thought that there could not be a war to end all wars, save a war that ended the human species. Apparently, this impossibility rests on a priori grounds. He did call for a unilateral reduction of nuclear weapons, but these weapons themselves are seen as a legitimate means of defense, it seems. We dare not use nuclear weapons, but we "also *cannot* see how to do away with" them (Hartshorne 1984c, 86—emphasis added). At the very least, one wonders whether Hartshorne, as a modal logician, can support this use of the term "cannot."

Throughout his career Hartshorne viewed power in Platonic fashion as the capacity to influence others *and* the capacity to be influenced by others. This led him to speculate about a world government that would make peace more likely, on the assumption that philosophical agreement among peoples regarding comprehensive doctrines is not a necessary condition for peace. In this regard he commended the American Catholic bishops for their efforts in the 1980s to decrease the levels of nuclear weapons, in particular, and violence, in general, without thereby imposing Catholic values on others. It must also be admitted that he always saw "righteous anger" as a dubious quality, especially in the context of the "ghastly absurdity" of nuclear weapons. But these admissions do not thereby negate his overall opposition to pacifism (Hartshorne 1984a, 235; 1984b, 128, 187–188; 1997, 22, 27, 49, 75–76, 222).

HARTSHORNE'S LIFE

The preceding theoretical considerations can be amplified through a selective treatment of Hartshorne's own life. I have saved this part of my analysis of Hartshorne's thought until the end so as to avoid the charge of delivering an *ad hominem* argument. That is, Hartshorne's position can stand on its own regardless of the details of his life. But a consideration of his life makes us aware of the difficulty of the task that confronts anyone who wishes to offer a theoretical defense of pacifism and to facilitate the FTP transition.

Although Hartshorne's relatives were mostly Episcopalians, some of them were Quaker. Thus it makes sense that, growing up in Pennsylvania, he attended Haverford College from 1915 to 1917, where Quaker meetings were mandatory. And it also makes sense, given this background, that Hartshorne had a lifelong admiration for witty, nonviolent methods of defusing tense situations and for people who had physical strength balanced by a pacific inner security. For a brief period, Hartshorne himself was a pacifist who regretted even *wanting* to strike another human being. This temporary pacifism was inspired both by Leo Tolstoy and by Hartshorne's first philosophy teacher, the Quaker Rufus Jones (Hartshorne 1990, 36–38, 51, 60, 79, 120, 345, 348).

From 1917 to 1919 Hartshorne was in the Army Medical Corps in World War I in France. Some scholars erroneously assume that he entered the medical corps due to his pacifism. But he had already abandoned pacifism by 1917. He saw conscription coming and then volunteered to join the medical corps, thereby avoiding being drafted into a fighting unit. Hartshorne himself admitted that this was an unheroic act; neither was it a calculated move in order to escape danger.

There were at least two reasons for his decision. First, he could not imagine himself as an officer, which was the position he would have been expected to obtain, given his social and educational background. He was not a "man of action" who could lead others into either real battle or even the mock battles of academic life; he was by disposition a "man of thought." Second, and more importantly for my purposes, even though he had already abandoned pacifism, Hartshorne was not able to imagine himself actually killing another human being. Although eventually he petitioned (unsuccessfully) to be transferred to a fighting unit, he was consistently impressed (as are pacifists) with the ominous character of the act whereby one human being knowingly kills another without consent. If only more just war theorists were similarly impressed, then progress could be made at the very least with respect to *jus post bellum* issues, in that even on a just war basis wars tend to drag on longer than they should (Hartshorne 1990, 123–126, 152).

As before, Hartshorne tantalizes the pacifist. He grants, in pacifist fashion, that conflicts are usually not exclusively the fault of one side;

Hartshorne admits this point even with respect to his own conflicts with colleagues at the University of Chicago. Although there is no real need to respond violently to momentary and not wholly unjustified anger, there *is* sometimes a need, he thinks, to respond violently to violent bullies (Hartshorne 1990, 346, 365).

But these situations are not nearly as frequent as militarists imagine. "The altruism that people have often shown in war needs to be shown from now on in trying to prevent war, to curb our human destructiveness." This observation, which reminds one of James' famous essay regarding the "moral equivalent" of war and the need to find types of pacific competition (James 1970; also see Dombrowski 2009), was triggered not only by the development of nuclear weapons but also by the misuse of conventional weapons in Vietnam, Central America, and elsewhere. That is, at the very end of his life Hartshorne came to see that, *just short of* pacifism, it nonetheless made sense to claim that "war itself has become the enemy" (Hartshorne 1990, 372, 400, 403).

THE ETERNAL OBJECT "PEACE"

If my argument thus far is persuasive, then pacifism is not contrary to theism; much less is it contrary to dipolar theism. I would like to further support the positive case for pacifism by appeal to what Hartshorne would call the abstract object or concept "peace" and to what Whitehead would call the eternal object "peace." That is, this section of the chapter signals a transition from Hartshorne to Whitehead, although the conceptual irritation signaled in the preliminary conclusion stated earlier will remain.

It should be noted that by "eternal object" Whitehead refers to anything that can be abstracted from experience and possibly recur. Thus, Whiteheadian eternal objects are pure potentials that could in principle characterize something actual. And we should not ignore the obvious fact that eternal objects are indeed objects rather than subjects and that objects exist only for subjects. They can be felt even if they do not feel. This realization serves the purpose of alerting us to the possibly misleading tendency of the word "eternal" to have us think in Platonic terms of the superiority of the eternal to the temporal. Nothing could be further from Whitehead's intent regarding eternal objects, in general, and regarding the eternal object "peace," in particular, which nonetheless can be ingredient in actual things in process (see Cobb 2007, 23–26).

As we have seen Hartshorne indicate, in agreement with Whitehead, "the ultimate power is the power of sensitivity," and "all power is sensitivity." This marks a radical departure from classical theism in that divine power is, above all else, not reliant on "brute force" but on love. Brute power may well be, at times, an instance of sensitivity for diverse actual occasions but only indirectly. Nonviolent *resistance* to evil (or more vaguely, pacifism) not only avoids the attenuated form of peace that Whitehead calls "anaesthesia" (*AI* 285) but has the advantage of being a more *direct* (and perhaps a more powerful) exhibition of sensitivity. Brute power is more indirect than nonviolent resistance because it kills to affirm life; it makes war to establish peace. Whitehead identifies the progress of humanity with transforming it so as to make the original Christian ideals practicable. The original Christians, he notes, thought the world would end soon; hence, they were not worried, as were Christians a few centuries later, with the preservation of society and with a "fortunate worldliness" (*AI* 15–16, 81–86).

An eternal object for Whitehead (or, to use Hartshorne's language, a universal or a concept or an abstract object) is not a detached, static, pure form with a life of its own, which is then imitated by actual occasions in the world. The eternal object "peace" enters into the real world *only* as a constitutive element in real becoming. Nonviolence is a way of becoming, specifically, a more direct way of becoming like the divine becoming (see the excellent article by Robert Kinast). Let me explain. The way the eternal object "peace" enters into the real world of becoming partially depends on the subjective form of the prehending actual occasion that brings it into the real world. There can be diverse prehensions of the same eternal object. Pacifism is only one way in which peace can be experienced, but it is the most appropriate way because of the great value-intensity it yields. Pacifism properly understood is not passive but is a disciplined attempt to attain what Whitehead calls "that Harmony of Harmonies which calms destructive turbulence and completes civilization" (*AI* 285). But Whitehead is also clear that, although the gentler modes of interaction have always been present, compulsion is sometimes necessary (*AI* 56, 69). That is, he seems to imply that the FTP transition can never be complete and that some "F" always remains, an implication that is perhaps supported by the consideration that the function of God as a principle of limitation in *SM* (and other books) requires a certain degree of coercion, even if the degree of coercion required is far less than that required by the omnicompetent God of classical theism.

The first step in the discipline of becoming like the divine peaceful becoming must be the removal of acquisitive urges due to preoccupation with self. That is, the initial locus of peace is the individual, who is an example of, and a contributor to, peace on a larger scale. In that the ultimate goal of becoming in process theism is to contribute intense value to God (including the value of present happiness), acquisitiveness gets in the way because hoarding is opposed to advancing, and preoccupation with self is repetitious, not creative. The selfish person prefers to travel along the already known and possessed paths of triviality. In a peculiar sort of way even this is violent: It is to try to have the past dominate the future. The other subjective forms of prehending peace include duty (where one feels obliged to be peaceful), compromise (where one is peaceful so as to attain something other than peace), or violence (where one coerces others for the sake of peace, as in the just war theory). Only the pacifist prehends peace *for its own sake*, without a compromised or attenuated prehension.

Violence consists in the determination of other actual occasions through dominance. In place of a contrast yielding mutual satisfaction there is conflict, a vying for control rather than a productive sort of creativity. Nonviolent actions alone preserve the desire to enhance the intrinsic value of every actual occasion. All of this is suggestive of God, whose primary contribution to the world for Whitehead and many process philosophers is the supply of its initial subjective aim. (This is not to say that this is all that God does, however. In addition to holding abstract eternal objects in mind and providing the initial subjective aim for each actual occasion, the process God also gives providential guidance not by coercion but by persuasion or as a lure; further, God preserves in memory objectified value.) From the perspective of humanity, God's initial aim can be variously interpreted, but Hartshorne and Whitehead agree that God's way is typified by persuasion rather than coercion. As we have seen Whitehead put the point, "God's role is not the combat of productive force with productive force, of destructive force with destructive force; it lies in the patient operation of the overpowering rationality of his conceptual harmonization" (*PR* 346).

God does not desire, it is safe to say, the repetition of yesterday's violence. Peace prehended in a pacifistic way approaches divine becoming. But once peace is prehended, alas, it perishes (at least for us); hence, it needs to be prehended often. Because acquisitiveness, preoccupation with self, and violence are all around us, the opportunities for such prehensions are not hard to find. But pacifism does not have to be approached exclusively as a reaction against something. Whitehead reminds us that youthful minds of any age can think ideally. The following passage not only sheds light on Whitehead's concept of peace, it also exhibits the overall tone of *AI*:

> At the heart of the nature of things, there are always the dream of youth and the harvest of tragedy. The Adventure of the Universe starts with the dream and reaps tragic Beauty. This is the secret of the union of Zest with Peace:—That the suffering attains its end in a Harmony of Harmonies. The *immediate* experience of this Final Fact, with its union of Youth and Tragedy, is the sense of Peace. In this way the World receives its persuasion towards such perfections as are possible for its diverse individual occasions. (*AI* 296—emphasis added)

This is one of those profound passages that is perhaps best left on its own, but I cannot resist the temptation of emphasizing that "the sense of Peace" consists in an *immediate* experience. Mediation through brute power always keeps us at least one additional step away from peaceful becoming. It should not be forgotten that Whitehead thought of Plato as the wisest in large measure due to his discovery of divine persuasion, in contrast to the absolute despotism of the God of the ancient Near East. Christianity's partial escape from the latter left it with scars (*AI* 81–86, 160–170).

The fact that the preceding quotation comes from *AI* should alert us to the fact that peace is in a tense relationship with *adventure*. Whereas adventure saves us from boredom and is fueled by the inevitable drive to novelty, peace saves adventure from cruelty and ruthlessness. Both adventure and peace are essential on a Whiteheadian view in that peace without adventure leads to what Whitehead labels "anaesthesia." To be precise, "peace is the disclosure of the ideal harmony toward which each occasion may tend without the vitality being lost" (Bixler 506, also

492, 498, 504–505, 508). Two extremes are to be avoided: tedium and painful conflict. In the end, Whitehead's stance points us toward a plea for tolerance (contra Stengers' interpretation) and for the "rule" of persuasiveness rather than toward a plea for the definitive rule of coercive power, as in the classical theistic template. As before, "omnipotence" is both meaningless (in that if each actual occasion is itself a dynamic center of power, no being, not even a divine one, could have *all* power) and harmful (in that if the *imitatio Dei* is one of the key religious ideas, human beings tend to imitate the supposed "perfect" coercive power found in an alleged omnipotent God).

Peace is precisely the sense that there are aims in the cosmos beyond our own and achievements beyond the passing sum of human attainments. This takes us across the religious threshold in that the discussion of these aims and achievements involves a consideration of God. Or again, peace is a direct apprehension of being related to that which is divine. This point is put most energetically in Cobb's idea that peace just *is* the vision of God, which requires a serene escape from the bondage of self-concern (Cobb 2007, 79–80, 144).

WHITEHEAD AND THE HOPE FOR PEACE

It should not escape our notice that Hartshorne offered a mild criticism of what he took to be Whitehead's treatment of "the Munich Principle," which was used by the appeasers in response to Hitler (Hartshorne 1983, 240, 321; also see Whitehead's AS). Apparently, Hartshorne's criticism here is based on his view that Whitehead was a bit too optimistic regarding human nature, although it should be remembered that Whitehead's famous break with Bertrand Russell was due in large measure to the latter's insensitivity (on Russell's own admission) regarding the death of Whitehead's son Eric in World War One. Indeed, it was this death that largely led Whitehead from mathematics to a career in philosophy, according to Russell (Russell 1956, 93, 100).

Here I would like to emphasize that my thesis regarding Hartshorne applies to Whitehead as well. Civilization, for Whitehead, consists in the process by which ancient ideals become practicable, but Whitehead was not a pacifist. Progress comes slowly, he correctly thinks, and the task of philosophy is to foster growth in mentality. From this we can infer that philosophy should at least lead us toward a consideration of pacifism, if not all the way to it. Whitehead even admits, as we have seen, that the task of philosophy reaches its zenith in the victory of persuasion over force. This remarkable idea has been the inspiration for the present book. Further, the three great periods in religious thought, for Whitehead, are: (a) the Platonic discovery of divine persuasion, (b) the exemplification of Plato's insights in a concrete way by Jesus, whose life does not exhibit coercive power—indeed, its power consists in an absence of violence and embodies the decisiveness of a supreme ideal such that Whitehead thinks that it is the crucial event for world history!—and (c) some of the intellectual developments of the Church Fathers. What is noteworthy here is Whitehead's omission of the Protestant Reformation, which he views as a "complete failure" regarding the concept of God, *except* perhaps for the Quaker view found in George Fox (*AI* 166; *RM* 57). Unfortunately, despite these moments of progress, the monopolar classical theistic notion of God as absolute despot has often prevented theology from teaching peace, as is witnessed in its frequent reliance on the last book of the Christian scriptures.

Solace is gained when we realize that countless generations are required in religious thought for people to become attached to profound ideas, as is exemplified in the long-delayed destruction of the institution of slavery in the West. So although Whitehead was not a pacifist, he all but admits that he was leaning in the direction of pacifism. He even talks of a "new epoch" being inaugurated with respect to war after World War Two (*DW* 288). Pacifists cannot help but find comfort in these words toward the end of Whitehead's life. That is, the elder Hartshorne as well as the elder Whitehead, although they do not entirely satisfy the pacifist in what they have to say about war, nonetheless tantalize. The hope is that eventually the practical implications of their view of God as persuasive rather than coercive will be fully realized.

If such a realization were to occur, it would signal the triumph of John Howard Yoder's view that pacifism is not "a cheaper or less dangerous or more shrewd way to impose one's will upon someone else" than violence. Rather, the renunciation of violence is a principled rejection of "the compulsiveness of purpose that leads [human beings] to violate the dignity of others" and to emulate a monopolar view of God as omnipotent tyrant. The Christian way to put the point (of course the point could be put analogously in a Jewish, Hindu, Buddhist, etc., way) is to say that "the cross is beginning to loom not as a ritually prescribed instrument of propitiation but as the political alternative to both insurrection and quietism" (Yoder 1972, 43, 243–244). That is, it is to be hoped that Yoder's achievements in pacifist theory will one day find their home in Hartshorne's and Whitehead's dipolar theism and in its attendant notion that divine persuasion is perhaps the greatest discovery in the history of metaphysics (see Dombrowski 1991a and Yoder's 1994 response; also Dombrowski 1987; Hartshorne 1948, 142).

A signal contribution from Whitehead regarding the subject matter of the present chapter is the idea that belief in divine omnipotence as a monopoly of coercive power is an instance of the fallacy of misplaced concreteness. It is only when we *abstract away from* all of the dynamic centers of power in the universe that we can then imagine that all power is found in God. Because these dynamic centers of power remain in their concreteness, however, belief in divine omnipotence rests on a *misplaced* concreteness. No doubt the continued appeal of divine omnipotence to theists is due to the understandable (if not justifiable) desire on the part of religious believers to exalt God by giving Him (once again, the male pronoun is needed here) *all* power. It is in this context that Whitehead wishes to avoid giving metaphysical compliments to God that backfire (*SM* 179). The view that makes sense metaphysically, and the only one that can help us develop a believable theology, is that there is a division of power in the universe. This shared responsibility is compatible with a view of God as social and living, which is ultimately at odds with the classical theistic view of God as *actus purus* and impervious to influence from others (Hartshorne 1941b, 516, 524, 527–528).

Although it is not one of the purposes of the present book to provide arguments for the existence of God (see Dombrowski 2006b), one such argument implied by Whitehead is relevant in the present context. If possibility is a property of existent things, one wonders about the locus for the general possibility of the universe. Either it might have been that nothing was possible (an alternative that is contradicted by the ancient Greek maxim adopted by Henri Bergson, Whitehead, and Hartshorne that "from nothing, nothing comes"), or there is a primordial power whose nonexistence is not possible and in whom possibility conceptually resides. Not much hope of an escape from this informal argument is found in speculation regarding an *omni*potent God who brings possibility itself into existence out of "absolutely nothing"; more intelligible is the view of God as a persuasive being, whose persuasiveness *to a point* cannot be resisted but beyond which can be rejected. "The goodness of God consists in this, that [God] never thwarts any desire, however perverse or trivial, without . . . sharing fully in every quality of feeling of pain or sorrow that the thwarting involves in the creatures" (Hartshorne 1941b, 553).

God's power cannot mean the gradual elimination of all evil in that ever-new causes of evil are operating in each present event. Partially free decisions plus social interdependence among the deciders is enough to account for tragedy in organic life. Although God does not secretly plan for evil so that good might eventually assert itself, God's persuasive power is such that some good can be squeezed out of evil once it arises (see Hartshorne 1941b, 553–555).

WAR AS PROTECTION

Whitehead's view seems to be that violence is justified only if it reduces the overall amount of violence *and* if it supports the growth of civilization (*DW* 90). But *can* it fulfill the latter condition? Consider the following description of war that he offers in a largely neglected essay: "War can protect; it cannot create. Indeed, war adds to the brutality that frustrates creation. The protection of war should be the last resort in the slow progress of mankind towards its far-off ideals" (AS 320). The notion of last resort in this quotation reminds one of traditional just war theory, which often contains last resort as one of its criteria. But clearly this characterization of war by Whitehead is also meant to dovetail with his major concerns in ethics, broadly conceived, which center on the advance toward civilized and civiliz*ing* ideals, such as peace. In historical phases of high tension and contagious emotion, as in the late 1930s in Europe, it is easy to lose sight of the ideals that war is alleged to indirectly serve. Whitehead's motto in March of 1939 was: isolation . . . unless isolation threatened long-term creative advance toward civilized ideals. He was aware of the fact that Polish history, for example, was tragic, but this in itself was not sufficient to justify a "crusade" in central Europe *prior to* a German attack (AS 309–312).

As with Hartshorne, Whitehead thought that the inflamed emotion that kept Hitler in power had the following implication: it would have been a "miracle" if Hitler would have been forced into inaction through a bluff. This seems to be an allusion on Whitehead's part to the appeasement mentioned earlier by Taylor, wherein Hitler was threatened with violence if he misbehaved, even if there was no intention to back up the threat. That is, the isolation that Whitehead defended in March of 1939 should *not* be equated with the idle threats of the appeasers but rather with *both* an opposition to a first strike against Hitler and the Nazis (actually encouraged previously by the Polish leader Józef Piłsudski), an opposition that perhaps led to Hartshorne's intimation that Whitehead was a bit soft on Hitler and the Nazis, *and* a bona fide threat to use violence if Hitler invaded Poland or other countries in Central Europe. He was firmly committed to the idea that the allies might be "forced into war by the wild lusts of dictatorial states to achieve domination" (AS 317, also 313).

WHITEHEAD'S LIFE

As with the previous discussion of Hartshorne's life, an understanding of the relationship between process thought and pacifism and an understanding of FTP is illuminated through a selective consideration of Whitehead's life. Both Hartshorne and Whitehead had fathers who were Anglican ministers; they also had Quaker ancestors, Whitehead's being a certain George Whitehead who is mentioned in George Fox's *Journal* (AN 3).

It is perhaps significant that Whitehead was never beaten as a child, nor did he punish physically his own children. Something of a crisis in his life occurred when, after being home-schooled by his father, he assumed a position of student leadership as a teen while he attended school at Sherborne. It was his task to "thrash" a disobedient student, who had to either submit to the thrashing or be expelled. Whitehead fulfilled his duty, albeit reluctantly. Like Hartshorne, Whitehead was by disposition a nonviolent, reflective person. A greater crisis occurred when his younger son Eric (the most fascinating human being Whitehead had ever met) was killed in World War One. We have seen that this was an event that Russell thought triggered Whitehead's turn toward philosophy, or at least toward the sort of philosophy for which he later became famous. It should also be noted that all three of Whitehead's children served in World War One (the eldest son throughout the whole war, his daughter in the Foreign Office, and Eric in the Air

Force), and the elder son narrowly escaped the bombing in London in World War Two (*DW* 149, 177–178, 274, 294; AN 9).

Although Whitehead was personally very familiar with the horrors of war, he was not a pacifist. In the 1930s he was worried by both Hitler's rearmament of Germany and the increasingly bellicose character of the German people, fueled by Wagnerian romanticism (*DW* 48, 73–75). As a consequence, he found himself at odds with both the Tories and the Labour Party. The former wanted peace for the wrong reason (to keep their wealth), whereas the latter's opposition to British rearmament was indirectly responsible for Italy's attack on Abyssinia. That is, both parties were (in different ways) wrong both to oppose rearmament and to conciliate dictators. In a comment that is every bit as startling as anything in Hartshorne on the topic, Whitehead is reported to have said that "the absolute pacifist is a *bad citizen*; times come when force *must* be used to uphold right, justice, and ideals" (emphasis added— *DW* 93–96). Like Hartshorne, Whitehead seems to equate appeasement with pacifism.

Three months after Hitler had attacked Poland, Whitehead thought it wise for the United States to stay out of the war so that Europe could find its own equilibrium, an equilibrium that did not occur at the end of World War One due to American intervention. Eventually, however, it seems that Whitehead welcomed American entry into World War Two in that, despite the typically peaceful nature of human beings (no police force would be large enough to keep public order if we were not basically peaceful), sometimes violence is needed on a massive scale in order to preserve civilized ideals. Germany under Hitler, who learned well the lessons of Niccolò Machiavelli, provided the occasion for defensive or protective violence such that, as before, pacifism in the face of Hitler would have been an indication of bad citizenship (*DW* 126–127, 129, 155–156).

Despite the fact that Whitehead traced the problems in Europe even as early as the time of the Roman Empire to the Germans (who toppled Rome), there is nothing uniquely violent about the Germans. Even in the middle of the war in 1943 Whitehead held that throughout the world there are a minority of people who actually *like* to dominate. However, the extent of German violence during the war was, he thought, remarkable. The staggering threat they posed to civilized life through their cruelty justified defensive war in response. No one, he seems to be arguing, should be forced to forfeit the right to avoid slavery (DW 123, 226–227, 287–288, 297). As a liberal in politics (AN 13), this was a matter of conviction for him.

Whitehead lived long enough to realize that World War One was the end of an era and long enough to hear about the dropping of atomic bombs on Japan in August of 1945. Despite some reticence to discuss these events in September of 1945, because they were too recent to be appraised, he nonetheless argued that, as a result of the dawn of the atomic age, humanity might well be on the verge of an age of liberation, an age that would exhibit a burst of creative energy that might lead to a new form of society. In Kantian fashion, he thought that if we do not move toward such a new form of society, we might commit omnicide. Further, he thought that because two world wars had all but destroyed Europe, the United States would have to take the lead in the establishment of this new society not only because of its military power but also, and primarily, because of its moral dynamism and sense of adventure (DW 173, 181, 255, 270–271, 344, 366; AN 10). I do not think that Whitehead hyperbolized when, toward the end of World War Two, he said that humanity faced the "greatest crisis" of its long history and that the crisis would not be averted through customary procedures and routines (DW 282).

The fact that Whitehead was a just war theorist from 1914 to 1916 is made clear in two letters he wrote to Bertrand Russell on August 28, 1914, and April 16, 1916 (both found at the Center for Process Studies archives). In these letters it is clear that he thought that it would have been "national suicide" for Great Britain to stay out of World War One and that by not fighting Great Britain would have brought about "the ruin of European civilization." The Allies fought to "save Western Freedom." He even goes so far as to say that those who refuse military service (unless they have a lifelong opposition to violence like the Quakers) violate a moral duty.

But it has been the purpose of the present chapter to argue that the routinized resort to violence and war to settle disputes is one of the habits that we will have to break in order to more closely approximate civilized ideals, or even to survive. Further, despite the defenses of just war theory in Hartshorne and Whitehead, there are strong conceptual grounds within their respective process philosophies to move away from just war theory and toward pacifism. Or again, I am not convinced that even defenders of a process or neoclassical concept of

God are fully aware of the extent to which the dipolar process God is at odds with the monopolar classical theistic God who lies behind just war theory.

Consider the remarkable, and still underappreciated, claim made by Whitehead to the effect that monopolar Christian theology is, for the most part, one of the "great disasters" of human history. One could have hoped for so much more from it. Admittedly, on the one hand, there is the admirable articulation of the concept of divine love, gentleness, and mercy. On the other hand, and problematically, behind the God of love lies God as an omnipotent despot, who, as we have seen, is even compared by Whitehead to Hitler. This is due to the common classical theistic belief that an omnipotent God enforces obedience such that the disobedient are given unending and cruel punishment. These contradictory views are found in Saints Augustine *and* Francis of Assisi, along with Luther and Calvin, among others. The God of the Hebrew scriptures not only lacks a sense of humor but also a sense of morality. The latter is evidenced in the command to Abraham to kill Isaac, contra the contorted Kierkegaardian attempt to put such a command in a more commendable light (*DW* 174–176, 189, 198; cf. Friesen).

In short, the despotic quality of the God of the Old Testament is carried over into the New (especially in the last book of the Christian scriptures), despite the progress evidenced in Galilean *agape*. Monopolar classical theistic philosophical and theological reflection continues (indeed, reifies) such despotism, even in the works of authors who otherwise are legitimately seen as reformers. The fact that Whitehead saw his own father as "an Old Testament man" alerts us to the fact that the problem here is personal and existential, not merely conceptual (*DW* 236, 277, 306, 339; also see *MT* 14–15 regarding homicide).

DIPOLAR THEISM, AGAIN

There is another important connection between the concept of God one chooses to defend and the issue of violence. Hartshorne and Whitehead are famous for their opposition to independent existence (the Greek *chorismos*) as allegedly found in Plato. There is no existent that is not interwoven with the rest of the universe, on their view. There is a serious problem with the opposite view. If one bifurcates the world into the civilized and the barbaric, contact with the civilized origin of the higher world might encourage those who have been in touch with this world to puff themselves up with a sort of pride. Only *they* understand ultimate reality, and hence they might come to think that only *they* can be trusted with a carte blanche to use violence. The self-appointed wise have historically convinced themselves that "a successful social system required despotism. This notion was based on the barbaric fact . . . that violence was the primary mode of sustaining large-scale social existence. This belief is not yet extinct" (IY 696–697, also 687). This belief is not yet extinct due in part to the continued influence of classical theism, with its bifurcated ("Platonic") universe. A counterpoint to this influence can be found in both neoclassical theism as well as in the pockets of pacifism that have sprung up historically, as in that variety of Cluny monasticism that was, as Whitehead notes, devoid of violence (IY 697).

Because the traditional monopolar conception of God as an active not passive, unmoved tyrant is inadequately related to the natural and cultural world that we live in, the God of the classical theist cannot be a dynamic God of peace but is at best an anesthetically abstract deity. The classical theist's God cannot commiserate with the tragic suffering that occurs in war, nor can this God persuade the bellicose world toward a more perfect state, because this God does not persuade but orders. Much less can the classical theistic God be persuaded. The neoclassical, process God *can* do all of these things. Hartshorne and Whitehead have unwittingly discovered that a pursuit of peace without the mediation of violence is a more fitting type of worship to give a dipolar God than brute power.

They give us the conceptual apparatus to think insightfully about, and hence the hope that there really would be an end to, the many centuries spent worshipping omnipotence more than love and static being rather than (everlasting) creative becoming. Although they were just war theorists throughout most of their lives, toward the end of their respective long lives Hartshorne and Whitehead came very close to the conclusion that the practical implication of their dipolar view of God involved nonviolence rather than violence. That is, each came to realize as a result of the atomic bomb that war itself had become the enemy and that God's role in human history was in the patient operation of the rationality of divine harmonization.

The longstanding transition from FTP, initiated by Plato, involves a coming to grips with the idea that mediation through brute power always keeps us at least one additional step away from peaceful becoming. The hope is that Hartshorne's and Whitehead's dipolar theism, and its attendant notion that divine persuasion is one of the greatest discoveries in the history of metaphysics, might eventually receive the theoretical and practical attention it deserves. Late in their lives Hartshorne and Whitehead take their readers to the edge of pacifism; my aim in this chapter has been to push these readers over the edge (cf. the insightful work by Neville).

POSTSCRIPT: IRAQ AND AFGHANISTAN

The purpose of this postscript is to explore the recent United States wars in Iraq and Afghanistan in light of just war theory, specifically in light of Michael Walzer's highly influential version of this theory that is in many respects similar to Hartshorne's and Whitehead's views on just war. Another purpose is to criticize these wars. What I will say here will supplement what I said earlier regarding the theme of pacifism and practicality. I will assume *for the sake of argument* what Walzer calls "the triumph of just war theory" (Walzer 2004, chap. 1). That is, I hope to show that even on the grounds of just war theory there are severe problems with the sorts of reasoning that lie behind these wars (see Dombrowski 2010).

The overall thrust of my view is to call into question the latter portion of the claim that the war in Iraq was a war of (ill-advised) choice, whereas the war in Afghanistan was and is a war of necessity. To say that the war in Afghanistan was and is *necessary* is to rule out in principle a pacifist mode of adjudicating disputes; hence, I will try to show why it was not and is not necessary. Because the thesis I wish to defend regarding the war in Afghanistan is developed in terms of its similarities to, and differences from, the war in Iraq, I will start with a brief summary of what I take to be the relationship between just war theory and the war in Iraq. Defenders of this war have offered at least four different justifications for the war:

(a) At times the war in Iraq was defended, whether explicitly or implicitly, in terms of the traditional *jus ad bellum* grounds of self-defense. The United States was attacked on 9/11, the argument goes; hence, it had a right to defend itself against its enemies. As is now well known, however, none of the named 9/11 attackers were from Iraq, nor did they receive financing from, or training in, Iraq. Although both Hartshorne and Whitehead show evidence of being amenable to this *sort* of just war reasoning in terms of self-defense, I assume that they would have agreed with me that, in the case of the Iraq war, there was not sufficient (or even any) evidence for the self-defense version of *jus ad bellum*.

The next two attempted justifications were not past-oriented but were future-oriented (see Walzer 2006, chap. 5; 2004, 146–147). Sadly, these two types of anticipatory violence are often confused:

(b) The war in Iraq was justified by some in terms of a *preemptive strike* against a state that had the ability to deliver a missile strike at Israel or Europe within forty-five minutes. Hence, it was argued, it would be foolish to wait to receive such a deadly blow from a dictator as oppressive as Saddam Hussein. That is, striking first can, in some instances, be morally defensible. Unfortunately for defenders of this view, the British intelligence on which the claim was based regarding forty-five-minute strike capacity was faulty. Here it should be noted that neither Hartshorne nor Whitehead show evidence of agreeing with this type of justification for war. In fact, in AS Whitehead explicitly rejects it, as we have seen.

(c) A preemptive strike against an immediate threat is somewhat different from a *preventive strike* in that the latter involves an appeal to alleged long-term threats. The claim was that Iraq was in the process of developing both nuclear weapons and chemical-biological weapons, such that to wait ten years, say, for such projects to reach fruition would be unjust to those who would be the victims of Saddam Hussein's future use of these weapons. Here there are at least two notable problems, as I see things:

(i) Once again, it turned out that there was no evidence for the development of weapons of mass destruction in Iraq. Some commentators have even suspected that United States government leaders may have lied about such projects in order to win popular support in the buildup to the war. I would here like to emphasize that contemporary philosophical attempts to defend the "noble" lie to citizens rest on Straussian or kindred conceptions of a philosophical elite who are (by self-proclamation) vastly superior to the unwashed masses who are lied to. The political liberalisms of Hartshorne and Whitehead, however, are directly opposed to the inegalitarian concept of politics on which the noble lie is based. Indeed,

I have no doubt that both Hartshorne and Whitehead would have seen the noble lie as odious (see Dombrowski 2004b; Morris).

(ii) But even more important from a theoretical point of view is the precarious nature of justification of preventive strikes, in general, in addition to the difficulties in such a justification in Iraq, in particular. Unlike the threat of violence that underlies the attempt to justify preemptive strikes, the unresolved character of future contingencies, especially contingencies in the distant future, makes preventive strikes especially difficult to justify. World War One is a prominent example of an utterly pointless war that was fought due to a series of miscalculations of anticipatory mobilization. Here the asymmetrical nature of time, wherein the past is radically different from the future, examined in detail by Hartshorne and Whitehead (see Hartshorne 1965b), can offer magisterial guidance to moral theory. This point will be of signal importance when Walzer's treatment of the war in Afghanistan is considered. The past is different from the future because it has already been determined, whereas the future is the region of determinables that are, moment by moment, rendered determinate by decisions made in the specious present.

(d) The war in Iraq was also claimed by some to be a war of *humanitarian intervention*. Here the problems are legion, on my view. Admittedly, Saddam Hussein was a brutal dictator, but it should not escape our notice that the worst of his human rights abuses happened when he was an ally of the United States in opposition to Iran. It is not clear that his brutality was worse than that of several other dictators around the world whose countries we did not decide to invade. Further, it seems to be a necessary condition of just humanitarian intervention that those who are liberated welcome their humanitarian saviors. But American troops were either not welcomed at all in Iraq or were welcomed only for the first few weeks of the war until Saddam Hussein was toppled from power.

For these and other reasons, I agree with Walzer that the war in Iraq was not necessary; it was a (bad) choice. By contrast, he thinks that the war in Afghanistan is "*certainly* a just one" (Walzer 2004, 137—emphasis added). My thesis is that this way of characterizing the war in Afghanistan should be called into question in that this war, too, is a war of choice. By eliminating any hint of necessity, one makes the intellectual world safe for the FTP transition. By contrast, to say that the war in Afghanistan was and is necessary is to erect a priori opposition to pacifism that is unwarranted.

The most notable difference from the perspective of just war theory between the war in Iraq and the war in Afghanistan is that in the latter case a plausible (if not a convincing) *jus ad bellum* claim could be made regarding self-defense, and this on the evidence that many of the alleged 9/11 attackers and the perpetrators of other terrorist attacks were trained in Afghanistan. Thus, it is something of a surprise to read Walzer saying that the justification for the war in Afghanistan is *not* primarily backward-looking. That is, it is not really a police action in that for the most part we do not know who the individuals were who ran the training camps and, as a result, there will not be Nuremberg-like trials for these individuals. Or, if there are Nuremberg-like trials, they will not be integral parts of the justice of the war.

Rather, Walzer defends the war in Afghanistan as largely a war of prevention (Walzer 2004, 137–138; also 2009). This fact should be more widely known. The justification for the war, he thinks, consists in the legitimate effort to stop preparation for future wars. To be precise, the Walzerian justification for the war in Afghanistan seems to be both backward-looking and *especially* forward-looking. It is because the United States received an attack in the past from an organization ensconced within Afghanistan, he implies, that it is legitimate for the United States and its allies to make sure that they do not receive another one in the future. On Walzerian grounds it seems that the insecure status of wars of prevention in just war theory, as evidenced in his own opposition to the attempted justification of the war in Iraq as a war of prevention (and, in a different context, in Whitehead's opposition in AS to anticipatory violence against Hitler and the Nazis), is mitigated in Afghanistan by the fact that the preventive implications of the invasion of Afghanistan are buttressed by the *jus ad bellum* claim to be fighting in self-defense.

I have argued in this postscript that there was no necessity to fight the war in Iraq. It was a war of choice. Indeed, it was a bad choice. There was no evidence to support the claim of self-defense. There was no evidence to support the case for a preemptive strike. There was no evidence to support the case for a preventive war; in fact, there are problems with preventive wars, in general, due to temporal asymmetry and the inability to predict in any detail the outcome to future contingencies when these are in the distant future, as process metaphysics makes clear. And we were not viewed in Iraq as liberators, which undermines any attempt to justify the war on humanitarian grounds. Finally, the noble lie is anathema to the sort of open society favored by process thinkers, including Hartshorne and Whitehead.

I am also claiming that the war in Afghanistan is a war of choice, despite Walzer's implicit (and Barack Obama's explicit) claim that it was and is a war of necessity. Further, I think that it was a bad choice in that on self-defense grounds the most that one could legitimate would be the destruction of the training camps, which was accomplished shortly after the start of military activities and with hardly any loss of life. To justify the *war* in Afghanistan one needs, in addition to a claim to be fighting in self-defense, future-oriented reasons that are part of a war of prevention argument. And it is precisely this sort of crystal ball prediction-making regarding the long-term future that is undermined by Hartshorne's and Whitehead's process metaphysics.

If one assumes for the sake of argument that the United States and its allies had a right (not a duty) to enter Afghanistan, at what point would a just end to their intervention be reached? Much depends on whether the goal is described in terms of a counterterrorism strategy or in terms of a counterinsurgency and state-building strategy. If the former alternative is chosen, then the goal was reached over a decade ago when the training camps were eliminated. If the latter alternative is chosen, then the end of the war has yet to be reached in that a democratic government has yet to be established.

One wonders in a Whiteheadian vein about what civilized ideals were fostered by support of the Karzai government, with its kleptocratic and antidemocratic tendencies. Transparency International on its website in 2009 rated Afghanistan 179th out of 180 nations in that apparently only Somalia was more corrupt. In addition to the moral difficulties in justifying the military defense of the Karzai government, there are familiar *realpolitik* considerations. Seth Jones, in his work *In the Graveyard of Empires*, details the difficulties exhibited in the counterinsurgency campaigns in Afghanistan of Alexander the Great, the British in the nineteenth century, and most recently the Soviet Union in the 1980s.

Because there are moral and *realpolitik* reasons to disassociate the war in Afghanistan from any claim to necessity, the theoretical stage is set for a consideration of real alternatives to war when dealing with terrorism. Once again, pacifists should nonviolently yet energetically resist the claim that we *must* fight for either moral or practical reasons or both (see Murphy).

Despite appearances, the prospects are bright when it is considered that worldwide both murder rates and the percentage of people killed in war are decreasing (see Pinker). And there is a growing realization, even among just war theorists, that those who fight are morally responsible not only for their *jus in bello* conduct *in* war but also for the *jus ad bellum* issue *of* war in general (see McMahan). As Walzer puts the point, especially in a democracy it is not exactly true that the buck stops with the president in that some bucks stop with each one of us (Walzer 2006, 40).

We are all familiar with the cliché "might makes right." It is to be hoped that the following saying will become better known: "the right makes its own might" (see Kreeft 2005, 90).

FIVE

Butler and Grievable Lives

THE ARGUMENT FROM MARGINAL CASES

The question Which lives are grievable? is a major concern for Judith Butler in at least two recent books: *Precarious Life* and *Frames of War*. Indeed, these two works can be seen, as Butler admits, as one extended response to this and related questions (e.g., When is life grievable?). It will be the purpose of the present chapter to respond to these questions by way of what has come to be known as the argument from marginal cases (hereafter, AMC). Sometimes this argument is also known as the argument from species overlap. I will not be merely reviewing or comparing the similarities and/or differences between Whitehead and Butler. Rather, I will be defending an argument that is, as I see things, a genuine attempt not only to clarify but also to develop and use some of the best aspects of these two thinkers in the effort to understand both MTO and FTP.

My hope is that an adequate response to the question Which lives are grievable? will be facilitated by a consideration of Whitehead and Butler *together* as their thought relates to AMC. (A recent conference at the Claremont Graduate School devoted to the relationship between Whitehead and Butler provides hope that this effort will be fruitful— see Faber, Halewood, and Lin.) At the end of the chapter I will clearly state my own response to this question, and I will explicitly summarize the ways in which Whitehead and Butler facilitate this response.

Granted, the context for Butler's questions—the American wars in Iraq and Afghanistan and an extension of her interest in these two wars so as to include a concern for the more general question regarding which lives are grievable—initially seems remote from the context of Whitehead's later, metaphysical books. We should remember, however, that it was largely Whitehead's grief over the death of his son in World War One that led him to devote his intellectual energies full time to philosophy and to questions that have at least a family resemblance to those asked by Butler.

There has recently been an explosion of interest in philosophy regarding our current environmental crisis, in general, and regarding the moral status of nonhuman animals, in particular. This interest often intersects with philosophical arguments in favor of nonhuman animal rights. The purpose of the present section is to present one such argument (indeed, one of the most important philosophical arguments in favor of nonhuman animal rights) and to argue for its philosophical soundness.

This line of reasoning is usually (and controversially) called AMC. It is a bit more complicated than another philosophical argument in favor of nonhuman animal rights, the more familiar argument from sentiency. This simpler argument looks something like this:

A. Any being that can experience pain or suffer has, at the very least, the right not to be forced to experience pain or suffer (or be killed) unnecessarily or gratuitously.

B. It is not necessary that we inflict pain or suffering (or death) on sentient nonhuman animals in order for us to have a healthy diet.

C. Therefore, eating sentient nonhuman animals is an example of unnecessary infliction of pain or suffering (or death) and ought to be avoided, that is, their lives are definitely grievable.

The intuitive appeal of the argument from sentiency is enough to convince many philosophical vegetarians. Whiteheadians who are convinced by it might speak in terms of *tragic loss*, and Butlerians who are convinced by it might speak in terms of the cogency of *mourning* with respect to the unnecessary suffering and death of nonhuman animals, as we will see. However, the realization that it is not necessarily rationality that is the criterion that must be met in order to deserve moral respect and to be grievable leads to further considerations that are treated in the argument that will be the focus of this chapter: AMC.

Defenders of this argument agree with almost everyone else regarding the criterion that must be met in order to be a moral agent (i.e., someone who can perform moral or immoral actions and who can be held morally responsible for his/her actions): rationality. At times it might be difficult to apply this criterion if the alleged moral agent is not obviously rational, but almost everyone agrees that rationality is the property that would be required in order to hold someone morally accountable for his/her actions.

The key question, however, is the following: What property needs to be possessed in order to be a moral patient or a moral beneficiary or a being who is grievable (i.e., someone who can receive immoral treatment from others, or who can have his/her rights violated, or who can be treated cruelly)? Here the issue is quite complicated and contentious. One of the complicating factors is that to speak without qualification of "properties" of "subjects" is both to run the risk of remaining within the subject-predicate mode of thought and to continue the fiction of a substantial self, which both Whitehead and Butler legitimately want to criticize. The proper task is to temporalize moral patiency status so as to avoid both of these defects, as we will see, while nonetheless paying sufficient attention to the infliction of unnecessary suffering or death that understandably results in a Whiteheadian sense of tragic loss or a Butlerian sense of mourning (see Dombrowski 1997a, 189–193). Tragic loss and mourning are understandable reactions to the failure to transition from FTP.

The most parsimonious response to this question also leads to a type of symmetry that some find attractive: Make *rationality* do double-duty by serving as the criterion for moral patiency status or grievability as well as for moral agency. But this response leads to disastrous consequences in that on its basis many human beings (the marginal cases of humanity) would not be moral patients and hence would not deserve moral respect or be grievable.

An understandable reaction to the difficulties involved in demanding a very high criterion for moral patiency status like rationality is to lower it significantly. For example, some religious believers (e.g., Albert Schweitzer and other "prolife" proponents in Christianity) wish to make *life* the criterion for moral patiency status. All life, we are told, deserves moral respect. But this response also leads to disastrous consequences in that on its basis we would not be morally permitted to mow, or even walk on, grass because living insects would be killed, cut out cancerous tumors because cancer cells are (unfortunately) quite alive and well, or even breathe if perchance we would suck in living organisms that would be killed, and so forth. What would we be able to eat on a consistent prolife basis? Schweitzer's own writings indicate what some of the absurd consequences would be (see Schweitzer). That is, AMC forces us to be a bit more specific than we have been thus far regarding the "O" in MTO, as we will see.

Defenders of AMC work their way, both theoretically and practically, to a place in between these two extremes so as to find a defensible criterion for moral patiency status or grievability in *sentiency*. On this basis all human beings deserve respect (even the most marginal of marginal cases still have a functioning central nervous system and hence are sentient), but nonhuman animals with central nervous systems, and hence sentiency, are also protected.

Before moving to the connection between AMC, on the one hand, and Whitehead and Butler, on the other, an ordinary language statement of the argument might be helpful:

(a) It is undeniable that members of many species other than our own have "interests," at least in the minimal sense that they feel and try to avoid pain, and feel and seek various sorts of pleasure and satisfaction.

(b) It is equally undeniable that human infants and some of the profoundly mentally impaired have interests in only the sense that members of these other species have them and not in the sense that normal adult humans have them. That is, human infants and some of the profoundly mentally impaired (i.e., the marginal cases of humanity) lack the normal adult qualities of purposiveness, self-consciousness, memory, imagination, and anticipation to the same extent that members of some other species of animals lack those qualities.

(c) Thus, in terms of the morally relevant characteristic of having interests, some humans must be equated with members of other species rather than with normal adult human beings.

(d) Yet predominant moral judgments about conduct toward these humans are dramatically different from judgments about conduct toward the comparable nonhuman animals. It is customary to raise the nonhuman animals for food, to subject them to lethal scientific experiments, to treat them as chattels, and so forth. It is not customary—indeed it is abhorrent to most people even to consider—the same practices for human infants and the mentally impaired.

(e) But lacking a finding of some morally relevant characteristic (other than having interests) that distinguishes these humans and non-human animals, we must conclude that the predominant moral judgments about them are inconsistent. To be consistent, and to that extent rational, we must either treat the humans the same way we now treat the nonhuman animals or treat the nonhuman animals the same way we now treat the humans.

(f) And there does not seem to be a morally relevant characteristic that distinguishes all humans from all other animals. Sentience, rationality, and so forth all fail. The assertion that the difference lies in the *potential* to develop interests analogous to those of normal adult humans should also be dismissed. After all, it is easily shown that some humans—whom we nonetheless refuse to treat as nonhuman animals—lack the relevant potential. In short, the standard candidates for a morally relevant differentiating characteristic can be rejected.

(g) The conclusion is, therefore, that we cannot give a reasoned justification for the differences in ordinary conduct toward some humans against some nonhuman animals (loosely based on Becker).

In one sense, the point of AMC is to ask for a more responsible use of apparently harmless terms like "all" and "only." Any morally relevant characteristic that is possessed *only* by human beings will not be possessed by *all* human beings. To try to escape from the ramifications of this observation by claiming, as many philosophers do, that all humans deserve moral respect because they *are* human, is clearly to beg the question. Exactly what morally relevant property is it that all humans, but only humans, possess that nonhuman animals do not possess?

I should note here my willingness to adjust any language I have used in this section that might be offensive. For example, to speak as I have of the "mental impairment" of some human beings is in one sense quite accurate, I think (other things being equal, we would wish our children to have brains and/or mental lives that function well), but it could be interpreted by some to imply a rational essence to humanity. Along with Whitehead and Butler, however, I am a critic of essentialism. Or again, to refer to the argument in question as that from "marginal cases" is a concession to standard usage among philosophers and it is not meant to imply that those who are different should be pushed to the margins. Actually, my obvious intent is quite the opposite. This is why "argument for moral consistency" or "argument from species overlap" might be better.

REFLECTIVE EQUILIBRIUM

A defense of AMC does not have to be based on the idea that there are independently existing facts out there that dictate our morality, as in some versions of natural law theory. (This point is crucial if we wish to understand Butler's contributions to AMC.) Rather, our values and obligations can legitimately be derived from facts if the facts to which they refer are intelligibly seen as the relevant ones, and if the values derived from these facts are defensible ones. Or again, a defender of AMC need not commit to the naïve view that facts wear their relevance on their face and that values can be immediately derived from them. That is, AMC is indeed an *argument* that gives reasons for the defensibility of the claims that nonhuman animals have basic rights due to their sentiency and that species membership is irrelevant when considering moral patiency status itself or grievability.

By way of contrast, critics of AMC like Elizabeth Anderson and Cora Diamond seem to move illegitimately from the claim that human decision-making is a necessary condition for there being rights to the claim that it constitutes a sufficient condition for there being rights. Another way to put the point is to say that Anderson and Diamond's views, in contrast to Butler's, as we will see, are overly nominalistic when they hold that beings acquire status as moral patients (entirely?) because *we* say that they deserve such status. Human beings on this view have the Orpheus-like and Wittgenstein-inspired ability to bring moral patiency status or grievability to life merely by saying that it should be so. The remedy for such an approach does not run to the other extreme, where it is assumed that moral patiency status is a fact "out there" waiting to be discovered. Rather, human beings are the measurers of nature, but not necessarily the measure; for they are the primary beholders of value in nature, but not necessarily the only holders of such value (to use Holmes Rolston's helpful language).

It is quite understandable why some people are sensitive to the possibility that others might exhibit insensitivity regarding marginal cases of humanity. This is because marginal cases of humanity have been treated deplorably in the past and because, for example, a United Nations statement declaring the rights of intellectually impaired beings did not occur until the 1970s, with many other historically marginalized groups receiving attention years before.

But as philosophers we must be on the alert to continue the Aristotelian project of treating similar cases alike and varying cases differently in proportion to their variances. James Rachels is on the mark in regard to AMC in stating that

> Aristotle knew that like cases should be treated alike, and different cases should be treated differently; so when he defended slavery he felt it necessary to explain why slaves are "different." Therefore, if the doctrine of [anthropocentrism] was to be maintained, it was necessary to identify the differences between humans and other animals that justified the difference in moral status. . . . [AMC is] . . . nothing but the consistent application of the principle of equality to decisions about what should be done . . . about our relation to the other creatures that inhabit the earth. (Rachels 196–197)

My defense of AMC, along with the amplifications of this argument by Whitehead and Butler, is compatible with the method of reflective equilibrium made famous by Rawls regarding theory of justice, and which is of use in ethics generally. The idea is that we should first carefully examine all of the relevant intuitions that we have and the judgments that we make, asking which are the most basic intuitions or which are considered judgments. Then we should investigate different theories that claim to organize these intuitions and judgments. Nothing is held to be fixed. The goal is to seek consistency and fit among both intuitions/judgments and theory when all are taken together as a whole. Or again, AMC follows the pattern of many contemporary arguments in applied philosophy in that it starts with considered opinion among reflective people, then moves to relatively unconsidered consequences. Thus, it makes sense to think that AMC could also be called the argument for moral consistency.

It is crucial in this method that we be able to revise our considered judgments, and even our intuitions, if such revision is required by a powerful theory. It is also possible that we might revise, or even reject, a theory in the face of considered judgments or intuitions. Neither component is fixed in advance. It is my hope that some small, yet real, contribution to ethics can be made by AMC. As a result of this theoretical argument, which has as its aim the familiar goal of logical consistency, closer attention should be paid to our common sympathetic intuitions in the face of: the suffering of nonhuman animals and the marginal cases of humanity, the basic rights of all human beings, as well as the special moral patiency status of rational beings. Both Anderson and Diamond should be seen by animal rightists as dialectical partners rather than as antagonists in the pursuit of this goal. That is, animal rightists can deliberate together with them, as derived from the Latin *deliberare*: to weigh in mind, to ponder, to thoroughly consider.

WHITEHEAD AND GRIEVABILITY

Before moving explicitly to Whitehead's contribution to an adequate response to the questions asked earlier regarding grievability, four preliminary points should be made.

(a) Whitehead's philosophy should be seen (along with Griffin's and Stengers' and Butler's) in the context of the long-term project in philosophy to *revolt against dualism*. This revolt has the implication that animals, in general (including human animals), are not understandable in abstraction from bodies. Likewise, bodies are not understandable in abstraction from experience of some sort, however miniscule; they are not machines. In Whiteheadian language, an actual occasion is a bipolar fusion of the physical and the appetitive or mental. Once Descartes separated mind and matter and viewed them as distinct substances, it was relatively easy for later mechanistic materialist philosophers to exorcise the Cartesian ghost from the machine due to the infamous problems regarding interaction and discontinuity in nature found in dualism, leaving human beings as mere machines. Descartes' mistake, from a Whiteheadian point of view, as Griffin has helped us to see, is both to view mind as a strictly "inside" realm that is temporal but not spatial and to view matter as a strictly "outside" realm that is spatial but not really temporal. That is, reductionistic materialism is not the only alternative to dualism (see *PR* 104, 108; *MT* 150; *AI* 210–213, 253, 259; *SM*, chap. 5). Whitehead's thought is integrally connected to the transition from MTO.

(b) This fusion of the physical and the appetitive or mental is spread throughout nature in something like a *scale of becoming*, which is the process version of the traditional scale of being. Whitehead (along with Butler 2009, 15–23) makes it clear that there are no airtight or essentialist boundaries in nature but rather heuristic or explanatory divisions. That is, the different modes of existence that comprise the scale of becoming "shade off into each other" (see *MT* 156–157; also see *PR* 50, 98, 102, 177–178). For example, due to the ubiquity of experience in nature, there is not even an absolute gap between the living and the nonliving in nature (see *PR* 102). Our experiences of the experiences of cells within our bodies shows us we are *integrally linked* to subhuman reality; hence, there is no need for a *bridge to* such reality.

(c) By implication, there is no absolute difference between human beings and nonhuman animals. Indeed, Whitehead helps us to relearn the old insight that human beings *are* animals. Because we live *within* nature, it should not surprise us that there is not even a sharp division among the levels of mentality in nature; hence, there is *human continuity with nonhuman animals*. Vertebrate animals with central nervous systems, in general, are dominated by mentality of some sort and, as a result, are personally ordered in terms of mental phenomena such as memory and expectation. Whereas, as is well known, primitive feeling pervades nature at the lower levels of reality, on a Whiteheadian view, "we have passed the Rubicon" when sense perception and its incipient mentality is acquired. Here "Rubicon" symbolizes a transition from the primitive feeling involved in sense *reception* to the more sophisticated experience involved in sense *perception*, which is a necessary condition for the mental lives of personally ordered animals who can explicitly identify error as such (see *PR* 113, also 34–35, 90, 104–108, 142, 168, 170, 178, 181, 312, 315; *MT* 65, 73, 113, 121, 156–159, 167–168; *AI* 4, 20, 177–178, 186, 205–206, 214–215, 247, 291).

To put the same point in different terms, we can distinguish between two sorts of sentiency. S1 refers to the microscopic sentiency that lies behind Griffin-like defenses of panexperientialism, whereas S2 refers to sentiency per se as found in human beings and other animals with central nervous systems. It is this latter sort of sentiency that is seen as the criterion for moral patiency status in AMC. Brian Henning has done exemplary work in articulating the sort of aesthetic concern (Whitehead would say, Quaker concern) S1 requires of us in that not

even microscopic organisms are machines incapable of internal relations or mattering. But this is a type of "mattering" that is quite different
(in degree if not in kind), but not absolutely different, from the moral
respect that is due to S2 organisms who can experience pain intensely,
indeed whose loss is tragic or grievable. No moral rights are claimed by,
or for, S1 organisms (see Dombrowski 1988a; Henning).

(d) Despite the considerable continuity between human beings
and nonhuman animals mentioned earlier, Whitehead is nonetheless
committed to the contrast between the high-grade mentality of (most)
human beings and "mere animal savagery." The contrast is a subtle one,
however, despite the startling language regarding savagery. The high-
grade functioning of (most) human beings in Whitehead is quite different from the traditional anthropocentric, essentialist claim that human
beings *are* rational. They are only intermittently rational; indeed, only
some of them are intermittently rational in that some of them are never
rational. Nonhuman animals with central nervous systems may be personally ordered series of occasions, with links to the past through memory, and hopes and expectations regarding the future course of their
lives, but they are apparently not self-consciously aware of themselves as
such. Our intermittent self-consciousness allows us a *partial transcendence of animality*. Most of our lives are spent aesthetically appreciating
the world in ways continuous with those of nonhuman animals. But
the partial transcendence of animality found in Whitehead, especially
in *MT*, is primarily due to the language in (most) human beings that
makes self-consciousness possible. Once again, there is continuity with
animal communication, but Whitehead poetically makes his point in
regard to partial transcendence by stating that on the sixth day of creation God gave (most) human beings speech and they thereby became
souls. Animals may enjoy the natural world, but only "we" really study
it, armed with our sophisticated uses of language and our concomitant
self-conscious awareness of ourselves as partially different from the rest
of nature (see *PR* 11–12, 79, 87, 104–109, 112–113, 319, 337; *MT* 3–5,
102–103, 120, 123; *AI* 48).

Given the preceding four points, there is much that a Whiteheadian could contribute in response to the Butlerian question Which lives
are grievable? Regarding the argument from sentiency, a Whiteheadian
could emphasize that higher animals with central nervous systems have
an enhanced mental pole and do not thoughtlessly or mechanically
adjust to causal factors affecting them. Life, in general, is the "clutch at

vivid immediacy" (*PR* 105), an immediacy that is especially noteworthy from an ethical point of view when it involves unnecessary or gratuitous infliction of pain or suffering. Although feeling of some minimal sort is spread throughout the universe (S1), in a Whiteheadian view, it is only with nonhuman animal sense perception that the Rubicon of sentiency per se (S2 in contrast to S1 microscopic sentiency) is crossed, as previously claimed. Further, nonhuman animal minds are temporally ordered; indeed, according to Whitehead, they are *personally* ordered societies in which the events of a nonhuman animal's life are connected to the past through memory and thrown toward the future through expectation. For these and other reasons, nonhuman animals rightly claim our "love and tenderness" in return. There is some "holiness" or "sacredness" in their beauty that civilized beings like ourselves cannot fail to notice (*MT* 120; also IY 690). This emphasis on what we *civilized* beings should notice (as Whitehead problematically uses this term in that it could play into the hands of a dualistic contrast with the savage) indicates that a Whiteheadian approach to nonhuman animals is as much a virtue approach as a rights-oriented one. However, as a political liberal Whitehead, in partial contrast to Butler, was not skittish regarding the language of rights, even if both of them share an affinity to a virtue approach.

Whitehead also helps us to understand the implications of AMC. There are no airtight boundaries (whether scientific or ethical) between species in that different modes of existence shade off into each other. Specifically, there is no absolute boundary between nonhuman animals and human beings at the very least because human beings *are* animals. Whitehead defends both hierarchy in nature *and* continuity and shades of difference between each hierarchical level: we live *within* nature, as do nonhuman animals. Further, we have seen that there is something hyperbolic in claiming that human beings *are* rational. Rather, some of them are rational some of the time and others (the marginal cases of humanity) are rarely or never rational. And some nonhuman animals exhibit remarkable mentality, such that we are tempted to think that they are either rational or are on the cusp of rationality. AMC makes it clear that there are ethical implications to the continuity (and overlap) thesis that Whitehead defends.

Some Whiteheadians resist the conclusions to the arguments from sentiency and marginal cases because a chicken, they allege, does not have a mental life that is very high and its momentary suffering just before its death is outweighed by all of the pleasurable moments it could have had in its life before the point of death; a life, by the way, that probably would not have come into being were it not for the practice of meat-eating (see Dombrowski 2001b regarding the positions of John Cobb and Clare Palmer).

But even if a nonhuman animal is killed painlessly, the loss involved is grievable on Whiteheadian (and Butlerian) grounds. The reason for this is that such a killing denies the nonhuman animal all of the future momentary experiences it would have had in *its* life (not ours). It should be remembered that it is young, vibrant nonhuman animals that are killed for the table, such that even if they are killed painlessly, we should (and many do) grieve the *unnecessary* loss of the rest of *their* lives. As in the argument from sentiency stated earlier, the words "unnecessary" or "gratuitous" are crucial here in the effort to move from FTP. We should note once again that Whitehead thinks that not only do nonhuman animals try to avoid pain, but they also engage in *self-preservation*, which seems to presuppose a sort of stable identity, albeit short of a substantial self, that is nonetheless stronger than that found in the view that there really is no enduring self whatsoever to be preserved. A process view of a self changing through time is nonetheless compatible with a genetic relatedness among the events in a temporal series that constitutes the same self; in fact, a personal society is one that *sustains a character* (PR 34–35, 176).

We should take Whitehead's example seriously where, in the Garden of Eden, Adam saw nonhuman animals before he named them, whereas children today can name nonhuman animals before they ever see them (*SM* 198). Granted, in this context Whitehead is discussing education, in general, but it is not too much of a stretch to apply his poetic performance of the Garden of Eden example to the education of real human beings regarding equally real nonhuman animals, in particular. That is, by extension, justifications of meat-eating are often very abstract, armchair (or better, dining room table) sorts of affairs that unthinkingly involve preaching what Whitehead calls the "Gospel of Force" (*SM* 206) rather than that of persuasion. Actually seeing what goes on in slaughterhouses moment by moment is an educational, albeit gruesome, affair that causes nothing short of grief, as almost anyone who takes the time to do so will quickly learn. As more people become aware of nonhuman animal sentiency (S2) and mentality, we can hope with Whitehead that "if mankind can rise to the occasion, there lies in front a golden age of beneficent creativeness" (*SM* 205). Or again:

> There is something in the ready use of force which defeats its own object. Its main defect is that it bars cooperation. Every organism requires an environment of friends, partly to shield it from violent changes, and partly to supply it with its wants. The Gospel of Force is incompatible with a social life. (*SM* 206)

One practical advantage of Whitehead's metaphysics is that it could enable us to give a more accurate analysis than has been given historically of quite ordinary propositions like (to use Whitehead's own example): "There is beef for dinner today" (*PR* 11). The process analysis would insist that "the point to be emphasized is the insistent particularity of things experienced and of the act of experiencing," in contrast to a very abstract description of the act of meat-eating wherein the point at which the cow suffers intensely is left out of the picture and hence is not grievable; that is, the cow appears only later in a creation *ex nihilo* wrapped in cellophane at the grocery store (see *PR* 43).

Whitehead notes that for a living organism to survive it needs food, even if there is no absolute distinction between living and "nonliving" organisms, as we have seen. The foods that are eaten are themselves societies of some sort. Whitehead's term for what is required in order for living organisms to survive is "robbery." The question is whether the robbery is to be a mere petty theft or a major heist. As he puts the point, "life is robbery. It is at this point that . . . morals become acute. The robber requires justification" (*PR* 105–106). It is noteworthy that in the paragraphs immediately following this passage Whitehead speaks of divine tenderness directed toward each actual occasion as it arrives in the evocation of intensities of experience.

It is commonly acknowledged that there is a romantic component to Whitehead's thought, as we will see, wherein the Wordsworthian dictum that "we murder to dissect" is taken quite seriously. Whitehead's philosophy (or better, the philosophy of organism), as he sees it, is an attempt to *enlarge ethical discourse* so as to include consideration of the nonhuman animals whom we rob or murder. No hyperbole is committed here on a Whiteheadian view. The goal should be to foster intensities of experience that are positive "adversions" or contributions to reticulative beauty rather than negative, painful "aversions," as in gratuitous killing of beings whose lives are grievable. Moral responsibility consists in owning up to the ways in which we use our power of self-motion to determine the course of events (*PR* 140, 204, 254–255; *SM*, chap. 5).

A nonhuman animal body is a nexus of many cellular events that can be treated as though it were one whole actuality. This one actuality when considered in reference to the publicity of things is a superject; but in reference to its own privacy it is a subject, a moment in the genesis of its own self-enjoyment. As Whitehead famously suggests, God is the "fellow-sufferer who understands" such self-enjoyment (*PR* 351). To put the point in different Whiteheadian terms, intense self-enjoyment has value for itself, for others, and for the whole. The key thing to notice in the present context is that human experience is but one, albeit especially exalted, sort of higher experience (S2), given the reigning doctrine of evolution that Whitehead supports (*PR* 287, 351; *MT* 111–112).

It may very well be the case, however, that the greatest contribution a Whiteheadian could make to the current debate regarding nonhuman animal entitlements would involve the emphasis Whitehead placed on what can be called reflective equilibrium. All of us, or almost all of us, recoil emotionally at the thought of (more so at the sight of!) a cow having its carotid artery slit. This emotional reaction needs to be reconciled with the justification we give for our eating practices (or robberies). The meat-eater, at the very least, is in a state of disequilibrium between *emotional* response and *rational* justification (*PR* 16). Granted, some momentary incoherence or disequilibrium or contrast is needed in order for novelty to emerge, but this is a far cry from leaving the tension between emotional response and rational justification in a permanent state of disequilibrium that tends toward dualism.

No doubt some Whiteheadians (e.g., Cobb—see Dombrowski 2001b) will reach a different conclusion. They will say that because human eating invariably involves robbery, we can eat what we wish as long as we do so "mindfully," by recognizing the loss in intrinsic value that occurs when we eat nonhuman animals.

Two comments are in order by way of response. (a) It is crucial that we not commit the fallacy of misplaced concreteness by thinking that it is the Platonic forms of Cowhood or Chickenness that suffer and die. It is individual cows and chickens, here and now, who are the loci of value in a Whiteheadian universe and it is their loss that is (or should be) grieved (see Dombrowski 1988a). (b) When these individuals are killed for food, their suffering and death are *unnecessary*, given the healthiness of a vegetarian diet, and hence the robbery involved is, as previously implied, a major heist rather than a petty theft. Granted, all of the pleasures the nonhuman animal experienced up until the point of death are not negated, in that they are preserved in the divine life, but neither are its sufferings negated, nor is the loss of *its* life (not ours) forgotten. It is unclear, to say the least, whether these meat-eating "contributions" (to use Hartshorne's terminology) to the divine life are the sorts that we would like to make when seen from the perspective of the adventure of ideas that spreads across the generations. That is, speciesism may very well eventually go the way of racism, sexism, and heterosexism in the transition from FTP.

Granted, "moral obligation" is not a characteristic way of speaking in Whitehead, and he apparently felt some distaste for overly zealous approaches to righteousness. But he is insistent that morality has to do with increasing generality of outlook and with concern for the longer rather than the more limited future. Further, he thinks that this generality of outlook requires a disinterested assessment of all available knowledge so as to fairly consider intrinsic value wherever it is found (see *AI* 346, 371, 375–376; *PR* 15; and Cobb 2007, 54, 64, 71–74).

BUTLER ON PRECARITY IN "PRECARIOUS LIFE"

My thesis in this and the following section is that Butler's thoughts on grievability can easily be brought into reflective equilibrium with Whitehead's. This is because the relationship between Butler's *Precarious Life* and *Frames of War*, on the one hand, and AMC, on the other, is rich. In the former book she is quite explicit about her desire to explore the implications of a nonviolent life, specifically with respect to those acts of violence that are not routinely reported in the press. The problem, as she rightly notes, is that there is a tendency to fail to see a subject-of-a-life *as* a life. Here her language is very close to Tom Regan's in his deontological defense AMC (also see Pluhar). Granted, Butler is ambivalent regarding liberal rights (for a reason to be discussed momentarily), sometimes putting the word "rights" in scare quotes and at other times speaking positively and without qualification about the sort of rights that liberals defend, including the right of autonomy (Butler 2004, xvii, 6, 12, 24–25, 139).

Throughout both of her works it is clear that Butler correctly rejects rationality as a criterion for moral patiency status. Further, the topics that interest her, like precarity and vulnerability, have a family resemblance to what I have called "sentience." Violence exposes vulnerability, on her helpful rendering of the problem; hence, we should be especially wary of violence when, through repeated iterations, it becomes a way of life, which is similar to Whitehead's language regarding the Gospel of Force. If I understand Butler correctly, she is not an absolute pacifist, but she does argue against what I have called the infliction of unnecessary or gratuitous suffering. Her way to put a similar point is in terms of inflicting violence against certain lives that are not considered as such. But which lives? it might be asked. Her answer: those that are grievable. Indeed, those lives that are not grievable (e.g., those of $S1$ microscopic organisms, those of plants) are not lives in the morally relevant $S2$ sense (Butler 2004, 28–34; also see 2009, 15–23), even if one grants that they are not machines.

Defenders of AMC can learn a great deal from Butler's claim that vulnerability is a precondition of the human, even of human beings who are severely mentally impaired, and it is the common bond of vulnerability that enables us to hear the cry of the human. Because women are especially vulnerable to violent attack, feminism in some sense has to include an opposition to violence (see Adams). But despite the fact that vulnerability is a precondition of the human, we should avoid a single definition of "the" human (say in terms of rationality or autonomy), while at the same time avoiding relativism, presumably because the latter jeopardizes the aforementioned liberal rights (Butler 2004, 42–43, 47, 90, 130, 147).

In *Precarious Life* there is nonetheless an ambivalence regarding the status of the other who is in a precarious state. At times the question regarding which lives are grievable bleeds into the question regarding which lives count as human. As I see things, these two questions are quite different, as Butler herself implies when she focuses on vulnerability. Or again, when she is understandably bothered when prisoners of war are treated like caged nonhuman animals, this in no way entails that treating nonhuman animals in these ways would be morally permissible. To reduce a rational human being to a nonhuman animal status, or to engage in bestialization, does not necessarily force the critic of such practices into a defense of anthropocentrism. When Butler suggests that we have yet to become human, she facilitates the realization that traditional anthropocentrists actually expected too little of us as rational human beings. The FTP goal should be the elimination of *all* attempts to normalize arbitrary and/or cruel infliction of unnecessary or gratuitous suffering: racism (including Orientalism), sexism, heterosexism, speciesism, and so forth (Butler 2004, 20, 73, 78, 100, 134).

BUTLER ON GRIEVABLE LIVES IN "FRAMES OF WAR"

The preceding considerations from *Precarious Life* are amplified in *Frames of War*. Here grievable lives should be more equally grievable than they have been historically and hence the need for broader *rights* of protection. Butler thinks that the problem is at least partially onto-logical, thereby avoiding the pitfalls of the overly nominalistic approach taken by Anderson and especially Diamond. Once the ontological status of a being facilitates a decision regarding its moral patiency status, however, it is nonetheless possible to speak of differentiated precarity and the need to allocate recognition differentially, although presumably not arbitrarily (Butler 2009, viii, 1–4).

I am a bit worried about Butler's assertion that recognition is a reciprocal notion, because I fear that we might run into problems simi-lar to those traditionally faced by social contract theorists when both nonhuman animals and mentally impaired human beings were consid-ered. Their abilities to reciprocate are either minimal or nonexistent. But this difficulty can be avoided in social contract theory through a revised Rawlsian original position where the participants are ignorant not only of their race, sex, sexual orientation, and class but also of their species (see Dombrowski 2001a, chap. 11). In any event, reciprocity *is* a crucial consideration, as Butler implies, when both parties are rational and politically autonomous (Butler 2009, 6).

More to the point is Butler's illuminating insistence that our exist-ing frames hide the precariousness of life and that there is a need for a more inclusive and egalitarian way to frame, and hence to recognize, precariousness. This new frame would enable us to really see the link between human and nonhuman animals. The criterion for moral alliance does not seem to be rationality for Butler, but something with a family resemblance to sentience, like precariousness and vulnerability and hence grievability (Butler 2009, 12–13).

To be precarious is to have one's life always in another's hands, an other who is often anonymous. "One's life" is integrally connected to grievability. Once again, we should ask, Which lives are grievable? Butler notes that plants are alive, but we do not usually grieve them. (I admit that aesthetic loss is great when, for example, a five-hundred-year-old Douglas fir is felled.) The reason, I suggest, is that plants as wholes do not exhibit sentience per se (S2), even if they are minimally sentient at the cellular level (S1). Pruning apple trees (wherein plant cells—S1—are destroyed) and decapitating cows (S2) are hardly morally equivalent actions. We cannot help but destroy cells, especially cancer cells. And we cannot help but destroy plants, at least if we want to avoid starvation. But more than our desire to survive is at stake here. We do not have a sense that plants, or simple animals without central nervous systems, are subjects-of-a-life; hence, their deaths are not grievable (Butler 2009, 14–18).

Butler acknowledges that this line of reasoning has implications as well for the abortion debate. Defenders of the "prolife" position try to convince us that fetuses are grievable. But Butler is astute to link this debate to the claim that nonhuman animals have rights. That is, if sentiency per se (S2) is a necessary and sufficient condition for moral patiency status, then fetuses in the early stages of pregnancy are not grievable, whereas late-term fetuses are. Nerve cells appear in the fetus long before they are linked together in a central nervous system, which makes the experience of intense pain possible (S2). In my view, Saints Augustine and Thomas Aquinas were wise to compare the moral status of the fetus in the early stages of pregnancy to the moral status of a plant (see Dombrowski 2000a). Given the developmental and processual character of the life of a fetus, we should be skeptical of those who use the same frame for the early fetus and for the fetus in the third trimester (Butler 2009, 16).

Debates regarding line-drawing at the onset of sentiency per se (S2) and vulnerability should not be confused with those surrounding high levels of sentiency, wherein it may be difficult to distinguish between mentally impaired human beings and many nonhuman animals. But this difficulty should not bother us if both are moral patients, as AMC shows. It would be a distortion of Butler's view, however, to say that she is primarily interested in drawing lines. Despite the aforementioned ontological dimension of the issues at hand, acknowledged by Butler herself, her overall stance is centered on the concept of decision (as in Whitehead, a literal de-cision, where some alternatives are cut off so that others remain to be framed). And the decisions we are dealing with, regarding which lives are not grievable and which ones are, should be understood as *social* practices. Likewise, if the grievable lives in question are those of persons, a *social* notion is involved (Butler 2009, 19–21).

Butler assumes here that her stance is opposed to liberalism, which she identifies with a sort of individualism. Although much depends on which liberal thinker she has in mind. Rawlsian liberals like myself identify liberal freedoms as not only individual but also associational. Admittedly, a just society is one where individuals should be free to choose their own conception of the good and their own comprehensive doctrine that enables them to make sense of the big issues in life. This is good, but a just society is also one that gives elbow room to various groups that allows them to flourish as they see fit as long as they are "reasonable" (as we have seen this technical term used in Rawls to refer to agreements that would be reached among people in a fair decision-making procedure). That is, there is nothing inherently "individualistic" in the pejorative sense of the term in justice as fairness (Butler 2009, 20, 31, 33, 148; also see Dombrowski 2001a; 2011).

Further, Rawls' difference principle is the analogue in justice as fairness to the most neglected of the three ideals of the French Revolution: fraternity (or sorority). In justice as fairness we agree to share each other's fate. In terms of the Rawlsian original position, it is crucial to note that the parties who *deliberate* there (there is no Hobbesian *bargaining* in the original position in terms of egoistic threat advantage) need not only rationality (as in the ability to follow arguments, etc.) but also reasonableness, which refers to a willingness to get along with others according to fair terms of agreement. In short, there is no reason to fear that Rawlsian liberalism is egoistic or problematically individualistic.

Ironically, Butler's stance is very much like that of justice as fairness when she emphasizes that precariousness should be minimized in egalitarian ways, even if, as previously claimed, there is no obligation to preserve all living things, including plant cells (S1). It is the differential, yet egalitarian, grievability of lives that is her major concern. In this regard, her stance has a family resemblance to the defender of AMC (Butler 2009, 21, 23, 26). Butler's signal contributions to AMC lie in her key ideas regarding framing and precariousness, which are found in the following instructive lines:

> One might . . . believe in the sanctity of life or adhere to a general philosophy that opposes violent action of all kinds against sentient beings, and one might invest powerful feelings in such a belief. But if certain lives are not perceivable as lives, and this includes sentient beings who are not human, then the moral prohibition against violence will be only selectively applied (and our own sentience will be only selectively mobilized). The critique of violence must begin with the question of the representability of life itself: what allows a life to become visible in its precariousness and its need for shelter, and what is it that keeps us from seeing or understanding certain lives in this way? (Butler 2009, 50–51)

She even goes so far as to suggest that we might focus less on identity politics so as to energize our framing of precariousness and our opposition to both torture and the social death that is slavery. In addition to the opposition to racism, sexism, and speciesism, Butler adds (in AMC-like fashion) opposition to "able-ism" so as to focus attention on those with disabilities (Butler 2009, 32, 38, 42, 52).

The fact that it is sentiency or vulnerability and not rationality that is operative in Butler's view of moral patiency status is evidenced in her reminder that the senses have to operate in the effort to minimize precariousness in egalitarian ways. Or again, she urges that to be ethical is to respond to suffering, in an appreciative response to Susan Sontag's last book entitled *Regarding the Pain of Others*. If philosophers persist in speaking of human beings as rational animals, as will likely be the case, it is nonetheless crucial to notice that it is *as animals* that we suffer. Hence, an ontology of human beings is not separable from that of sentient animals, in general. As in AMC, overlap between the two groups is to be expected. New frames can emerge that help us to realize that grievability is the precondition of sentient life (Butler 2009, 52, 54, 63, 75–76, 88, 98, 139).

According to Butler, these new frames are perhaps more likely made through a serious consideration of Emmanuel Levinas' view that the "face" (in at least one sense of the term) demands an ethical response (Butler 2009, 77; also see 2004, xviii, 8, 130). A stunning example of this is provided by Aldo Leopold, who ceased killing wolves for the National Forest Service when he came upon a wolf he had shot but that had not yet died:

> We reached the old wolf in time to watch a fierce green fire dying in her eyes. I realized then, and have known ever since, that there was something new in me in those eyes—something known only to her. . . . I was young then, and full of trigger-itch; I thought that because fewer wolves meant more deer, that no wolves would mean hunters' paradise. But after seeing the green fire die, I sensed that . . . the wolf [did not agree] with such a view. (Leopold 130)

But these new frames are not assured, say if we become inured even to a photograph of a face of a child burned by napalm (Butler 2009, 69).

Once again, although Butler (like Whitehead) is skeptical in regard to complete nonviolence, and although she seems to enjoy a healthy *agon* in her writing (see Dombrowski 2009), we should nonetheless be attentive to different sorts of gratuitous violence as they are committed against "merely" sentient beings as well as human persons (Butler 2009, 165–166). Although we have been formed in habits of violence, our norms are iterable and in process and hence are, at least in principle and in the long run, subject to change. This provides hope for the Whiteheadian transition from FTP. If the generalized condition of precariousness and interdependency is made more visible, and is framed more carefully for us so that we may really see vulnerability, a more nonviolent, a fairer, world is possible. Further, a Butlerian (and Whiteheadian) list of virtues would have compassion toward the top of the list. And she reminds us that no group has a monopoly on being persecuted; hence, no group has a monopoly on deserving compassion. With this the stage could be set for the realization that nonviolence is a result of the apprehension of equality in the midst of precariousness (Butler 2009, 168, 170, 180–182). If this is not AMC, it is a very close relative to it.

WILD ANIMALS AND ENVIRONMENTAL ETHICS

There are two topics that I would like to examine before concluding the present chapter. The first of these involves the difference between our moral obligations to domestic animals and those, if there are such, to wild animals, such as the wolf described earlier by Leopold. Focusing on this difference provides a bridge from moral obligations to individual animals to a Whiteheadian environmental ethics, in general, as developed by several scholars, especially Cobb and Henning. Although process thinkers have contributed significantly to environmental ethics, this bridge is a much needed new one. The second topic, to be treated in the following section, involves a more detailed look at our moral obligations to nonrational human beings. Both topics are integral to the FTP transition.

Debates in philosophy regarding animal ethics have understandably centered around the question of *harm*: Do animals have rights not to be harmed? Do human beings have duties not to harm animals? Along with Palmer (2010) it makes sense to focus as well on questions regarding when we may *assist* animals: When is it permissible to assist animals? Are we ever duty-bound to assist animals? The distinction between domesticated and wild animals looms large in how we should respond to these questions. It makes sense to claim that we have a prima facie duty not to harm domesticated animals, but because we have bred them to be docile and vulnerable to us, we also have a prima facie duty to assist them when they are in trouble. By contrast, although we have a prima facie duty not to harm wild animals, we do not generally have a duty to assist them when they are in trouble. This lack of a duty to assist wild animals Palmer calls the laissez-faire intuition (LFI).

However, there are at least three different versions of LFI: strong, weak, and relational. In strong LFI we should neither harm nor assist wild animals because by assisting them we might be reconstituting them in our own image and hence be stripping them of their wildness. In weak LFI we should not harm wild animals, but it might be permissible to assist them if we could alleviate their pain while allowing them to be who they are. In relational LFI we should not harm wild animals, but there might also be duties to assist them generated by our causing the destruction of their habitat. Relational LFI is especially congenial to the process-relational stance found in a Whiteheadian view. Further, Whitehead's and Palmer's relational approach is close to the rights-based approach of Regan in his defense of AMC. This view is relational in the sense that the permissibility of assistance, or even the duty to assist, depends on what sort of relationship we have to the wild animal in question (e.g., whether we are the ones who have caused the trouble the wild animal is in).

Consider several examples: coyotes displaced by a new suburban subdivision, the endangered status of polar bears, the question of assistance to neighborhood squirrels, possible duties to restrain housecats when birds are attacked, possible duties to rescue dumpster kittens, the status of massive numbers of wildebeests who die in migration, the question as to whether one should intervene with respect to preventable disease in mountain goats, and so on. From a process theistic point of view, the way to put the tension between animal rights and environmental ethics is to say that an omnibenevolent God must not only love *each* sentient being but *all* of them.

I will not attempt to deal with these examples, which are ably treated by Palmer. But I would like to note that an adequate treatment of these examples would require awareness of both perpetrator and beneficiary versions of reparations theory in the effort to understand the concept of past harms to animals, harms that bear directly on whether we have duties to assist. Even if we are not the ones who deprived the coyotes of their habitat, if we benefit from such deprivation, we may have a duty to assist. Or again, recent work on agent-centeredness by virtue ethicists can be used profitably to understand agent-relatedness, which is crucial in the effort to understand when one has a duty to assist. In this regard one wonders about what sort of person could remain indifferent to the plight of a polar bear who has to swim hundreds of miles in order to find safe haven for her cubs.

I confess that for years I have been struggling to bridge the gap between my defense of animal rights, especially through AMC, and the sorts of concerns that are crucial in environmental ethics. The effort to bridge this gap is much facilitated by relational LFI as defended by Palmer, which I think should also be the view of process-relational thinkers. That is, the permissibility of assistance, or the duty to assist, cannot be determined in abstraction from a consideration of the relations human beings have with animals. If we have domesticated them, then we have a duty to assist them. However, if they are almost entirely unrelated to us, as in the case of almost fully wild animals, then we have no duty to assist; in some cases, it might not even be permissible to assist. In between are an increasing number of animals who are in the "contact zone." Our acquired relations to animals who enter into, or who are pushed into, the contact zone entail acquired duties.

In an influential article written a generation ago, J. Baird Callicott called attention to what he called "a triangular affair." That is, the conceptual battle is not merely between anthropocentrists and environmentalists but also includes animal rightists, who are neither anthropocentric nor unqualified supporters of the ecoholism that is assumed by many to be required in a defensible environmental ethics. Callicott himself modified his view somewhat so as to facilitate rapprochement between environmental ethics and nonhuman animal rights. I would like to push further so as to claim that a reticulative vision of the nonhuman animal rights stance *is itself* a defensible environmental ethics. Although I will not offer a detailed defense of this claim here, I will indicate three points that should indicate to the reader what such a defense would look like. These three points will deal with three different sorts of sentiency.

First, there is a certain primacy to the interests of those who are sentient per se (S2) because they can experience intense pain and can be harmed. Pain *hurts*. In one sense this point is obvious, but in another sense ethical theory is still trying to catch up with this insight.

This means that a defensible version of environmental ethics would have to take seriously the conditions necessary for the flourishing of sentient and rational human beings, with their only partial transcendence of animality. In the legitimate move away from anthropo*centrism* we should not forget that one of the reasons why we want a defensible environmental ethics is to enable human beings, including myriads of future generations of them, to flourish. More colloquially, we ought not throw away the baby with the dirty anthropocentric bathwater. There is nothing shallow about this concern for human beings, especially when it is realized in a Whiteheadian way that in the quest for a beautiful world we need to be concerned not only with the greatest unity in the midst of the greatest diversity but *also* with (rather than instead of) high-grade intensity of experience (see Dombrowski 2004a). Sentient and rational human beings add something significant to the aesthetic value of the world; hence, we ought to try to ensure that they continue to do so.

But a defensible environmental ethics would also have to take seriously the conditions necessary for the flourishing of domesticated animals. The two arguments stated previously regarding nonhuman animal rights (the argument from sentiency and AMC) indicate the significant changes that would have to occur in order to approximate reflective equilibrium with respect to domesticated animals. Further, these two arguments have consequences far beyond those that involve domesticated animals themselves. If our duties to domesticated animals were more widely acknowledged and protected by law, radical environmental changes for the good would be evidenced. For example, when it is considered that it takes between fifteen and twenty pounds of grain to produce one pound of meat in the beef industry, one realizes how wasteful it is environmentally to eat beef. Analogous arguments could be developed regarding pork and poultry. It is a commonplace among animal rightists, but still curiously ignored by others, that switching to a vegetarian diet is more environmentally efficacious than switching from a gas-powered car to a hybrid or electric vehicle.

A more defensible treatment of domesticated animals would also have a positive effect on wild animals. If the United States became a vegetarian nation, for instance, there would be far less land needed in cultivation such that vast stretches of the Midwest and elsewhere could be turned into national parks and national forests. Here the great numbers of domesticated animals would gradually go down in that there would be less of a need to breed them, but there would be a gradual increase in wild or semi-wild animals who could roam freely. Or again, it is widely noted that deforestation is a problem worldwide, especially deforestation of tropical rainforests in Brazil and Indonesia and elsewhere. It is not widely noted, however, that such deforestation largely occurs so as to make room for cattle ranchers.

In short, all of the major environmental problems (deforestation, climate change, aquifer depletion, desertification, etc.) are connected to, indeed are made worse by, the institution of meat-eating. By carefully attending to the conditions required for S2 animals (of whatever species) to flourish, we would be responding positively to the demands of well-informed and morally reflective environmentalists. The thesis of the present section is thus very much in conformity with the Thoreauvian dictum that in wildness is to be found the preservation of the world (see Dombrowski 1986).

Of course, the nonhuman animal rights approach cannot do all of the work of environmental ethics. For example, this work is enormously facilitated by widespread commitment to children's health and women's rights. This is because when parents, especially mothers, are confident that their children will survive, they have fewer of them. And when women attain political autonomy and economic security, they do not perceive the need to bear a large number of children. That is, although the solution to environmental problems hinges on slowing human population, it is crucial to do so in ways that are compatible with justice. An asymptotic approach to justice is enhanced when we note the conceptual link between sexism and speciesism in that both tend to rely on the (mistaken) assumption that rationality is the criterion for moral patiency status, with women (incredibly) seen as failing to meet the proposed criterion in some way.

It is to be hoped that what I have said thus far in this section is sufficient to dispel any suspicion that the environmentalism I am defending lacks depth. As we move from respect for sentient and rational human beings to sentient domesticated animals, the range of our duties gets wider and the depth of such concern grows because, as a result of including domesticated animals within the scope of moral concern, it becomes clear that environmental issues are vitally important not because their resolution would be conducive to the flourishing of disembodied Cartesian cogitos (if such were to exist), but rather because they would enhance the flourishing of sentient animals, including ourselves *as animals*. Likewise, the range and depth of our environmental ethics grows still further when we attend to the needs of not only human beings and domesticated animals but also to the needs of wild animals. This is because by attending to the necessary conditions for the flourishing of wild animals—polar bears and halibut and Western meadowlarks—we are: (a) led to think globally if not cosmically, and (b) led to consider carefully the quality of air, water, soil, temperature, climate, and so forth, as these impact the flourishing of animals, in general, whether human or nonhuman, both domestic and wild (see Scarborough et al.).

In the Whiteheadian transition from mechanism to organism, there is an abandonment of both the Cartesian idea that nonhuman animals are mere machines and the related idea that the only intrinsic values to be found in nature are located in human beings. As before, there is both intrinsic value in us *and* continuity in nature. Of course, there is also conflict among the values in nature, as becomes especially evident when the phenomenon of predation is considered. Although I will not treat this complex issue in any detail, I would like to make two brief points: First, because lions are not rational enough to be moral agents, their killing of a gazelle is of a different moral quality than the human killing of a sentient animal at the abattoir, and second, in the Whiteheadian quest for a more beautiful world, it should be clear that the beautiful should not be equated with the pretty. That is, prettiness is only one sort of beauty, as is sublimity (see Dombrowski 2004a).

There are at least two sorts of aesthetic disvalue or evil, on a Whiteheadian view, both of which lead to a world that is uglier than need be. One sort involves destruction or violence and the other sort is anesthesia, wherein one settles for a lesser value when a higher one was easily available. Nonhuman animal rights on a Whiteheadian basis are obviously key components in the effort to block the former. But it is not often noticed that by avoiding unnecessary or gratuitous violence we also counteract anesthesia. There always was something suspect about attempts to exalt humanity via violence inflicted on nonhuman animals. In fact, the reverse seems to be the case. By humbling ourselves to take stock of our own sentient animality, we are exalted (see 2 Corinthians 12: 9). Or again, Jesus reminds us that God cares even for the fall of a sparrow (Matthew 10: 28), a claim that was not lost on Hamlet (act 5, scene 2).

Second, on a Whiteheadian basis animal rights environmentalism can avoid the familiar charge that although the animal rights stance avoids anthropocentrism, it is nonetheless "sentient-centric." This avoidance is due to the fact that minimal sentiency (S1), if not morally considerable sentiency in the sense of acutely experienced gratuitous pain, pervades nature. Indeed, we should be attentive to, exhibit (Quaker) concern for, the ubiquity of S1 value in nature as part of the aesthetic drive to contribute to the beauty of the world, with "beauty" referring to both high-grade intensity of experience *and* unity-in-the-midst-of-diversity in a panexperientialist world wherein minimal experience is pervasive.

Henning is surely correct to emphasize that Whitehead's widely noted critique of *ontological* dualism is integrally connected to his less widely known critique of *axiological* dualism. In effect, process panexperientialism includes the claim that there is a continuum of *value* in nature. Although there are debates among process thinkers regarding how microscopic experience and hence value in nature is aggregated or compounded, it seems clear that all process thinkers have to steer clear of two extremes. If one leans too hard in the direction of giving a

Whiteheadian society a unity proper to itself, one runs the risk of moving too close to the classical concept of substance; however, if one offers a strictly reductionist description of a Whiteheadian society, such that it is constituted *solely* in terms of the interplay of its constituents, then one runs the risk of making a whole nothing but an aggregate that is the mere sum of its parts (see Bracken).

As I see things, both poles in this tension (not contradiction) need to be acknowledged and preserved. Hence, I think that, despite the obvious advantages of ecoholism, it is a view that should be defended with a grain of salt. As we have seen, a tree, even a glorious redwood, is a democracy in Whitehead (e.g., *AI* 205–206) in that its principle of unity is not nearly as real as the principle of unity found in an animal (of whatever species) with a central nervous system. That is, sentient animals have a level of coordination of diverse parts that is quite remarkable (indeed, it is Rubicon-crossing!) in contrast to the level of coordination found in a plant, say, at one end, and in the level of coordination found in an ecosystem, on the other. But the ubiquity of S1 in nature means that it is inaccurate to say that the rest of nature is merely meant to serve the interests of S2 beings. Rather, *all* concrete singulars have value not only for others and for the whole but also to some extent *for themselves.*

And third, the value for the whole mentioned by Whitehead is called "contributionism" by Hartshorne, which is a label that can easily cause confusion, especially if it is assumed that the goal of process theists is to give over everything to God, hence leaving us and the rest of the natural world impoverished. Theological fascism fueled by a belief in divine omnipotence, after all, would be just as bothersome as environmental (or political) fascism. We have seen that, at one point, Whitehead is alleged to have compared the classical theistic omnipotent God with Hitler (*DW* 174–176, 189, 198)! Hartshorne's language regarding God as a Platonic World Soul is particularly helpful here in that if we conceive of God as the mind or soul not for this or that particular body but for the body of the entire universe, then we and other animals are by analogy cells in the divine life. We can refer to the World Soul in terms of divine sentiency or S3. The advantage of this interpretation of value for the whole is that healthy cells are good in themselves and do not lose their individual worth when they contribute to the entire body, in this case to the cosmic divine body. That is, what we can contribute to God is our own happiness, our own refusal to settle for anesthesia, and our own dogged attempt to live nonviolently.

To use Henning's helpful language that he has adopted from White-head, the obligation to contribute to the greatest possible universe of beauty (importance) is at odds with neither the obligation to maximize intensity and harmony among one's own experiences (self-respect) nor the obligation to facilitate the same in others (love). These goals, in turn, require the avoidance of wanton destruction of natural value (peace) and the expansion of the breadth and depth of aesthetic horizons (education).

A bit more needs to be said here about the relationship between an animal rights stance and environmental ethics. My overall view is like Dale Jamieson's in claiming that an animal rights view *is* an environmental ethic. There is nonetheless a tension (not a contradiction) between my defense of moral patiency status in S2 beings and my defense of the Whiteheadian idea that all concrete singulars have value of some sort, however minimal. This tension is best dealt with in terms of the claim that the continuity of value in nature that goes all the way down is nonetheless compatible with the existence of certain thresholds that are crossed that lead to qualitative changes. An analogy for the S2 threshold provided by a functioning central nervous system can be found in water being gradually heated (or cooled) until a qualitative change occurs at 212 degrees Fahrenheit (or 32 degrees Fahrenheit). A Whiteheadian can see value of some sort as ubiquitous yet reject biotic egalitarianism.

One way to finesse this point would be to say that only S2 organisms are subjects-of-a-life who deserve rights, whereas S1 organisms, although they are to be seen as objects of concern, are not possessors of rights. Another way to finesse it would be to say that moral patiency status pervades nature, but S2 organisms have it to a qualitatively higher degree than S1 organisms. I find the latter way of speaking somewhat cumbersome in that it puts our emotions into disequilibrium with our rational understanding. To cite an odd, yet instructive, example: Beer lovers enjoy visiting breweries and bread lovers enjoy visiting bakeries, yet I have never met a meat-eater who enjoyed going to slaughterhouses. Cutting down hops in their prime just does not bother us emotionally, whereas cutting down cows does. Clearly, there is a qualitative difference between S2 organisms and S1 organisms, even when this difference is seen against the backdrop of the continuity thesis and of the escape from dualism. Hartshorne and others are surely correct, however, to emphasize that, because of the defensibility of panexperientialism and of the continuity thesis, there will always be something rough about the S2-S1 distinction; hence, such a distinction ought not to degenerate into an absolute bifurcation.

MARGINAL CASES, AGAIN

It will be profitable to return once again to a consideration of marginal cases, this time in light of a recent defense of the intellectually disabled by Licia Carlson, whose Foucaultian approach is in many ways congenial to Butler's. Carlson attempts to "unmask" AMC, which, by her own admission, is different from refuting it. To unmask an argument is not to show that it is wrong or useless (Carlson 13–17) but to show the function it serves, especially the nontheoretical function it serves in upholding existing power relations. And existing power relations are unfavorable to the intellectually disabled. To be clear, Carlson is not necessarily opposed to the claim that animals have rights (although like Whitehead and Butler she never asserts this claim explicitly), but she is opposed to "using" the intellectually disabled in the cause of defending the rights of animals.

In order to understand the unmasking of AMC, it is important to know that Carlson is primarily influenced by Foucault (Carlson 4–13). As a result, she rejects the medical model for intellectual disability and accepts the social model. In the latter, although some individuals may have medical *impairments*, if these lead to *disabilities*, such results are due to social decisions. To take an analogy from the physical, if one has impaired legs, this need not be a disability in a wheelchair-friendly society. Or more precisely, Carlson seems to go even further than the social model by affirming a Butler-like postmodern model of intellectual disability, which deconstructs the very notion of an individual with impairments.

In Carlson's view, when human beings who are intellectually impaired are viewed as marginal cases, there is only a limited possibility that they will be treated justly (Carlson 10, 197). Here the defender of AMC is likely to think that an important distinction is needed between viewing those who are intellectually impaired as marginal human beings and viewing them as marginal moral patients *when rationality is used as the criterion for moral patiency status.* One should be bothered by the former. But the intellectually impaired *are* marginal moral patients when rationality is used as the criterion for moral patiency status. This is precisely why defenders of AMC reject rationality as the criterion for moral patiency. Because of the danger of the former alternative, however, it might be better to refer to the argument in question as that from species continuity and/or species overlap, as we have seen.

A similar sort of partial agreement and partial disagreement between Carlson and the defender of AMC can be found regarding the animality of those who are intellectually impaired. At times she seems to be saying that *any* comparison of the intellectually impaired and animals is dehumanizing to the intellectually impaired. But this assumes certain speciesist attitudes toward animals. Human beings themselves *are* animals (as Whitehead especially indicates); hence, "animality" does not have to be a pejorative term.

Although it may be correct that AMC is peculiar to philosophers, it should be noted that biologists and others from the time of Charles Darwin to the present have been thoroughly familiar with the thesis that there is not only continuity but also overlap between the affective and intellectual abilities of animals and those of human beings. Or again, in one sense the intellectually impaired cannot be "animal*ized*" if they are already (along with the intellectually accelerated) animals.

Carlson is at her best from a process perspective when she emphasizes the idea that we should not think of intellectual impairment as a static fact but as part of a process. Nor should we equate intellectual impairment with its most severe cases (Carlson 36–45). Many moderately intellectually impaired human beings can, over the course of time, transition into mild cases, however "moderate" and "mild" are defined. My own adopted and intellectually *delayed* son is an example of this transition.

Carlson is also insightful in suggesting that those who are only mildly intellectually impaired should be listened to when they tell us how they would like to be treated (Carlson 128). Of course, defenders of AMC are also prone to point out that animals can communicate in their own ways, too. Who really doubts that a normally compliant cow, who nonetheless resists going into the abattoir, is trying to tell us something? One can imagine a context in which the myths and perceptions regarding *both* intellectually impaired human beings and animals are unmasked together. This project would seem to be congenial to both Whitehead and Butler.

It is correct for Carlson to think that intellectually impaired human beings, even those who are severely impaired, are nonetheless moral patients. The point to AMC, however, is to argue that if they are moral patients, then animals at comparable (or higher) affective and cognitive levels should also be seen as moral patients, assuming that some fair manner of determining affective and cognitive functioning can be developed. However, I am not sure it is informative to say, as Carlson does, that fellow human beings deserve respect because they *are* human beings (Carlson 148–157). One needs to avoid begging the question as to why all humans deserve respect; this point to a certain extent affects Butler as well.

It is true that some philosophers will say that it is a fundamental, brute fact, amenable to no further explanation, that all humans deserve respect. But even if it is true that justification has to stop somewhere, I am not convinced that it has to be here. That is, as I see things on a Whiteheadian basis, there are some things even more basic than humanity in morality, most notably S2 sentiency or Butlerian vulnerability. This does not necessarily mean that all intellectually impaired human beings suffer, however, as Carlson ably argues (Carlson 168).

Carlson follows rather closely the aforementioned view of Diamond (and that is partially resisted by Butler), a view that is influenced by Wittgenstein and that is surprisingly close to the Foucaultian view. The idea here is that we create moral patiency status by caring for the intellectually impaired and by baptizing them into the moral (human) community. Here I think that both Wittgensteinians and Foucaultians should be resisted. Some nonarbitrary reason is required to determine who gets to be baptized as a moral patient and who is left bereft of moral patiency status. Otherwise we could just as easily not "baptize" them, the way racists and sexists have traditionally left blacks and women, respectively, outside of the class of moral patients.

What defenders of AMC can most profitably learn from Carlson is that those with intellectual impairment ought not be seen as mere conscripts for the purpose of advancing animal rights (Carlson 131–148). They are ends-in-themselves with inherent value and who have their own purposes. However, defenders of AMC do not have to follow Carlson in thinking that the oppression of intellectually impaired human beings and the oppression of animals have to be assessed separately, especially when it is considered that members of both groups are moral patients largely as a result of their sentience (S2) rather than as a result of their (nonexistent or minimal) rationality.

Further, rapprochement with Carlson can be reached regarding her very insightful treatment of the need for cleanliness in intellectually impaired human beings (Carlson 152). Once moral patiency status itself is determined in a nonspeciesist manner, defenders of AMC need not object to additional species-dependent duties being added, as in the duty to attend to the hygiene needs of intellectually impaired human beings but not to those needs, if there are such, of pigs. In fact, the latter may actually *like* to roll in the mud so as to cool off or to "clean" themselves of bugs. But this is quite different from making moral patiency status itself a function of species membership. The important thing is that the added duties owed to intellectually impaired human beings not be used to erase the duties we have to animals or to impede the FTP transition.

Another way to put my point is to say that an intellectually impaired human being has the same interests regarding pleasure and pain as an animal, but *in addition* this human being has a species-dependent interest in cleanliness. Although the intellectually impaired human being may or may not be *interested in* cleanliness, it is surely the case that it is *in the interest of* the intellectually impaired human being to be clean. I agree with Carlson when she includes all human beings in the realm of moral considerability, but I am not convinced that such inclusion is due solely, or even primarily, to either species membership or social relations that are (allegedly) peculiar to human beings.

To admit that intellectually impaired human beings have more rights than animals at comparable affective and cognitive levels is not to say that they have more theoretically secure rights, say the right not to be forced to suffer or be killed unnecessarily or gratuitously. The defender of AMC can appeal here to the age-old idea in moral theory that negative duties (e.g., the duty not to be cruel) have a certain priority over the positive ones. This in no way, however, is meant to eradicate or even trivialize the positive duties (e.g., the duty to attend to the hygiene needs of intellectually impaired human beings). My point here is to commend Carlson for pointing the way, through her comments about cleanliness, to this important distinction, which once again would seem to be congenial to Whitehead's and Butler's views.

I think that Carlson's antipathy is, or at least should be, directed at utilitarianism. The utilitarian version of AMC, wherein *both* intellectually impaired human beings (along with intellectually accelerated human beings?) *and* animals can be sacrificed for the sake of an aggregative good, is indeed deeply troubling. Hence, it is unfortunate that the defender of AMC she refers to most frequently is Peter Singer (Carlson 137–145). Within the utilitarian version of AMC, one is understandably tempted either to retain our present attitudes toward animals and change (i.e., lower) our attitudes toward the intellectually impaired (as in R. G. Frey) or to change our attitudes toward both animals and the intellectually impaired (as in Singer). In either case Carlson is correct to think that utilitarians are insensitive to the intellectually impaired.

But the problem here is not with AMC but rather with the aggregative logic of utilitarianism and with its failure to respect the distinctness of moral patients. By contrast, consider an animal *rights* version of AMC similar to the one defended by Regan and others (in contrast to utilitarian "rights"):

(a) Humans, including the intellectually impaired, belong to the class of rights holders.

(b) However, given the most reasonable criterion for the possession of rights, one that enables us to include the intellectually impaired, this same criterion will require us to include sentient (S2) animals in this class.

(c) Therefore, if we include the intellectually impaired in the class of rights holders, we must also include sentient (S2) animals.

The rights of those who are intellectually impaired cannot be accounted for on the basis of rationality, sophisticated language use, and so on. If we say that the intellectually impaired have rights because we stipulate that they do (the apparent view of a Foucaultian like Carlson and a Wittgensteinian like Diamond), we account for neither the existence of nor the strength of our intuition that the intellectually impaired can be violated. If sentiency (S2) is a sufficient condition for moral patiency status, as I think it is, we can explain why we think that the intellectually impaired can be the victims of gross injustice (hence, a defender of AMC need not be insensitive to them) and why morally reflective people (including meat-eaters!) cringe when they imagine cows being cut down in the slaughterhouse.

Of course, not everyone shares my views. Some (at times, both Butler and Carlson) seem to be skeptical of the claim that the intellectually impaired and animals have *rights*. But it has been my experience that such skepticism is always accompanied by a nervous twitch. The twitch is due to the fact that the infliction of pain is morally relevant if *anything* is morally relevant; hence, it is risky to leave undefended the right not to have pain inflicted on one unnecessarily. Once again, however, Carlson is to be thanked for alerting us to the fact that once the minimal rights of the intellectually impaired and animals are acknowledged (e.g., the right not to receive gratuitous suffering or the right to life), it is still permissible to put in place additional protections regarding the intellectually impaired. As I see things, partial affections are legitimate in morality as long as they are ancillary to, rather than replacements for, impartial ascription of basic rights (see Dombrowski 1997a; also see 1984a; 1984b; 2000b; 2006a; 2008).

The difficulty involved in pinning down exactly what process ethics can contribute to ethical theory can actually be seen as one of its strengths. Once one becomes convinced of the need for a sort of "moral eclecticism" (Fleischacker 232), process ethics looks more appealing because of its systematic (yet fallible) attempt to bring all of the relevant theoretical considerations to bear in the effort to achieve reflective equilibrium. The emphasis in process ethics on education (Henning 146) has led several scholars to emphasize connections with virtue ethics, its prominent place for the maximization of value of all sorts has led Palmer and others to see its similarities to utilitarianism, and the important place in it for the irreplaceability of individuals capable of high-grade experience leads us to consider seriously its close connection to deontology. Although Henning is rightly skeptical of any claim to the *absoluteness* of deontology in process ethics, this skepticism is perfectly compatible with deontological considerations being necessary if not sufficient conditions for a defensible environmental ethics from a process perspective (Henning 178–180). Further, Palmer was surely correct in noting that my own version of process ethics is deontology-heavy, but the stance I am taking is nonetheless amenable to rapprochement not only with Palmer but also with an appropriately qualified ecoholism (Palmer 1998, 104–107).

If intrinsic value is on a continuum, as process thinkers hold, then we should not be surprised to learn that continuum-thinking is nonetheless compatible with there being moral thresholds that make a significant difference. That is, continuum-thinking is not at all at odds with threshold-thinking. As before, think of water gradually being heated to 212 degrees Fahrenheit, when a qualitative change occurs as it evaporates into air, likewise regarding water being gradually cooled to 32 degrees when it turns to ice. It is hard for me to imagine how to reach reflective equilibrium in a sort of biocentric egalitarianism that is, at the very least, vulnerable to compelling *in extremis* cases. It is clear that some beings are more morally significant than others. Who really doubts that one should swat the tsetse fly that is about to bite one's granddaughter? The two most significant threshold points, as I have treated them, are the rise of the central nervous system and hence sentiency (S2) and hence moral patiency status, on the one hand, along with the rise of rationality and hence moral agency status, on the other. We ignore these thresholds at our (reflective equilibrium) peril.

WHICH LIVES ARE GRIEVABLE?

The question Which lives are grievable? can be reformulated as the following: Who counts as a who (Butler 2009, 163)? If my defense of AMC, my effort to interpret Whitehead and Butler in light of AMC, and my attempt to supplement AMC in light of Butlerian concepts (framing, vulnerability, precariousness, grievability, mourning, etc.) are sound, I believe the following can be said by way of response to these questions, and herein lie signal contributions of AMC to the understanding of FTP:

All human lives are grievable. As a result of the reasoning found in AMC, the lives of sentient nonhuman animals with central nervous systems are also grievable (along with late-term fetuses who are sentient once a central nervous system starts to function toward the end of the second trimester). Other living organisms (single-celled organisms, plants, early fetuses, and other "lower" animals that exhibit S1 but not S2) are not grievable in that they are not subjects-of-a-life. Because they are not subjects-of-a-life, there is no reason to grieve their passing, although the destruction of plant life can have a deleterious effect on beings who are subjects-of-lives, and the destruction of plant life can lead to aesthetic disvalue.

There is obviously a difference between gargling with a mouthwash that "kills germs on contact" and violating the Geneva Conventions' prohibition against the killing of prisoners of war. The goal is to asymptotically approach reflective equilibrium between intuition and theory when all of the relevant considerations are on the table for discussion, including those that relate to more difficult cases. It has been my hope that a consideration of AMC, on the one hand, and Whitehead and Butler, on the other, has taken us closer to this goal.

To be precise, although Whitehead sometimes overemphasizes human transcendence of animality (especially in *MT*), and although he is a bit sketchy regarding his idea that our survival requires robbery, he is clear that the robbery requires justification. And such a justification is greatly facilitated by a careful consideration of his views. In his critique of dualism, Whitehead insightfully defends the thesis that there is a scale of becoming in nature wherein at each level members of adjacent categories shade off into each other. This leads to the view that human beings have continuity with nonhuman animals and that they have continuity with us, as in the Whiteheadian view that the series of occasions that make up a sentient animal's life can be personally ordered. Thus, as a result of Whitehead (and Butler), it is more understandable that rationality not be seen as the criterion for moral patiency status and that the unnecessary suffering or death criticized in AMC be seen as a tragic loss. Even we are only intermittently rational; hence, once essentialism is rejected (by both Whitehead and Butler), we are in a better position to affirm the proposition that species membership itself is irrelevant regarding the attribution of basic rights.

Whitehead helps us to see that the main ethical implication of the continuity and overlap thesis is an insistent particularity that he calls the clutch at vivid immediacy, especially at the moment when unnecessary or gratuitous suffering or death are inflicted. It is not Cowhood in general that suffers, but *this* cow here and now. The overall thrust of Whitehead's view of ethics consists in an *enlargement* of value discourse so as to include value for oneself, value for others, and value for the whole (God). Part of this enlargement consists in the effort to reach an equilibrium between emotional response to injustice and the traditional bounds of rational justification.

Likewise, despite some features of Butler's thought that run counter to AMC (her skittishness regarding rights in general, and in regard to political liberalism in particular, and in her view that recognition requires reciprocity), the overall weight of her view in *Precarious Life* and *Frames of War* is not only supportive of but enhances AMC in important ways. Like Whitehead, she does not assume that rationality is basic to what I have called moral patiency status. Instead, we more easily approach reflective equilibrium in moral theory by looking for such a status among several Butlerian phenomena that have a family resemblance to each other: precarity, vulnerability, sentiency, and hence grievability and mourning.

In an effort to avoid both essentialism and nominalism (in that the problem is, after all, partly ontological), Butler insightfully explores the implications of a nonviolent life. The chief impediment of such a life is the failure to even see a subject-of-a-life as such. This failure is largely due to the fact that existing frames tend to hide the precariousness of certain subjects-of-a-life. But because these frames are habitual social practices that are iterable, they are changeable over the course of time, a view that should be congenial to process thinkers of all sorts. That is, our violent habits are not inevitable and are especially subject to alteration at the moment when one is faced with another face, here and now, in a common bond of vulnerability. AMC is intended to facilitate thinking about a more egalitarian view, which is nonetheless compatible with a partially differentiated precarity, that can arise as a result of these face-to-face meetings. In short, the FTP transition is greatly facilitated by this argument.

SIX

Wordsworth, Whitehead, and the Romantic Reaction

WHITEHEAD ON WORDSWORTH

Something more needs to be said about the connection I noted in the introduction between MTO and FTP. To put my thesis in the strongest terms: I think that there is logical entailment between the two, such that once one views the mind-body problem and the MTO transition from a panexperientialist point of view, one *cannot help* but facilitate the FTP transition. Machines can be pushed around and manipulated, even exploited, and we do not much mind, but organisms, because they feel and hence are capable of internal relations, matter. Force may be needed when dealing with machines, but persuasion is more appropriate when dealing with organisms. There is a very strong tendency, once one transitions MTO to ask questions like: Is it ever morally permissible to intentionally kill human organisms? What are our responsibilities regarding sentient organisms of any species? Are there responsibilities *regarding* microscopic (S1) organisms in addition to those *to* sentient (S2) organisms? The purpose of the present chapter is to strengthen the case for the close connection between MTO and FTP.

This case has been anticipated before and its name is "romanticism." This label, like "democracy" and "liberalism," can mean many different things, so it will be crucial for me to isolate the specific meaning I have in mind. In this effort I will rely on Whitehead's (and Hartshorne's) own reliance on Wordsworth in the attempt to support both the MTO and FTP transitions and the connection between the two. Whitehead himself tells us that Wordsworth was a "major interest" in his life (AN 6).

The *locus classicus* for process thinkers regarding the subject matter of the present chapter is chapter 5 of *SM*, titled "The Romantic Reaction." In this chapter Whitehead follows up on his thesis that in the seventeenth and eighteenth centuries a scheme of scientific concepts was developed that was congenial to Augustinian theology. Both Catholic Jansenism and Protestant Calvinism had a view of the human person as helpless and supine before irresistible divine grace. The mechanistic science of the modern period led to a view of human beings as helpless before the mechanism of nature, which was likewise irresistible. Whitehead's insight lies not merely in noticing these two types of helplessness, but in his argument that they are alike in being "the monstrous issues of limited metaphysics" (*SM* 75).

Scientific mechanism has endured with more force than the Augustinian view, although both of these stances deserve criticism. For example, Whitehead wonders about how one can be a mechanist once one notices that there are organisms in existence with their various powers of self-motion. Note that it is not so much the existence of consciousness that poses problems for mechanism but autokinetic living organisms of whatever sort. Mechanists cannot help but be halfhearted in their approach to living organisms, a halfheartedness that tends to distract us from the importance of organisms, at best, or that encourages us to treat organisms as machines, at worst. Civilization itself is enfeebled as a result of mechanism. Of course, even theism can survive (if not flourish) in a mechanistic universe, but its "God" tends to resemble William Paley's famous (or infamous) divine mechanic for natural mechanism. Whitehead's response, which influences Griffin's appealing approach, is once again to say that "the only way of mitigating mechanism is by the discovery that it is not mechanism" (*SM* 76); instead, in panexperientialist fashion, any "mechanism" is really an aggregate of more fundamental organisms.

Although literary figures tend to largely ignore or misunderstand developments in science, Wordsworth and other romantic writers consciously and often in an informed way reacted against mechanism (see the insightful work by Middleton). Wordsworth was moved, on Whitehead's interpretation, by moral repulsion: mechanism dangerously leaves something out (*SM* 77). The argument that runs as follows highlights this danger: (a) molecules (and stars) blindly run, (b) human bodies are collections of molecules, (c) hence, human beings are not responsible for their actions. The view that mental experiences are determined by mechanical laws convinced one of the greatest minds of the nineteenth century, John Stuart Mill (see Mill, books 5–6, "On the Logic of the Moral Sciences"). Volitions are determined by motives and motives are the result of mechanical antecedent conditions that determine us. And Whitehead alleges that Mill's view is generally accepted by contemporary scientists.

The way to contradict this view is not by way of vitalism, which is really a type of dualism. Vitalism accepts the mechanistic account of "inanimate" nature, but it also suggests that mechanism is partially mitigated in the case of living organisms. Whitehead finds the gap here between living and dead somewhat vague. More plausible, he thinks, is the view that mechanistic materialism, if it applies at all, does so with respect to very abstract aggregate entities like telephones and rocks. In his words:

> The concrete enduring entities are organisms, so that the plan of the *whole* influences the very characters of the various subordinate organisms which enter into it. In the case of an animal, the mental states enter into the plan of the total organism and thus modify the plans of the successive subordinate organisms until the ultimate smallest organisms, such as electrons, are reached. Thus, an electron within a living body is different from an electron outside it, by reason of the plan of the body. (*SM* 79)

This view is by no means an abandonment of science, although it might seem to be such if one identifies a mechanistic account of nature with a scientific one.

As we have seen, Whitehead sometimes in *SM* confuses the reader by calling his view "organic mechanism," a confusion that is eliminated in *PR* in terms of the label "philosophy of organism." This latter designation better suggests Whitehead's and Wordsworth's response to the "perplexity which haunts the modern world" (*SM* 81), a perplexity treated earlier in terms of Griffin's panexperientialist response. Whitehead thinks it significant that John Milton's *Paradise Lost* is addressed to the classical theistic God and Alexander Pope's *An Essay on Man* is addressed to Lord Bolingbroke, but Wordsworth's *The Excursion* is addressed to nature. But unlike mechanists, who study nature through scientific abstractions (mass, extension, etc.), Wordsworth studied it through experiential particulars. As the philosopher John Smith was fond of pointing out, the problem with the British empiricist philosophers in their various defenses of mechanism was that they were ironically insufficiently empirical. They did not really pay attention to experience.

Wordsworth's absorption in nature is evident at every turn. Indeed, Whitehead sees him as a "genius" who was "drunk with nature" (*SM* 83), despite the fact that he was well read and philosophically inclined. Although at times Wordsworth transfers his distaste of mechanism to repulsion to science itself, this transference is understandable when the hegemony of mechanism is considered. Wordsworth's famous line from "The Tables Turned" illustrates this repulsion: "We murder to dissect." Although this line is amenable to many different interpretations, it is easy to see why it is something of a rallying cry for animal rightists who are opposed to treating animal research specimens as mere machines. Here the tight relationship, even causal connection, between MTO and FTP is most evident: It is only when animals are seen as machines that vivisection and dissection can be morally permissible. If we concentrate on them as living, sentient (S2) organisms, then intentionally causing them to suffer or be killed unnecessarily or gratuitously is nothing less than murder (!), on Wordsworth's view as emphasized by Whitehead (*SM* 15, 83; *PR* 140).

If one asks in Wordsworthian fashion, What exactly is it in nature that mechanism leaves out? Whitehead has us note that the question should be asked in the interest of science itself, otherwise science will be insufficiently empirical. What is left out is the tonality of the particular instance, the experience of a living organism at a particular moment, the brooding presence of the hills, the connaturality that occurs when one laughs with the daffodils ("I Wandered Lonely") or when one finds in the primrose thoughts that lie "too deep for tears" ("Intimations of Immortality"). The overarching hope is that there could be a panexperientialist science wherein abstraction could be fallible, reformable, and in process.

The important facts of nature elude mechanism. Wordsworth's greatest poem, according to Whitehead, is the first book of *The Prelude*, which is pervaded by the haunting presences of nature, as we will see momentarily. One of the reasons to consider these presences,

Whitehead urges, is the negative one of alerting us to how paradoxical both dualism and mechanistic materialism really are. If philosophy consists in a critique of abstractions, as Whitehead thinks, then the testimony of poets, especially Wordsworth, have to be taken very seriously because it is more likely that they, rather than philosophers, will be able to articulate concrete feelings and intuitions. And the more articulate they are, the more we notice the gulf between feeling or aesthetic intuition, on the one hand, and mechanism, on the other. As Whitehead emphasizes (*SM* 199), "there is no substitute for the direct perception of the concrete achievement of a thing in its actuality. We want concrete fact with a high light thrown on what is relevant to its preciousness."

However, Whitehead has no desire to retreat to a subjectivist world in that this world would concomitantly signal a retreat to dualism, which, as we have seen Griffin argue, is easily reduced to mechanistic materialism once the ghost in the machine is exorcised. What we want is an accurate description of a "common world" (*SM* 87–89). Here we see more precisely what Whitehead means by "the romantic reaction" and how some popular conceptions of romanticism have given it a bad name. One often hears that the romantics wanted to recover human subjectivity or to bolster human subjectivity against the rising tide of mechanistic materialism (see McFarland). But this sort of language flirts with dualism, and, by implication, facilitates mechanistic materialism itself once the rare human subjects are either exorcised or deconstructed. Romanticism need not play into the hands of its intellectual opponents, however. What is meant by "romanticism" in the present context is a rethinking of nature itself and an effort to do justice to it in a nonmechanical fashion.

Whitehead even calls the sort of romanticism to be defended a type of objectivism: Our naïve experience (what Griffin would call "hardcore common sense") tells us that we exist *within* a natural world that influences us, our historical knowledge tells us that a vast natural world—including distant galaxies—existed before human beings came into existence on this planet, and our instinct for action tells us that the world transcends us as human subjects and requires a response from us in order to insure survival. It is very difficult for us to hold that the experienced world is merely an attribute of our own subjectivity (*SM* 89–90).

The intrinsic reality of an event is termed its "value" by Whitehead. In the first instance "value" refers to individuality, to the intrinsic nature of an event, a subjective or psychological quality whereby an organism *feels* (see Bixler 500). But in *MT* and elsewhere Whitehead is clear that there are three types of value: the value of an individual, the value of diverse individuals for each other, and the value of the whole (God). The poetic view of the world fostered by Wordsworth is permeated by value in all three senses and Wordsworth was obsessed with them, indeed he worshipped them, according to Whitehead. It would be a misreading of Wordsworth to assume that this leads to pantheism in that pantheism does not exhaust the types of divine world-inclusiveness that are possible. That is, there is also, at the very least, the panentheistic alternative defended by Hartshorne wherein God includes the world of value but is not exhausted by it, as would be the case in pantheism (see Dombrowski 1985; 1988a, chap. 6; 1988b; 1988c). Further, whereas pantheism seems to exclude any sense of God as a person, it is clear that Wordsworth (and Whitehead) personalizes God and Nature, indeed sees the divine as benevolent (Pite 192; Levine). This lends support to the claim that he was a panentheist, even if he was not aware of this designation. In the present context it is crucial to cement the link between "romanticism" as the term is used here and value: "The nature-poetry of the romantic revival was a protest on behalf of the organic view of nature, and also a protest against the exclusion of value from the essence of matter of fact. . . . The romantic reaction was a protest on behalf of value" (*SM* 94).

TWO POEMS

It will be helpful to illustrate Wordsworth's contributions to the MTO and FTP transitions through passages from one of his most famous poems, "Intimations of Immortality," and from the poem that Whitehead thinks is his greatest (indeed, Whitehead thinks that it is Wordsworth's greatest poem "by far"—see *SM* 83): the first book of *The Prelude*.

The opening stanzas of the immortality ode introduce a theme that is central to romanticism: the idea that things are not as they should be and that originally they were much better. This "original" ideal need not be interpreted literally, however. In fact, much harm can be done if this hermeneutically unsophisticated position is allowed to go through. If this "original" purity is taken literally, then there is a danger-ous tendency for romantic thinking to be pushed in a conservative or reactionary direction as part of an effort to restore some sort of imagined primeval perfection. Think of right-wing German romanticism in the hands of various followers of Friedrich Nietzsche and Richard Wagner and Heidegger in the mid-decades of the twentieth century.

But Whitehead tellingly does not interpret Wordsworth in these terms. "The glory and the freshness of a dream" that is destroyed by mechanistic materialism is a dream that occurs in the present. When Wordsworth says that "there hath past away a glory from the earth," he is, in effect, referring to a falling away from the panexperientialist ideal as discussed here in chapter 1. This ideal was *prefigured* by Plato, as we have seen, but he never attained it; hence, we need not call for a literal return to Plato or to his antidemocratic politics. In fact, without cell theory or twentieth-century physics, Plato could not have fully attained the panexperientialist ideal. That is, there is no necessary connection between *philosophia perennis* and political conservativism. Regarding Wordsworth's own nineteenth-century contributions to *philosophia perennis* interpreted panexperientially, it should be noted that he uses Platonic concepts throughout the immortality ode. He alludes to a Platonic form of Treeness that unifies our experiences of a multiplicity of particular trees: "of many, one." He also makes reference to Platonic anamnesis, which, once again, need not be interpreted literally: "shadowy recollections, / Which, be they what they may." But these uses of Plato are perfectly consistent with an overall thrust toward the future that is compatible with the overall structure of process metaphysics: One learns from the greatest thinkers from the past *so that* one can do the best job possible of rendering future determinables determinate in the clutch of vivid immediacy in the present.

In the opening stanzas of the immortality ode Wordsworth has birds experience joy in their singing, in contrast to the mechanistic view that the only reasons for birdsong are to defend territory and to attract a mate. As before, however, one wonders why they sing when territory is not threatened and when mating season is over if not because they *like* to sing (once again, see Dombrowski 2004a, chap. 4; Hartshorne 1973). And beasts of all sorts (whom Wordsworth refers to as "blessed creatures") "keep holiday" in their quotidian "bliss" and "jubilee." "The visionary gleam" and "the glory and the dream" are really experienced by us when we vicariously feel their enjoyments. Right *now* we can have intimations not only of the way things are but of the way they could (or better, should) be.

Not in "entire forgetfulness" do we partially succumb to mechanism. Rather, "trailing clouds of glory do we come / From God who is our home." The glorification of childhood in the immortality ode is, once again, not to be taken literally. It is the child*like* that leads us away from mechanism's "shades of the prison house." For example, children have to *learn* that it is permissible to harm animals in that they tend initially to balk at the suggestion that hamburgers are slaughtered cows. An adult who is childlike in the honorific sense provides an "Eye among the blind" with respect to a "Presence which is not to be put by." The one who experiences this presence is called the "best Philosopher" by Wordsworth. Here again we are reminded of Whitehead's similar claim on the last page of his last book that "the purpose of philosophy is to rationalize mysticism" (*MT* 174).

By stanza 9 we find Wordsworth asserting with a certain degree of confidence: "O joy that in our embers / Is something that doth live, / That nature yet remembers / What was so fugitive!" This "something that doth live" is discovered as a result of "obstinate questionings / Of sense and outward things, / Fallings from us, vanishings." Joyfully singing birds reappear toward the end of the poem in stanza 10, which contains the most famous lines of the poem:

> Though nothing can bring back the hour
> Of splendor in the grass, of glory in the flower;
> We will grieve not, rather find
> Strength in what remains behind;
> In the primal sympathy
> Which having been must ever be;
> In the soothing thoughts that spring
> Out of human suffering;
> In the faith that looks through death,
> In years that bring the philosophic mind.

Note that it takes years to become a childlike best philosopher.

The hope in the poem is that our momentary glimpses into the life of things and our occasional experiences of being a living part of an organic whole will gain over us a sort of "habitual sway." If such were our habit it would not seem odd to utter the following: "Thanks to the human heart by which we live, / Thanks to its tenderness, its joys, and fears, / To me the meanest flower that blows can give / Thoughts that do often lie too deep for tears." Whitehead notes this last line of the immortality ode as a prime example of "the tonality of the particular instance" (*SM* 83).

These same themes are found in the first book of *The Prelude*, which has surprisingly largely been ignored by Whitehead scholars, despite Whitehead's praise of it. To set the context, Wordsworth planned a systematic, philosophical poem with three parts titled *The Recluse*, of which only the second part, *The Excursion*, was finished. *The Prelude*, itself an enormous poem, is meant as an autobiographical preparatory work in front of *The Recluse*. The analogy here is that of an ante-chapel that is entered before one goes into a Gothic cathedral (Wordsworth 494). But in Whitehead's view we need not go beyond the vestibule provided by the very first book of *The Prelude* in order to appreciate Wordsworth's contribution. Whitehead seems to have something very particular in mind. We should also note in this context that, according to Nicola Trott, this cathedral metaphor in Wordsworth is subservient to a river metaphor. In Heraclitean fashion, Wordsworth's own works as well as the natural world they describe are "forever in process," a movement that is described as "rivery" (Trott 11–14).

The most well-known lines of this part of *The Prelude* concern an incident (a "spot of time") from Wordsworth's boyhood. One summer evening he found a little boat within a rocky cave that was tied to a willow tree. In an "act of stealth" the young Wordsworth untied the boat and pushed from the shore for some "troubled pleasure." He was proud of his skill as a rower until at one point his view was fixed on the summit of a craggy ridge, then he "lustily" dipped his oars into the lake once again as the boat moved through the water like a swan. What happened next is quite remarkable:

> When, from behind that craggy steep till then
> The horizon's bound, a huge peak, black and huge
> As if with voluntary power instinct
> Upreared its head. I struck and struck again,
> And growing still in stature the grim shape
> Towered up between me and the stars, and still,
> For so it seemed, with purpose of its own
> And measured motion like a living thing,
> Strode after me. With trembling oars I turned,
> And through the silent water stole my way

Back to the covert of the willow tree;
There in her mooring-place I left my bark,—
And through the meadows homeward went, in grave
And serious mood; but after I had seen
That spectacle, for many days, my brain
Worked with a dim and undetermined sense
Of unknown modes of being; o'er my thoughts
There hung a darkness, call it solitude
Or blank desertion. No familiar shapes
Remained, no pleasant images of trees,
Of sea or sky, no colours of green fields;
But huge and mighty forms, that do not live
Like living men, moved slowly through the mind
By day, and were a trouble to my dreams.

One is initially reminded of Augustine's analogous transgression as a boy (in book 2 of the *Confessions*) when he threw stolen pears at pigs. In neither case do we have a sense that they were really bad kids. But the lessons drawn from these incidents are quite different, which is not surprising given Augustine's dualism and his classical theism, in contrast to Wordsworth's panexperientialism and panentheism, respectively.

First, throughout the text in question we are confronted with a *reenchanted nature*, to use language from Griffin. The boy Wordsworth is visited by a breeze that is "half-conscious," the fraction being the poetic way, I assume, of talking about microscopic sentiency (S1). Here Wordsworth and Whitehead meet: Whereas the latter looks to the former for language appropriate for the tonality of concrete particulars, the former has an aspiration for "some philosophic song / Of truth." Not only do they meet, they complement each other.

One of the most notable features of the preceding quotation is the way in which Wordsworth's reenchanted nature is characterized by immense, sublime forces. As the boy pulls away from the shore the first summit appears, but then as he gets further along a different, ominous peak appears, seemingly growing in stature and alive and chasing the rower. Earlier in the first book of *The Prelude* Wordsworth says in a similar vein that he "heard among the solitary hills / Low breathings coming after me." But he was not harmed. Rather, he was given food for thought, both conscious and unconscious (dreamlike). He tells us he was left in solitude, which reminds us once again of one of Whitehead's definitions of religion in *RM* as "what the individual does with his own solitariness" (16). Note that Whitehead does not define religion as solitariness but as what one *does* with one's solitariness. Perhaps one will vow to make the world a better place once one realizes in solitude the solemnity of life (see Dombrowski 2015).

This reenchantment of nature, obviously conducive to the MTO transition, also facilitates the FTP transition in that Wordsworth admits that there is a "grandeur in the beatings of the heart," as in the boy Wordsworth in his encounter with the "gloomy hills." But there is also the grandeur in the beating heart of "the hunted hare," with "melancholy not unnoticed." There is a "bond of union between life and joy," or between life and suffering, depending on how the living being in question is treated. "Obscure feelings," he suggests, can nonetheless be "majestic in themselves." In sum, "I held unconscious intercourse with beauty / Old as creation, drinking in a pure / Organic pleasure."

Second, in addition to the theme of a reenchanted nature, the other major theme that may have recommended so positively the first book of *The Prelude* to Whitehead may have been its *obvious and alternative religiosity*. I have noted previously a remark that anachronistically seems to be directed at Stengers, where Whitehead reminds us that "the chequered history of religion and morality is the main reason for the widespread desire to put them aside in favour of the more stable generalities of science. Unfortunately for this smug endeavor . . . the impact of aesthetic, religious and moral notions is inescapable" (*MT* 19). Wordsworth, like Whitehead, attests to "a higher power" that can be approached or experienced in the "hermitage" of nature (see the instructive book by Schilbrack). It is no accident that in his "yearning toward some philosophic song / Of Truth," mentioned previously, truth is spelled with a capital "T."

And Wordsworth, like Whitehead, is skilled at making some of his most important points through allusion to scripture, which is metaphorically (or better, spiritually) interpreted. He speaks of his desire to "seek repose / In listlessness from vain perplexity, / Unprofitably travelling toward the grave, / Like a false steward who hath much received / And renders nothing back" (see Luke 16: 1–13). This is the "wise passiveness" also discussed in the poem "Expostulation and Reply." Or again, in the first book of *The Prelude* he says (also see Genesis 3: 19) that "Dust as we are, the immortal spirit grows / Like harmony in music; there is a dark / Inscrutable workmanship that reconciles /

Discordant elements, makes them cling together / In one society." There is indeed a *uni*verse, a material world that is hylomorphically animated by a divine spirit, contemplation of which is "sanctifying."

A question from the philosopher Erazim Kohak takes us to the heart of the matter religiously:

> Shall we conceive of the world around us and of ourselves in it as *personal*, a meaningful whole, honoring its order as continuous with the moral law of our own being and its being as continuous with ours, bearing its goodness—or shall we conceive of it and treat it, together with ourselves, as *impersonal*, a chance aggregate of matter propelled by a blind force and exhibiting at most the ontologically random lawlike regularities of a causal order? (Kohak 124–125)

Wordsworth and Whitehead (despite the latter's skepticism regarding the Platonic World Soul that is adopted by Hartshorne) opt for the former.

The troubled dreams of the rower treated in the first book of *The Prelude* reinforce the process view that each of us is the partial product of our own moral decisions made in the past that partially determine our own futures. As Duncan Wu puts the Wordsworthian and Whiteheadian point, "our actions, though momentary, are of enduring significance" (Wu 32–33).

THE FUNCTION OF SYMBOLS AND REASON

Strange as it sounds, Whitehead's support for the romantic reaction is part of an effort to retrieve the medieval period's fascination with symbolism. This does not mean that he wants to endorse nineteenth-century historicism, very often associated with conservative romanticism, wherein every character should be primarily studied in its embryonic stage. In fact, the true roots of symbolism, contra historicism, are to be found in the prehuman, for example in tulips, which turn toward the light in their own very primitive way. Symbolic reference is an *organic process* wherein it is as true to say that the word "tree" symbolizes real trees as it is to say that for a poet like Wordsworth a walk in the woods suggests the appropriate words: symbolic reference has a double character (*SY* 1, 5–6, 12).

Whitehead is clear that symbolic reference in general can be erroneous; hence, it makes sense to urge that Wordsworth's symbolic reference should be approached critically. The problem itself is symbolized by Aesop's fable regarding the dog who dropped a piece of food in order to grasp at its own reflection in a pool of water. Whitehead wants to emphasize the fact that what the dog lost in terms of food was gained in terms of growth in imagination (see Stronge). A stone conforms to the conditions set by its external environment to a considerable degree, less so with respect to the aforementioned tulip, and much less so in the case of Aesop's dog. These examples from the nonhuman are crucial in the effort to counteract the hegemony of Humean perception in the mode of presentational immediacy, which, although almost exclusively the property of human beings, is comparatively empty when contrasted with the deep significance of perception in the mode of causal efficacy. Our enhanced imaginative powers, as nurtured by Wordsworth, are ironically needed in order to come to understand the otherwise ineffable natural forces that lean on us at every turn. As Whitehead puts the point: "The world, given in sense-presentation, is not the aboriginal experience of the lower organisms, later to be sophisticated by the inference to causal efficacy. The contrary is the case. First the causal side of experience is dominating, then the sense-presentation gains in subtlety" (*SY* 49). Of course, it is in a way true to say that a rock is nothing but a society of molecules; nonetheless, it is by no means trivial to notice that social life is not peculiar to humans. In fact, *our* social life together, in contrast to a rock's, is not infrequently interrupted by discord. At times we are even divided by the different types of nature poetry found in various cultures as words from a distant past are used to do symbolic work: "eagle" and "bear" and "cedar," for example, can be used for symbolic purposes that are quite efficacious (*SY* 64, 67).

Whitehead thinks it premature to claim that Wordsworth *invents* the meanings of his symbols if such meanings are already there implicitly, ready to be expressed. The symbols in his poetry themselves help us to *discover* their meaning. Granted, "hardheaded" thinkers want facts, not symbols, in that they (erroneously) assume that in the dogged pursuit of facts we can dispense with symbols altogether. Whitehead is not so sure about this, especially when he quotes the Latin proverb to the effect that "nature, expelled with a pitchfork, ever returns." At the very least, the object of symbolism enhances the *importance* of what is symbolized (*SY* 57, 60–63).

By contrast, the mechanist view that science is a mere neutral description of things observed, although apparently clear, turns science into something that lacks importance. Integrally connected to Whitehead's very important Wordsworthian romanticism is a different concept of the function of reason from that found in mechanism. This function is to promote the flourishing of living organisms, which I have tried to symbolize in the present book in terms of the MTO and FTP transitions. Once one sees the hazards in drawing a sharp distinction between living things and "inorganic" matter, one can then better understand the upward trend of evolutionary history, a trend that is evidenced in two different, yet complementary, kinds of reason: (1) the reason of Plato, the reason of the gods that is concerned with both abstract understanding of the real and aspiration toward apparently unreachable ideals; and (2) the reason of Ulysses, the reason of the foxes that utilizes a practical and/or technical methodology that, as enshrined in modern mechanism, can be quite a problem: "Some of the major disasters of mankind have been produced by the narrowness of men with a good methodology. Ulysses has no use for Plato, and the bones of his companions are strewn on many a reef and many an isle" (*FR* 12, also 4, 54). As we will see, the point is not to disparage Ulysses, however.

One often hears that the romantic thinkers opposed reason and emotion, but for Whitehead the antithesis of reason is not emotion. It is the fatigue that sets in when novelty seems to evaporate (which is actually impossible, given the reality of temporal advance). What Whitehead seems to especially admire in romantic poetry, in addition to its insistence on a panexperientialist take on concrete particularity, is its attempt to resuscitate appetition and final causality in nature. The point is not to oppose Ulysses and Plato but rather to realize that "a satisfactory cosmology must explain the interweaving of efficient [Ulysses-like] and of final [Platonic] causation" (*FR* 28, also 23, 32). Such a realization is facilitated through Whitehead's (and Wordsworth's) view of each occasion of experience as dipolar: mental experience integrated with physical experience, with "mental" here referring to something much more primitive than consciousness. What he has in mind is emotional purpose and the (Platonic) power to strive.

Of course, in reality the separation between the two sorts of reason is not as sharp as indicated previously. Although practical reason extends far back into our animal pasts, speculative reason grows out of it. We might not notice this, given the fact that speculative reason was not clearly identifiable historically until a few thousand years ago in the period when all of the world's great religions were formed. Modern mechanism, however, counterintuitively did *not* develop out of practical reason; rather, it too arose out of the advanced speculative reason of the medieval and early modern periods. Galileo was a Platonist, after all. In fact, the truly earth-shattering technological implications of modern science came rather late (as in the improved steam engine of 1769), a few decades before Wordsworth wrote his great poetry. The point here is that an error in speculative reason can only be adequately countered by a better exercise in speculative (Platonic) reason itself. Whereas some modern thinkers (e.g., Thomas Hobbes) made bodies fundamental, and others (e.g., Berkeley) made minds fundamental, a better response to dualism is not necessarily found in Kant, who in his first critique reduces our knowledge of the whole system of nature to mere appearance. It is true that he was moved by the starry heavens above and the moral law within, but these signal not the success of his overall philosophy but its obvious shortcomings. In sum, Wordsworth and other romantic thinkers in their reactions to mechanism prepare the way for Whitehead's and Hartshorne's genuine advances (see *FR* 40–41, 48, 59–60; also see Malone-France 2007; Cappon 1982; 1983; 1985).

There is clearly the perennial danger of looking *through* a poet's verse to something conceptual beyond it, rather than looking *at* it, as Stephen Gill emphasizes. But there is also the opposite danger of ignoring difficult passages in a philosophical poet that one does not understand or of claiming that what is philosophical in a poet's work contributes nothing to its success. Among these passages are those in Wordsworth that point to an active principle in every existing thing (*The Excursion*, book 9, etc.) or that suggest a (S3) spirit for the entire universe (*The Prelude*, books 1, 2, 6, etc.). Whitehead's panexperientialism, analyzed earlier through the work of Griffin, as well as Hartshorne's doctrine of the World Soul, help to make sense of what Gill sees as especially difficult and challenging verses in Wordsworth. That is, process thinkers encourage us to be attentive to *all* the forms that life can take, as alluded to often in Wordsworth's works (e.g., "An Evening

Walk"). As Gill insightfully puts the point, what is needed is a *bridge* between philosophy and poetry. I am alleging that Whitehead and Wordsworth help us to build this bridge and that it would be difficult to build it without teamwork between the two; Wordsworth's poetry *articulates* that to which Whitehead's philosophy merely *points*. However, poetry should be seen not merely as a vehicle for knowledge but a species of knowledge itself that is particularly concerned, once again, with concrete feelings that are easily overlooked in the prosaic world that we normally inhabit (see Gill; also Hamilton 219, 227).

The philosophical aspect of Wordsworth's poetry is intimately connected to his relationship with Samuel Taylor Coleridge, who, like Wordsworth, had difficulty in feeling without thinking or thinking without feeling. The strong feelings elicited by Wordsworth lead some of his readers to actually think of themselves as Wordsworthians and hence subject to the criticism analogously leveled at some Whiteheadians that they are members of a secret school or cult (because religious—once again, see Stengers 2011, 6). But a belief in a persistent divine presence in an unfallen nature is not so esoteric that it is unintelligible to those outside of Wordsworth's or Whitehead's immediate circles. In fact, Whitehead is especially popular these days with Chinese and Japanese scholars (see, e.g., Yang). The principle that reality flows, which was to have been the theme of Coleridge's never-written epic "The Brook," can be generally understood, as can the tenet that there is an active principle alive in all things, a presence that disturbs us with the joy of elevated thoughts, to put the point in Wordsworth's own terms from "Tintern Abbey." Although Wordsworth's adherence to the principle of "One Life" appears to have faded in his later years as he became more conservative, his attempt to awaken readers to the inexhaustible treasures of the supposedly ordinary things of nature never faded (see Perry; Gill).

HARTSHORNE ON WORDSWORTH

Although Hartshorne's favorite poems from Wordsworth are different from Whitehead's, as we will see, he is equally indebted to Wordsworth, in particular, and to English romantic poetry, in general (see Hartshorne 1980). In fact, Hartshorne admits that he may have learned more from Wordsworth than from Whitehead (!), a claim that will no doubt surprise many scholars (see Hartshorne 1970, xvii). A summary of the indebtedness of Hartshorne's process thought to Wordsworth can be found in the following five points:

First, animate nature in general (even in plants) is characterized by S1 feeling (see later regarding the "budding twigs"). Here the MTO transition is quite clear.

Second, what is often called "inanimate" nature is not really inanimate. The example from Wordsworth that Hartshorne cites comes from the immortality ode: "The moon doth with delight / Look round her when the heavens are bare." Of course, on process grounds it is the microscopic parts of the moon that exhibit at least microscopic sentiency (S1). Once again, the MTO transition is apparent, if not as clearly as in the previous point (also see Hartshorne 1923, 233–236; 1970, 301).

Third, as a whole Nature expresses one living, indeed mindlike, reality and all the lesser lives are constituents of this reality. Herein lies the basis for romantic religiosity and its powerful effect on both Whitehead and Hartshorne.

Fourth, the evidence in favor of the truth of the previous three claims is to be found in experience, specifically in our perceptions of nature when we attend to them carefully. Whitehead and Hartshorne look to Wordsworth for linguistic support for their versions of process phenomenology. We (at least most of us) *experience* ourselves as parts of an intelligible, meaningful whole (also Hartshorne 1997, 56, 70, 165).

And fifth, many "civilized" people are skeptical of the preceding four claims because after childhood it is harder for them to attend to direct experience, or at least as we grow up we tend to let go of the capacity to accept the panexperientialist message of direct experience. That is, we tend to either be driven by practical concerns or be dominated by mechanistic assumptions, particularly the assumption that most of the universe is dead matter and that there is not even feeling *in* plants, much less *in* rocks (Hartshorne 1980, 81; also 1934, 104).

The two poems from Wordsworth that Hartshorne thinks best exemplify the preceding points are "Lines Written in Early Spring" and "The Simplon Pass," the latter found in Wordsworth both as an independent poem and as part of the sixth book of *The Prelude*.

Consider the treatments of birds and plants in the former poem. Of birds: "The birds around me hopped and played, / Their thoughts I cannot measure:— / But the least motion which they made, / It seemed a thrill of pleasure." Of plants: "The budding twigs spread out their fan, /

To catch the breezy air; / And I must think, do all I can, / That there was pleasure there." Wordsworth is clear that birds have thoughts, but he cannot measure them well against a human standard except to say that they must be playful and associated with pleasure, indeed with a certain thrill. He does not attribute thought at all to plants, but he does attest to pleasure in the budding *twigs*, which I assume is the poetic way of pointing toward striving *in* plants if not to plants as wholes. Previously, we saw him use quantification by way of fractions to make a similar point regarding what I have called S1 in plants rather than animal-like S2. There is no implausible claim in the poem to having *direct* intuition of the inner lives of birds or plant cells. Rather, our most direct contact with nature comes by way of our feeling the feelings of the cells in our own bodies. In the lines regarding birds, note the words "around *me*," "*I* cannot," and "seemed." Then in the lines regarding plants see "*I* must think, do all *I* can," or to put a different emphasis on these lines, "I *must* think."

Our nerve cells are living individuals and these cells transmit to us other cellular feelings that are local in character. The feelings of an individual, as evidenced in the previous paragraph, involve a comprehensive pooling of, as well as participation in, cellular feelings. We have no other avenues to nature, hence the word "must." So in our very bodies we have evidence of feeling that goes far below birds. It is not so much panexperientialism that is a construct as it is the concept of nature as being composed of dead, insentient matter. It is M rather than O in MTO with which we are unfamiliar. *As* experienced, nature consists of feelings. In different terms, beings are in happenings, not the other way around.

Granted, the lines cited from "Lines Written in Early Spring" deal with parts of nature (birds, plants) that are clearly animate. Regarding "inanimate" nature, consider "The Simplon Pass," which memorializes Wordsworth's trip through the Alps:

> Brook and road
> Were fellow-travelers in this gloomy Pass,
> And with them did we journey several hours
> At a slow step. The immeasurable height
> Of woods decaying, never to be decayed,
> The stationary blasts of waterfalls,
> And in the narrow rent, at every turn,

Winds thwarting winds bewildered and forlorn,
The torrents shooting from the clear blue sky,
The rocks that muttered close upon our ears,
Black drizzling crags that spake by the wayside
As if a voice were in them, the sick sight
And giddy prospect of the raving stream,
The unfettered clouds and region of the heavens,
Tumult and peace, the darkness and the light—
Were all like workings of one mind, the features
Of the same face, blossoms upon one tree,
Characters of the great Apocalypse,
The types and symbols of Eternity,
Of first, and last, and midst, and without end.

The first task is to respond to those who would suggest that these lines constitute one long commission of the pathetic fallacy. *Of course* winds are not literally "bewildered and forlorn," nor is Wordsworth trying his hand as an amateur meteorologist. The question concerns one's experience of wind and one's experience of a closed-in space in the mountains as gloomy. The thesis here (although I risk murdering the poem by dissecting it in this way) is that as animals we always enjoy or suffer the world. As rational animals we also sometimes think it. The natural world reaches us only through feelings.

In a plant there are feelings (prehensions or graspings) in the cells even if there is little or no feeling in the plant as a whole, which lacks a central nervous system. Analogously, there may be primitive feeling in the molecules, atoms, or subatomic particles in a wind, cloud, or rock. Single cells can feel and act as individuals even though they do not have central nervous systems, and it is through cellular feeling that we experience the world. We are well aware of subhuman experience in that it is found in our own bodies; thus, "if we really know ourselves, we know a lot about nature" (Hartshorne 1980, 85).

If one rejects the effort to generalize dynamic experience or feeling (the aforementioned Platonic power to receive influence and the power to creatively advance in response to such influence) as the very stuff of nature, one is apparently condemned to have one's "knowledge" of nature be purely abstract and arithmetical/geometrical, as Whitehead as a mathematician realized. On the basis of such a rejection, either there is no internal power to experience (mechanism) or there are only a relatively few beings who have the power to experience, given the immensity of nature (dualism). Wordsworth helps us to see that one pays too great a price for such a rejection: The world is not as boring and lifeless as mechanists/dualists think.

Wordsworth's poetry obviously enables us to better appreciate the MTO transition. However, Hartshorne thinks that it also helps us to see the connection between what I have called the MTO and FTP transitions:

> I am confident that, if culture does not collapse in fearful catastrophe, there will, centuries hence, still be knowledge-able human beings who will be saying, with Wordsworth, that life and feeling, in a variety of forms, pervade and constitute nature. . . . It is plausible to explain the entire idea of mere lifeless, insentient matter as a fiction. . . . Atoms and particles seem animate enough, as now described. They exhibit spontaneous motion. . . . The cosmic machine of the 18th century has become the "cosmic dance" of the 20th. (Hartshorne 1980, 85–86)

The possible catastrophes that he has in mind are environmental, biological, military, political, or some combination of all of these.

The theistic implications of the final lines in "The Simplon Pass" quoted earlier are certainly compatible with process theism, even if Wordsworth did not have Whitehead's or Hartshorne's technical vocabulary to rely on. Hartshorne was so enamored with these lines that he took the title to his intellectual autobiography (*The Darkness and the Light*) from them. Contrary to what many scholars might think, even regarding theism the evidence is often found in experience in addition to rationalistic argumentation. It is not uncommon for us to experience ourselves as *fragments*. But to really experience oneself as a fragment is to indirectly experience oneself as part of the whole of which one is a fragment. Divine world-inclusiveness, however, does not have to be interpreted in pantheistic terms if pantheism is opposed to the view of God as personal (see Levine). Wordsworth, like Whitehead and especially like Hartshorne, describes God in personal terms: "one mind," "the same face," and so forth, once again contra Stengers' interpretation.

Admittedly, Wordsworth speaks of divine "eternity" rather than "everlastingness," which unwittingly continues the Boethian view of

God as outside of time altogether rather than as sempiternally existing throughout all of time. Once again, Wordsworth would not have had this theoretical distinction at his disposal. It also should be admitted that some of Wordsworth's religious beliefs, especially late in life, were very conservative politically; nonetheless, they always seem to offer friction to the classical theistic view. For example, on the pervasive classical theistic view that God does not (indeed cannot) change, the happinesses of creatures are superfluous additions to a divine reality that is already fully actualized; on this view God is an unmoved mover who cannot be moved even by the sufferings of creatures. This is not Wordsworth's or Whitehead's or Hartshorne's view, wherein the happiness or unhappiness of creatures, and not only human creatures, *matters* to the greatest conceivable being-in-becoming. If God were the only agent with creative power, God would be the only individual, but God is not the only individual; hence, there must be other centers of creative power, and God as omnibenevolent could not remain unmoved or indifferent to them.

Consider the following lines from "Tintern Abbey," which both Whitehead and Hartshorne alluded to at different points in their careers:

> And I have felt
> A presence that disturbs me with the joy
> Of elevated thoughts; a sense sublime
> Of something far more deeply interfused,
> Whose dwelling is the light of setting suns,
> And the round ocean and the living air,
> And the blue sky, and in the mind of man:
> A motion and a spirit, that impels
> All thinking things, all objects of all thought,
> And rolls through all things.

Granted, the presence that disturbs Wordsworth rolls through all things, dwells in setting suns, in the oceans, in the air, and in human cogitation. But this self-moving presence also *impels* all thinking things, implying that this presence has some sort of independent existence of its own.

The issue of pervasive experience or feeling in nature, along with the powers associated with experiencing or feeling beings, is not a trifling matter. If there were merely lifeless, insentient matter, then there would not really be any intrinsic value (which requires experience or feeling); hence, nature would simply be there for us to use as a mere means to an end outside of itself. The fact that we often treat the world as if it were there to be exploited rather than loved indicates that this view itself is a powerful one (see Hartshorne 1980, 88). To try to find a defensible religious view of nature is to swim in the other direction.

CONCLUSION

The position I defend can be seen as romantic in the sense that it involves, negatively, a moral repulsion to mechanism and, positively, a panexperientialist attempt to respond to the perplexity that haunts the modern world. This perplexity concerns the question regarding how to account for the organic on dualist-mechanist assumptions. Romantic panexperientialism is a type of naturalism; indeed, it consists in an attempt to rethink the very concept of nature in light of the perplexity created by dualism-mechanism. Such a rethinking is not opposed to science but is, in part, engaged in for the sake of science itself. The goal regarding science is to have it become more empirical by enabling it to take seriously and to appropriate the data of concrete experience.

The organic view of nature I defend, in addition to its superiority to dualism-mechanism, is a protest against the exclusion of value in nature. The inclusion of value in nature, however, does not signal a retreat into human subjectivity, a retreat that flirts with dualism and *a fortiori* with mechanism. Rather, romantic panexperientialism seeks a *common world* wherein creatures, both human and nonhuman, are seen to exist within an objective nature that precedes us. (This is epistemological objectivity; metaphysically, the world is made up of subjects, pulses of dynamic power.) Further, the "original" purity from which we have deviated in our violence toward members of our own species, in our violence toward members of other animal species, and in our exploitation of supposedly "inanimate" nature, is not to be taken literally. This "original" ideal is conceptual, not historical, as Plato anticipated a long time ago. This clarification enables us to avoid the bellicose defects found in right-wing versions of romanticism.

It makes sense to suspect that the arguments from sentiency and marginal cases discussed in the previous chapter are crucial to the success of the present book. I doubt if any rational, morally sensitive person can be a consistent mechanist when cutting into the unanesthetized flesh of a living animal with a central nervous system. It is only when we act *as if* organisms are machines that current practices regarding animals can be permitted. Once one sees the soundness of these two arguments, however, one can then move more easily upward to abhorrence to the intentional killing of members of our own species who do not request to be killed and downward to a consideration of the value found in microscopic organisms. Once the grip of mechanistic anthropocentrism is loosened, one can more easily consider the merits of panexperientialism and, ironically, of theocentrism. Conversely, by rejecting these two arguments, we murder to dissect: ourselves, other animals, and the natural world itself.

In a previous context I defended Cobb's claim that, despite the fact that Whitehead's philosophy is not centered on the concept of God the way Hartshorne's philosophy is, Whitehead's overall vision is religious through and through (Cobb 2007, 145). At present I would like to say something similar regarding Whitehead's romanticism, which goes back at least as early as 1919 in *EC*, which is supposedly before he was interested in God or in philosophical issues other than those that concerned mathematics and physics. Just as it makes sense to resist Stengers' view that the process God (or at least the consequent nature of God) pops up rather arbitrarily in Whitehead, hence easily jettisoned, so also it makes sense to resist those who wish to distance Whitehead from Wordsworth's romanticism.

Throughout his philosophical career Whitehead was convinced that biological phenomena did not belong in a different category from other natural phenomena. What this means is that in order to articulate a unitary view of nature, either organisms must conform to the (allegedly) inorganic or the (allegedly) inorganic must conform to organisms. Whitehead and Hartshorne and Griffin courageously defend the latter hypothesis. In fact, Whitehead holds that the former hypothesis is "a metaphysical fairy tale" in that at every turn living experience rebels romantically against the exclusion of the organic. Further, this fairy tale has been associated since the time of Newton, Whitehead thinks, with a view of absolute space and time that is nothing less than "a metaphysical monstrosity." Whitehead could not be clearer, nor could he be more emphatic, in his rejection of the philosophy characterized by "mind watching things" in empty space (*EC* 3–9).

Whereas we *prehend* momentary *events*, we *re-cognize* relatively permanent *objects* that retain a character throughout the transition from one momentary event to the next. In *EC* Whitehead views the whole scientific enterprise as an attempt to organize our knowledge of the circumstances in which these recognitions occur. He is also astute to notice that ordinary thought (in human beings as well as in nonhuman animals) tends to confusedly waver between events and objects. This wavering has obvious practical import: We sometimes focus on the prisoner in the dock as the one who performed the deed, and at other times we emphasize the fact that the unlawful event occurred in the irrevocable past in a moment of passion. Both concerns are understandable such that process philosophy should not be interpreted as involving a hostility to endurance (*EC* 57, 65–66, 88).

I have contended in the present book that the MTO transition is crucial not only to understand Whitehead but also to deal successfully with several of the most crucial ethical problems that we face. In Whitehead's language, "the mechanical rigidity . . . of the traditional views" regarding the material world gets in the way not only of an adequate response to the mind-body "problem" but of an ethically responsible approach to the world as well. Once again, we experience the world organically; indeed, the ultimate data of science are our awarenesses of living events in process. I have readily admitted that the Griffin-like, Wordsworth-like panexperientialism I have defended in the present book will strike some as romantic in the pejorative sense of the term, but I take solace in Whitehead's realization that "all novel theories emerge with a childlike simplicity which they ultimately shed" (*EC* 95, also 72–73).

It should not escape our notice that Whitehead asks with such childlike simplicity, "Are there any material objects in nature?" (*EC* 182). What he has in mind is the idea that an alleged material object like a drop of water, when empirically magnified, looks much like a swarm of flies in a room. Or again, although softcore common sense is content with the solidity of the walls of a room, and although this solidity impresses those like lawyers who are driven by softcore common sense, we now know that much more is going on in the walls than softcore common sense assumes. Granted, in Aristotelian fashion, we start empirically with a figure that is sensed, then we derive a geometrical figure from this, but this derivation does not necessarily establish the case for "materialism." As before, what we want to preserve from

Aristotle (mathematical abstraction, *kinesis*) is not to be confused with what is best left behind (the hegemony of substance-accident thinking). From at least 1919 until the end, Whitehead thought that *process* "is the fundamental idea" (*EC* 202, also 190, 201, 204; IY 683).

It is also to Whitehead's credit that he notices that *rhythm* is an essential feature of the organic: Crystals have it to such a minimal degree that they might understandably initially strike us as inorganic, and fog might understandably strike us as patternless and unrhythmic. But there are both gradations of rhythm and an important distinction between rhythmic parts and an unrhythmic mechanical whole. It is here where Whitehead, even in *EC*, invokes Wordsworth in partial contrast to two other writers who might otherwise be seen as allies.

One of the subtler rhythms of nature involves the interplay of sound and silence. In lines that catch Whitehead's attention, Alfred Tennyson (in "The Princess," part 4) expresses this rhythm in a way that could, in isolation, be interpreted as congenial to contemporary religious skepticism:

> Blow, bugle, blow, set the wild echoes flying,
> And answer, echoes, answer, dying, dying, dying.

Henri Bergson interprets the same rhythmic phenomenon in terms of the dualistic pulsation between *élan vital* and relapse back into mechanism. Wordsworth adds depth to our understanding of the rhythm in question (by avoiding both religious skepticism and dualism) in a poem titled "The Solitary Reaper" (see *EC* 199–200):

> The music in my heart I bore,
> Long after it was heard no more

It is only organisms who can preserve value through memory; hence, it is only they who can overcome the greatest of evils (*PR* 340): the transiency of that which is good.

BIBLIOGRAPHY

Adams, Carol. 1990. *The Sexual Politics of Meat*. New York: Continuum.

Akers, Keith. 2000. *The Lost Religion of Jesus: Simple Living and Nonviolence in Early Christianity*. New York: Lantern Books.

Allan, George. 2008. "A Functionalist Reinterpretation of Whitehead's Metaphysics." *Review of Metaphysics* 62: 327–354.

Anderson, Elizabeth. 2004. "Animal Rights and the Values of Nonhuman Life." In *Animal Rights: Current Debates and New Directions*. Ed. Cass Sunstein and Martha Nussbaum. Oxford: Oxford University Press.

Anscombe, G. E. M. 1979 [1961]. "War and Murder." In *Moral Problems*. 3rd ed. Ed. James Rachels. New York: Harper and Row.

Armstrong, Susan. 1976. "The Rights of Nonhuman Beings: A Whiteheadian Study." PhD dissertation. Bryn Mawr College.

Auxier, Randall, and Mark Davies, eds. 2001. *Hartshorne and Brightman on God, Process, and Persons*. Nashville: Vanderbilt University Press.

Barrett, Nathaniel. 2009. "The Perspectivity of Feeling: Process Panpsychism and the Explanatory Gap." *Process Studies* 38: 189–206.

Becker, Lawrence. 1983. "The Priority of Human Interests." In *Ethics and Animals*. Ed. Harlan Miller. Clifton: Humana.

Bixler, J. S. 1941. "Whitehead's Philosophy of Religion." In *The Philosophy of Alfred North Whitehead*. Ed. P. A. Schilpp. LaSalle: Open Court.

Bracken, Joseph. 2015. "A Case of Misplaced Concreteness?" *Process Studies* 44: 259–269.

Butler, Judith. 2004. *Precarious Life: The Powers of Mourning and Violence*. New York: Verso.

———. 2009. *Frames of War: When Is Life Grievable?* New York: Verso.

Callicott, J. Baird. 1989. *In Defense of the Land Ethic: Essays in Environmental Philosophy*. Albany: State University of New York Press.

Cappon, Alexander. 1982. *About Wordsworth and Whitehead*. New York: Philosophical Library.

———. 1983. *Aspects of Wordsworth and Whitehead*. New York: Philosophical Library.

———. 1985. *Action, Organism, and Philosophy in Wordsworth and Whitehead*. New York: Philosophical Library.

Carlson, Licia. 2010. *The Faces of Intellectual Disability*. Bloomington: Indiana University Press.

Chalmers, David. 1996. *The Conscious Mind*. Oxford: Oxford University Press.

Christian, William. 1959. *An Interpretation of Whitehead's Metaphysics*. New Haven: Yale University Press.

Clarke, W. Norris. 2007 [1979]. *The Philosophical Approach to God*. Revised ed. New York: Fordham University Press.

Cobb, John. 1982. *Process Theology as Political Theology*. Manchester: Manchester University Press.

———. 2007 [1965]. *A Christian Natural Theology: Based on the Thought of Alfred North Whitehead*. 2nd ed. Louisville: Westminster John Knox Press.

Cobb, John, and Charles Birch. 1981. *The Liberation of Life*. Cambridge: Cambridge University Press.

Daniels, Norman. 2003. "Democratic Equality: Rawls's Complex Egalitarianism." In *The Cambridge Companion to Rawls*. Ed. Samuel Freeman. New York: Cambridge University Press.

Dennett, Daniel. 1991. *Consciousness Explained*. Boston: Little, Brown.

Desmet, Ronny, and Bogdan Rusu. 2012. "Whitehead, Russell, and Moore: Three Analytic Philosophers." *Process Studies* 41: 214–234.

Diamond, Cora. 2004. "Eating Meat and Eating People." In *Animal Rights: Current Debates and New Directions*. Ed. Cass Sunstein and Martha Nussbaum. Oxford: Oxford University Press.

Dikotter, Frank. 2010. *Mao's Great Famine*. New York: Bloomsbury.

Dombrowski, Daniel. 1984a. *The Philosophy of Vegetarianism*. Amherst: University of Massachusetts Press.

———. 1984b. "Vegetarianism and the Argument from Marginal Cases in Porphyry." *Journal of the History of Ideas* 45: 141–143.

———. 1985. "Wordsworth's Panentheism." *The Wordsworth Circle* 16: 136–142.

———. 1986. "Thoreau, Sainthood, and Vegetarianism." *American Transcendental Quarterly* 60: 25–36.

———. 1987. "Pacifism and Hartshorne's Dipolar Theism." *Encounter* 48: 337–350.

———. 1988a. *Hartshorne and the Metaphysics of Animal Rights.* Albany: State University of New York Press.

———. 1988b. "McFarland, Pantheism, and Panentheism." *History of European Ideas* 9: 569–582.

———. 1988c. "Panpsychism." *The Wordsworth Circle* 19: 38–45.

———. 1991a. *Christian Pacifism.* Philadelphia: Temple University Press.

———. 1991b. "Hartshorne and Plato." In *The Philosophy of Charles Hartshorne.* Ed. Lewis Hahn. LaSalle: Open Court.

———. 1997a. *Babies and Beasts: The Argument from Marginal Cases.* Chicago: University of Illinois Press.

———. 1997b. *Kazantzakis and God.* Albany: State University of New York Press.

———. 2000a. *A Brief, Liberal, Catholic Defense of Abortion.* Chicago: University of Illinois Press.

———. 2000b. *Not Even a Sparrow Falls: The Philosophy of Stephen R. L. Clark.* East Lansing: Michigan State University Press.

———. 2001a. *Rawls and Religion: The Case for Political Liberalism.* Albany: State University of New York Press.

———. 2001b. "The Replaceability Argument." *Process Studies* 30: 22–35.

———. 2004a. *Divine Beauty: The Aesthetics of Charles Hartshorne.* Nashville: Vanderbilt University Press.

———. 2004b. "On the Alleged Truth about Lies in Plato's *Republic.*" *Polis* 21: 93–106.

———. 2005. *A Platonic Philosophy of Religion: A Process Perspective.* Albany: State University of New York Press.

———. 2006a. "Is the Argument from Marginal Cases Obtuse?" *Journal of Applied Philosophy* 23: 223–232.

———. 2006b. *Rethinking the Ontological Argument: A Neoclassical Theistic Response.* New York: Cambridge University Press.

———. 2008. "Nonhuman Animal Rights." In *Handbook of Whiteheadian Process Thought.* Vol. 1. Ed. Michel Weber and Will Desmond. Frankfurt: Ontos Verlag.

————. 2009. *Contemporary Athletics and Ancient Greek Ideals*. Chicago: University of Chicago Press.

————. 2010. "Just War Theory, Afghanistan, and Walzer." *International Journal of Applied Philosophy* 24: 1–7.

————. 2011. *Rawlsian Explorations in Religion and Applied Philosophy*. University Park: Pennsylvania State University Press.

————. 2012a. "The Face of Suffering." *Journal of Animal Ethics* 2: 235–241.

————. 2012b. "Review of Clare Palmer, *Animal Ethics in Context*." *Journal of Animal Ethics* 2: 113–115.

————. 2012c. "Which Lives Are Grievable?" In *Butler on Whitehead: On the Occasion*. Ed. Roland Faber, Michael Halewood, and Deena Lin. Lanham: Lexington Books.

————. 2013a. "Griffin's Panexperientialism as *Philosophia Perennis*." In *Reason and Reenchantment*. Ed. John Cobb, Richard Falk, and Catherine Keller. Claremont: Process Century Press.

————. 2013b. "The Process Concept of God and Pacifism." *Sophia* 52: 483–501.

————. 2013c. "Stengers on Whitehead on God." In *Philosophical Thinking and the Religious Context*. Ed. Brendan Sweetman. New York: Bloomsbury Academic.

————. 2015. "Religion, Solitariness, and the Bloodlands." *American Journal of Theology & Philosophy* 36: 226–239.

————. Forthcoming. "Plato and Panpsychism." In *A History of Panpsychism*. Ed. William Seager. New York: Routledge.

Edelman, Gerald, and Giulio Tononi. 2000. *A Universe for Consciousness*. New York: Basic Books.

Eslick, Leonard. 1955. "The Platonic Dialectic of Non-Being." *New Scholasticism* 29: 33–49.

Faber, Roland, Michael Halewood, and Deena Lin, eds. 2012. *Butler on Whitehead: On the Occasion*. Lanham: Lexington Books.

Felt, James. 2001. *Coming to Be: Toward a Thomistic-Whiteheadian Metaphysics of Becoming*. Albany: State University of New York Press.

Fleischacker, Samuel. 2011. "The Virtues of Eclecticism." *Process Studies* 40: 232–252.

Ford, Marcus, ed. 1987. *A Process Theory of Medicine*. Lewiston: Edwin Mellen Press.

Frey, R. G. 1983. *Rights, Killing, and Suffering*. Oxford: Blackwell.

Friesen, Philip. 2010. *The Old Testament Roots of Nonviolence.* Eugene: Wipf and Stock.

Gamwell, Franklin. 2005. *Politics as a Christian Vocation.* New York: Cambridge University Press.

Gill, Stephen. 2003. "The Philosophic Poet." In *The Cambridge Companion to Wordsworth.* Ed. Stephen Gill. New York: Cambridge University Press.

Griffin, David Ray. 1976. *God, Power, and Evil.* Philadelphia: Westminster Press.

———. 1991. *Evil Revisited.* Albany: State University of New York Press.

———. 1998. *Unsnarling the World Knot: Consciousness, Freedom, and the Mind-Body Problem.* Berkeley: University of California Press.

———. 2000. *Religion and Scientific Naturalism: Overcoming the Conflicts.* Albany: State University of New York Press.

———. 2001. *Reenchantment without Supernaturalism: A Process Philosophy of Religion.* Ithaca: Cornell University Press.

Gunton, Colin. 1980. *Becoming and Being: The Doctrine of God in Charles Hartshorne and Karl Barth.* Oxford: Oxford University Press.

Hamilton, Paul. 2003. "Wordsworth and Romanticism." In *The Cambridge Companion to Wordsworth.* Ed. Stephen Gill. New York: Cambridge University Press.

Hartshorne, Charles. 1923. "An Outline and Defense of the Argument for the Unity of Being in the Absolute or Divine Good." PhD dissertation. Harvard University.

———. 1934. *The Philosophy and Psychology of Sensation.* Chicago: University of Chicago Press.

———. 1935. "An Economic Program for Religious Liberalism." *The Christian Century* (June 5): 761–762.

———. 1937. *Beyond Humanism.* Chicago: Willett, Clark, and Co.

———. 1941a. *Man's Vision of God.* New York: Harper Brothers.

———. 1941b. "Whitehead's Idea of God." In *The Philosophy of Alfred North Whitehead.* Ed. P. A. Schilpp. LaSalle: Open Court.

———. 1942. "A Philosophy of Democratic Defense." In *Science, Philosophy, and Religion.* Ed. Lyman Bryson and Louis Finkelstein. New York: Conference on Science, Philosophy, and Religion in Their Relation to the Democratic Way of Life.

———. 1948. *The Divine Relativity.* New Haven: Yale University Press.

————. 1953a. *Philosophers Speak of God*. Chicago: University of Chicago Press.

————. 1953b. *Reality as Social Process*. Boston: Beacon Press.

————. 1962. *The Logic of Perfection*. LaSalle: Open Court.

————. 1965a. *Anselm's Discovery*. LaSalle: Open Court.

————. 1965b. "The Meaning of 'Is Going to Be.'" *Mind* 74: 46–58.

————. 1970. *Creative Synthesis and Philosophic Method*. LaSalle: Open Court.

————. 1972. *Whitehead's Philosophy*. Lincoln: University of Nebraska Press.

————. 1973. *Born to Sing*. Bloomington: Indiana University Press.

————. 1974. "Beyond Enlightened Self-Interest." *Ethics* 84: 201–216.

————. 1980. "In Defense of Wordsworth's View of Nature." *Philosophy and Literature* 4: 80–91.

————. 1981. "The Ethics of Contributionism." In *Responsibilities to Future Generations: Environmental Ethics*. Ed. Ernest Partridge. Buffalo: Prometheus Books.

————. 1983. *Insights and Oversights of Great Thinkers*. Albany: State University of New York Press.

————. 1984a. *Creativity in American Philosophy*. Albany: State University of New York Press.

————. 1984b. *Existence and Actuality: Conversations with Charles Hartshorne*. Chicago: University of Chicago Press.

————. 1984c. *Omnipotence and Other Theological Mistakes*. Albany: State University of New York Press.

————. 1987. *Wisdom as Moderation*. Albany: State University of New York Press.

————. 1990. *The Darkness and the Light*. Albany: State University of New York Press.

————. 1997. *The Zero Fallacy and Other Essays in Neoclassical Philosophy*. Ed. Mohammed Valady. LaSalle: Open Court.

————. 2001. *Hartshorne and Brightman on God, Process, and Persons*. Ed. Randall Auxier and Mark Davies. Nashville: Vanderbilt University Press.

————. 2011. *Creative Experiencing: A Philosophy of Freedom*. Ed. Donald Viney. Albany: State University of New York Press.

Henning, Brian G. 2005. *The Ethics of Creativity*. Pittsburgh: University of Pittsburgh Press.

James, William. 1970 [1910]. "The Moral Equivalent of War." In *War and Morality*. Ed. Richard Wasserstrom. Los Angeles: Wadsworth.

——. 1985 [1902]. *The Varieties of Religious Experience*. Cambridge: Harvard University Press.

Jamieson, Dale. 1998. "Animal Liberation Is an Environmental Ethic." *Environmental Values* 7: 41–57.

Johnson, A. H. 1943. "The Social Philosophy of Alfred North Whitehead." *Journal of Philosophy* 40: 261–271.

Jones, Seth. 2010. *In the Graveyard of Empires: America's War in Afghanistan*. New York: W. W. Norton.

Kant, Immanuel. 1900 [1766]. *Dreams of a Spirit-Seer*. Tr. and ed. Emanuel Goerwitz and Frank Sewall. New York: Macmillan.

Keynes, John Maynard. 1920. *The Economic Consequences of the Peace*. New York: Harcourt, Brace, and Howe.

Kim, Jaegwon. 1993. *Supervenience and the Mind*. Cambridge: Cambridge University Press.

Kinast, Robert. 1981. "Non-Violence in a Process Worldview." *Philosophy Today* 25: 279–285.

Kohak, Erazim. 1984. *The Embers and the Stars: A Philosophical Inquiry into the Moral Status of Nature*. Chicago: University of Chicago Press.

Kreeft, Peter. 2005. *The Philosophy of Tolkien*. San Francisco: Ignatius Press.

Latour, Bruno. 2011. "Foreword." In Isabelle Stengers, *Thinking with Whitehead: A Free and Wild Creation of Concepts*. Tr. Michael Chase. Cambridge: Harvard University Press.

Leclerc, Ivor. 1972. *The Nature of Physical Existence*. New York: Humanities Press.

Leopold, Aldo. 1949. *A Sand County Almanac*. New York: Oxford University Press.

Levine, Michael. 1994. *Pantheism*. London: Routledge.

Loomer, Bernard. 1976. "Two Conceptions of Power." *Process Studies* 6: 5–32.

——. 2013. "The Size of the Everlasting God." *Process Studies Supplements* 18: 1–45.

Lucas, George. 1989. *The Rehabilitation of Whitehead*. Albany: State University of New York Press.

Malone-France, Derek. 2007. *Deep Empiricism: Kant, Whitehead, and the Necessity of Philosophical Theism*. Lanham: Lexington Books.

——. 2012. *Faith, Fallibility, and the Virtue of Anxiety*. New York: Palgrave Macmillan.

Marsh, James. 1999. *Process, Praxis, and Transcendence*. Albany: State University of New York Press.

Mash, Roy. 1987. "How Important for Philosophers is the History of Philosophy?" *History and Theory* 26: 287–299.

McFarland, Thomas. 1985. *Originality and Imagination*. Baltimore: Johns Hopkins University Press.

McGinn, Colin. 1991. *The Problem of Consciousness*. Oxford: Blackwell.

McHenry, Leemon, and Christine Holmgren. 2012. "Quine and Whitehead on Ontological Reduction: Properties Reconsidered." *Process Studies* 41: 261–286.

McMahan, Jeff. 2009. *Killing in War*. Oxford: Clarendon Press.

Merton, Thomas. 1968. *The Springs of Contemplation*. New York: Farrar, Straus and Giroux.

Middleton, Darren. 2002. *God, Literature, and Process Thought*. Burlington: Ashgate.

Mill, John Stuart. 1950 [1881]. *John Stuart Mill's Philosophy of Scientific Method*. New York: Hafner.

Morris, Randall. 1991. *Process Philosophy and Political Ideology*. Albany: State University of New York Press.

Murphy, Timothy. 2013. "The Pacifism of Duane Friesen." *Process Studies* 42: 110–131.

Murray, John Courtney. 1960. *We Hold These Truths: Catholic Reflections on the American Proposition*. New York: Sheed and Ward.

Nagel, Thomas. 1986. *The View from Nowhere*. New York: Oxford University Press.

———. 2003. "Rawls and Liberalism." In *The Cambridge Companion to Rawls*. Ed. Samuel Freeman. New York: Cambridge University Press.

Neville, Robert. 1978. *Soldier, Sage, Saint*. New York: Fordham University Press.

Nozick, Robert. 1974. *Anarchy, State, and Utopia*. New York: Basic Books.

Palmer, Clare. 1998. *Environmental Ethics and Process Thinking*. Oxford: Clarendon Press.

———. 2010. *Animal Ethics in Context*. New York: Columbia University Press.

Perry, Seamus. 2003. "Wordsworth and Coleridge." In *The Cambridge Companion to Wordsworth*. Ed. Stephen Gill. New York: Cambridge University Press.

Pinker, Steven. 2011. *The Better Angels of Our Nature: Why Violence Has Declined.* New York: Viking.

Pite, Ralph. 2003. "Wordsworth and the Natural World." In *The Cambridge Companion to Wordsworth.* Ed. Stephen Gill. New York: Cambridge University Press.

Pluhar, Evelyn. 1995. *Beyond Prejudice: The Moral Significance of Human and Nonhuman Animals.* Durham: Duke University Press.

Popper, Karl. 1972. *Objective Knowledge.* Oxford: Clarendon Press.

Rachels, James. 1990. *Created from Animals: The Moral Implications of Darwinism.* Oxford: Oxford University Press.

Rawls, John. 1996 [1993]. *Political Liberalism.* Paperback ed. New York: Columbia University Press.

———. 1999a. *The Law of Peoples.* Cambridge: Harvard University Press.

———. 1999b [1971]. *A Theory of Justice.* Revised ed. Cambridge: Harvard University Press.

Regan, Tom. 1983. *The Case for Animal Rights.* Berkeley: University of California Press.

Riffert, Franz. 2012. "Analytic Philosophy, Whitehead, and Theory Construction." *Process Studies* 41: 235–260.

Rolston, Holmes. 1988. *Environmental Ethics.* Philadelphia: Temple University Press.

Rorty, Richard. 1979. *Philosophy and the Mirror of Nature.* Princeton: Princeton University Press.

———. 1999. *Philosophy and Social Hope.* New York: Penguin.

Royce, Josiah. 1908. *The Philosophy of Loyalty.* New York: Macmillan.

Russell, Bertrand. 1956. *Portraits from Memory.* New York: Simon and Schuster.

Scarborough, Peter, Paul Appleby, Anja Mizdrak, Adam Briggs, Ruth Travis, Kathryn Bradbury, and Timothy Key. 2014. "Dietary Greenhouse Gas Emissions of Meat-Eaters, Fish-Eaters, Vegetarians and Vegans in the U.K." *Climate Change* 125.2: 179–192.

Schilbrack, Kevin. 2004. *Thinking Through Rituals.* New York: Routledge.

Schmidt, Thomas. "Reflective Secularization and Public Reason." Unpublished.

Schweitzer, Albert. 1992. *Reverence for Life.* Tr. Reginald Fuller. Cooper Station: Irvington Publishers.

Seager, William. 1991. *Metaphysics of Consciousness.* London: Routledge.

————. 1995. "Consciousness, Information, and Panpsychism." *Journal of Consciousness Studies* 2: 272–288.

Searle, John. 1992. *The Rediscovery of the Mind*. Cambridge: MIT Press.

Shields, George. 2012. "Whitehead and Analytic Philosophy of Mind." *Process Studies* 41: 287–336.

Shields, George, and Donald Viney. 2003. "The Logic of Future Contingents." In *Process and Analysis*. Ed. George Shields. Albany: State University of New York Press.

Sia, Santiago. 2004. *Religion, Reason, and God: Essays in the Philosophies of Charles Hartshorne and A. N. Whitehead*. New York: Peter Lang.

Simons, Henry. 1934. *A Positive Program for Laissez-Faire*. Chicago: University of Chicago Press.

Singer, Peter. 1979. *Practical Ethics*. Cambridge: Cambridge University Press.

Skrbina, David. 2005. *Panpsychism in the West*. Cambridge: MIT Press.

Smart, J. J. C. 1979. "Materialism." In *The Mind-Brain Identity Theory*. Ed. C. V. Borst. London: Macmillan.

Smith, John. 1978. *Purpose and Thought: The Meaning of Pragmatism*. New Haven: Yale University Press.

Snyder, Timothy. 2010. *Bloodlands: Europe between Hitler and Stalin*. New York: Basic Books.

Sontag, Susan. 2003. *Regarding the Pain of Others*. New York: Farrar, Straus and Giroux.

Stengers, Isabelle. 2002. *Penser avec Whitehead: Une libre et sauvage creation de concepts*. Paris: Editions du Seuil.

————. 2011. *Thinking with Whitehead: A Free and Wild Creation of Concepts*. Tr. Michael Chase. Cambridge: Harvard University Press.

————. 2014. "A Constructivist Reading of *Process and Reality*." In *The Lure of Whitehead*. Ed. Nicholas Gaskill and A. J. Nocek. Minneapolis: University of Minnesota Press.

Strawson, Galen. 1994. *Mental Reality*. Cambridge: MIT Press.

————. 2006. "Being Realistic: Why Physicalism Entails Panpsychism." *Journal of Consciousness Studies* 13: 3–31.

————. 2008. *Real Materialism and Other Essays*. New York: Oxford University Press.

Stronge, Paul. 2012. "The Flow of Meaning: A. N. Whitehead and Roy Wagner on Symbolism." *Process Studies* 41: 42–63.

Stump, Eleonore, and Norman Kretzmann. 1981. "Eternity." *Journal of Philosophy* 78: 429–458.

Sturm, Douglas. 1979. "Process Thought and Political Theory." *Review of Politics* 41: 375–376.

Taylor, A. J. P. 1962. *The Origins of the Second World War*. New York: Atheneum.

Tennyson, Alfred. 1969. *The Poems of Tennyson*. 2nd ed. Vol. 2. Ed. Christopher Ricks. Essex, UK: Longman.

Trott, Nicola. 2003. "Wordsworth: The Shape of the Poetic Career." In *The Cambridge Companion to Wordsworth*. Ed. Stephen Gill. New York: Cambridge University Press.

Viney, Donald. 1985. *Charles Hartshorne and the Existence of God*. Albany: State University of New York Press.

Walzer, Michael. 2004. *Arguing About War*. New Haven: Yale University Press.

———. 2006 [1977]. *Just and Unjust Wars*. 4th ed. New York: Basic Books.

———. 2009. "Is Obama's War in Afghanistan Just?" *Dissent* (Dec. 3): http://dissentmagazine.org/online.php?id=314.

Weitzman, Martin. 1984. *The Share Economy*. Cambridge: Harvard University Press.

Whitehead, Alfred North. 1920. *The Concept of Nature*. Cambridge: Cambridge University Press.

———. 1939. "An Appeal to Sanity." *Atlantic Monthly* 163 (March): 309–320.

———. 1941a. "Autobiographical Notes." In *The Philosophy of Alfred North Whitehead*. Ed. P. A. Schilpp. LaSalle: Open Court.

———. 1941b. "Immortality." In *The Philosophy of Alfred North Whitehead*. Ed. P. A. Schilpp. LaSalle: Open Court.

———. 1941c. "Mathematics and the Good." In *The Philosophy of Alfred North Whitehead*. Ed. P. A. Schilpp. LaSalle: Open Court.

———. 1947. *Essays in Science and Philosophy*. New York: Philosophical Library.

———. 1954. *Dialogues of Alfred North Whitehead*. Ed. Lucien Price. New York: Mentor Books.

———. 1958 [1929]. *The Function of Reason*. Boston: Beacon Press.

———. 1961 [1933]. *Adventures of Ideas*. New York: Free Press.

———. 1966 [1938]. *Modes of Thought*. New York: Free Press.

————. 1967 [1925]. *Science and the Modern World*. New York: Free Press.

————. 1978 [1929]. *Process and Reality*. Corrected ed. Ed. David Ray Griffin and Donald Sherburne. New York: Free Press.

————. 1985 [1927]. *Symbolism*. New York: Fordham University Press.

————. 1996 [1926]. *Religion in the Making*. New York: Fordham University Press.

————. 2007 [1919]. *An Enquiry Concerning the Principles of Natural Knowledge*. New York: Cosimo Classics.

Wilson, Catherine. 2008. "Kant and Leibniz." *Stanford Encyclopedia of Philosophy*. http://plato.stanford.edu.

Wolterstorff, Nicholas, and Robert Audi. 1997. *Religion and the Public Square*. Lanham: Rowman & Littlefield.

Wordsworth, William. 1981. *Poetical Works*. Ed. Thomas Hutchinson and Ernest De Selincourt. Oxford: Oxford University Press.

Wright, Quincy. 1965. *A Study of War*. 2nd ed. Chicago: University of Chicago Press.

Wright, Sewell. 1977. "Panpsychism and Science." In *Mind in Nature*. Ed. John Cobb and David Ray Griffin. Washington, DC: University Press of America.

Wu, Duncan. 2003. "Wordsworth's Poetry to 1798." In *The Cambridge Companion to Wordsworth*. Ed. Stephen Gill. New York: Cambridge University Press.

Yang, Fubin. 2010. "The Influence of Whitehead's Thought on the Chinese Academy." *Process Studies* 39: 342–349.

Yoder, John Howard. 1972. *The Politics of Jesus*. Grand Rapids: Eerdmans.

————. 1994. "How Many Ways Are There to Think about War?" *Journal of Law and Religion* 11: 83–108.

INDEX OF NAMES

Made in the USA
Middletown, DE
22 May 2023

31232885R00123